# Domestic Violence in Diverse Contexts

Overwhelmingly, it is women who are the victims of domestic violence and this book puts women's experiences of domestic violence at its centre, whilst acknowledging their many diverse and complex identities.

Concentrating on the various forms of domestic abuse and its occurrence and manifestations within different contexts, it argues that gender is centrally implicated in the unique factors that shape violence across all these areas. Individual chapters outline the experiences of:

- mothers
- older women
- religious women
- refugee women
- rural women
- Aboriginal women
- lesbians
- women with intellectual disabilities.

Exploring how domestic violence across varying contexts impacts on different women's experiences and understandings of abuse, this innovative work draws on post-structuralist feminist theory and how these ideas view, and potentially allow, gendered explanations of domestic violence. *Domestic Violence in Diverse Contexts* is suitable for academics and researchers interested in issues around violence and gender.

**Sarah Wendt** is Senior Lecturer in the School of Psychology, Social Work and Social Policy, and co-director of the Research Centre for Gender Studies at the University of South Australia.

**Lana Zannettino** is Senior Lecturer in Sociology in the School of Nursing and Midwifery at Flinders University, South Australia.

# Routledge Advances in Health and Social Policy

# Domestic Violence in Diverse Contexts

A re-examination of gender

## Sarah Wendt and Lana Zannettino

Routledge
Taylor & Francis Group

LONDON AND NEW YORK

First published 2015
by Routledge
2 Park Square, Milton Park, Abingdon, Oxon OX14 4RN

and by Routledge
711 Third Avenue, New York, NY 10017

*Routledge is an imprint of the Taylor & Francis Group, an informa business*

© 2015 Sarah Wendt and Lana Zannettino

*British Library Cataloguing-in-Publication Data*
A catalogue record for this book is available from the British Library

*Library of Congress Cataloging-in-Publication Data*
Wendt, Sarah, author.
Domestic violence in diverse contexts : a re-examination of gender / Sarah Wendt and Lana Zannettino.
     p. ; cm. -- (Routledge advances in health and social policy)
Includes bibliographical references.
I. Zannettino, Lana, author. II. Title. III. Series: Routledge advances in health and social policy.
[DNLM: 1. Domestic Violence. 2. Feminism. 3. Internationality. 4. Women. WA 308]
RC569.5.F3 , W 46 2015
616.85′822–dc23                                        2014013054

ISBN: 978-0-415-53010-1 (hbk)
ISBN: 978-1-315-75189-4 (ebk)

Typeset in Baskerville
by HWA Text and Data Management, London

# Contents

# About the authors

**Sarah Wendt** has a background in social work. She is currently a senior lecturer in the School of Psychology, Social Work and Social Policy, and co-director of the Research Centre for Gender Studies at the University of South Australia. Sarah has made significant contributions to the field of domestic violence. She wrote *Domestic Violence in Rural Australia* (2009), and has been published in numerous high-ranking, international academic journals including *Health and Social Care in the Community*, *International Social Work*, *Journal of Social Work*, *British Journal of Social Work*, *Journal of Rural Studies*, *Affilia: Women and Social Work* and *Australian Social Work*. Her current research projects explore the impact of domestic violence on women's citizenship, the role of religion in domestic violence, and service provision for Aboriginal communities experiencing family violence.

**Lana Zannettino** has a background in social work. She is currently a senior lecturer in Sociology in the School of Nursing and Midwifery at Flinders University, South Australia. Lana has made significant contributions to the field of domestic violence and gender theorising, including being published in several high-ranking, international academic journals such as *Violence Against Women*, *Gender and Education*, *Australian Feminist Studies* and *Child and Family Social Work*. Her current research projects explore the impact of encampment on domestic violence in refugee communities, and the sexual health care needs of young refugee women. She currently serves as one of the Commonwealth's nominated non-government representatives on the Implementation Panel for the National Plan to Reduce Violence Against Women and their Children 2010–2022.

# Acknowledgements

The stories described in this book could not have emerged without the participation of women who gave their time and effort to be interviewed by us about their experiences of domestic violence. We remember their courage, strength and willingness. Similarly, we acknowledge human service workers who help and assist women, men and children experiencing domestic violence and especially those who gave their time to be interviewed for the purposes of this research.

We thank the University of South Australia and Flinders University for support and time given to write this book. In particular, we would like to thank Kathryn Evans, who assisted us during literature searching, Kate Leeson for her editing services and Katrina Pestka for interviewing women living with intellectual disabilities. We would like to thank the following colleagues and experts in their fields who gave their time to read and comment on respective chapters: Professor Irene Watson, Professor Jude Irwin and Sandra Seymour. We also thank our colleagues for the many passionate discussions and vibrant conversations about our shared commitment to researching violence against women and their children to ultimately make a difference, especially Dr Nicole Moulding, Dr Fiona Buchanan and Deirdre Tedmanson. Thank you to Professor Suzanne Franzway for her mentorship and discussions about gender.

Finally, Sarah would like to personally thank her husband Greg and two sons Curtis and Mitchell for supporting, encouraging and loving her throughout this writing journey. Lana would like to personally thank her partner Herman and two daughters Isabella and Melanie for their constant love and support throughout this endeavour and all others.

# 1 Introduction

## Introduction

We identified the need for this book from a number of factors we have observed in well over a decade of research in the area of domestic and family violence. First, we have been around long enough to have seen the evolution of feminist theory and knowledge in academia, and its impact on theorising and knowledge development in the area of domestic violence. In a broad brush stroke, this evolution can be characterised as a shift from a focus on male structural power or patriarchy as the aetiology of domestic violence, to a focus on social constructions and identities, which, if they do not outright reject the existence of patriarchy as a stable reality or truth, see it as incapable of accommodating those aspects of identity such as class, race, ethnicity, sexuality and geographical location that disrupt and reshape the development and meaning of violence and abuse in women's lives. In the last few years, however, we have witnessed a critique of this shift in feminist theorising, which has garnered a renewed interest in patriarchy and gender oppression in theorising about domestic violence. In this way, there has been a circuitous nature to the evolution of feminist theorising, not only in domestic violence but in theorising women's lives more generally. This circuitous evolution in feminist theorising has prompted us to re-examine the centrality of gender in domestic violence, both as a concept and as an element of lived experience.

Second, our empirical research with women has compelled us to recognise the diversity of women's lives and the ways that this diversity can variously impact on women's experiences of violence and abuse. This recognition made us think again about the centrality of gender in women's lives – how significant, for example, is gender in shaping the lives of refugee women affected by domestic violence, many of whom have fled persecution and spent years in camps? And, should we impose gender as a central category of analysis in researching the lives of these women? The same could be asked of Aboriginal women, mothers, religious women, women with intellectual disabilities, lesbians, and so on.

This book, therefore, stems from a deep questioning of ourselves as researchers and as feminist theorists in the field of domestic violence against a backdrop of evolving and often contested feminist theorising in the academe. What we are certain of, however, is our commitment to feminism, both as a movement and as a theoretical construct, and a firm belief in its capacity to improve the lives of women. Such a capacity has been well evidenced over the last fifty years, beginning with the success of second-wave feminism in putting the 'private' and hidden problem of domestic violence and other forms of violence against women and girls on political, legal and social agendas. The recognition that domestic violence is a significant social problem that is both a criminal offence and violation of human rights in some countries is the outcome of substantial political activity by feminists from the 1960s onwards. In terms of feminism in academia, we hold the view that a key strength of feminist theorising is its contested nature and history – without contestation there is no possibility for critique and development of new ideas. In this book, we view ourselves as participants in and contributors to this contested terrain, with an aspiration to build on existing knowledge with new vigour and insight. In short, in this book we seek to advance feminist analyses of domestic violence in order to shed new light on the role and operation of gender in the lives of diverse communities of women. In so doing, we hope to identify and mobilise those social transformations that are necessary to put an end to domestic violence for all women.

## What is domestic violence?

This book focuses on women's experiences of domestic violence. The two questions that need answering at the beginning of this book are what do we mean by domestic violence, and why do we focus on women? The World Health Organization (WHO) states that violence against women is the most pervasive yet under-recognised human rights violation in the world (Ellsberg & Heise, 2005). The United Nations defines violence against women as any act of gender-based violence that results in, or is likely to result in, physical, sexual or psychological harm or suffering to women, including threats of such acts, coercion or arbitrary deprivation of liberty (United Nations, 1993). Domestic violence is an act of gender-based violence. Domestic violence reflects what Johnson (2011, p. 290) names as intimate terrorism or a pattern of violent coercive control. Domestic violence, as we use the term in this book, involves the combination of physical and/ or sexual violence with a variety of control tactics such as economic, emotional, social (constant monitoring) and spiritual abuse, the use of children and pets, and threats and intimidation. To demonstrate this definition in lived experience we draw on an interview with a woman aged 49 who left her partner after thirty years of marriage. She had two children and was interviewed twenty months after leaving the relationship:

> I started with my partner when I was about 17 years old. I was about 18 when I was studying a course. I was having lots of fun and actually making friends for the first time. He got jealous and kept on threatening and getting aggressive and threatening to kill himself if I didn't stay with him and disconnected me from my friends. This happened throughout our relationship years later … making sure I never had connections with friends. If he got mad or angry

he would throw plates and stuff around the house. With him it was all more verbally aggressive ... he didn't really hit me ... but then a few times he put knives to my throat. I would have to make sure the kids were always quiet otherwise he would get upset and starting shouting abuse at us all ... This all just sort of progressed along the way I think.

(2013)

Johnson and Ferraro (2000, p. 952) name the distinguishing features of domestic violence as a pattern of violent and non-violent behaviours that indicates a general motive to control, and almost all perpetrators are male. The indication 'almost all' is used here to acknowledge that this type of violence has been identified in lesbian relationships and that some women terrorise their male partner but, as Johnson (2011) has argued and distinguished over time, the primary perpetrators in heterosexual couples are men, and gender plays an important role.

Domestic violence as defined and outlined above has been the most visible in feminist theory, which has argued that partner violence is primarily a problem of men using violence to maintain control over 'their women', a control to which they feel they are entitled and that is supported by a patriarchal culture (Johnson & Ferraro, 2000, pp. 948–9). The purpose of this book is to examine and contribute to advancing this feminist analysis of domestic violence. It is important to make the point here, however, that feminist analyses are not monolithic or homogenous – there are a range of feminist theories and positions, some of which have been more pervasive than others in explicating the precursors to, and dynamics and effects of, domestic violence in women's lives. In recognition of the heterogeneous nature of feminist theorising more broadly and in relation to domestic violence in particular, in this book we will visit and re-visit a range of feminist positions in order to interrogate their currency and applicability in contemporary contexts of domestic violence.

## Why focus on women?

Gender affects every aspect of our lives, and violence is highly gendered. Walby (2011, p. 41) points out gender-based violence against women is violence that is directed against a woman *because* she is a woman, or violence that affects women disproportionately. The research on domestic violence spans decades and consistently shows that women experience abuse from known men in their lives, particularly their intimate partners. The risk to women from their current partners has been found to be three times greater than for men, and women are more likely to endure a wide range of violent behaviours, be injured and have a weapon used against them by their partners or ex-partners. Women are more likely to experience multiple incidents and the impacts tend to be worse (Mooney, 2000). These experiences of domestic violence explain women's higher levels of fear relative to men. It is through fear that men are able to control women's behaviour, movements and freedom (Yodanis, 2004). We write this book using women's experiences of domestic violence and we concentrate on the various forms of abuse, its occurrence and manifestations within and across different community groups.

It is well recognised that domestic violence is often 'hidden' because of the nature and impact of such abuse, and so levels of domestic violence are thought to be underestimated. Despite this, population-based surveys have been conducted around the world to ascertain the prevalence of domestic violence. The WHO Multi-Country Study on Women's Health and Domestic Violence (Garcia-Moreno et al., 2006; Abramsky et al., 2011) documented the widespread nature of intimate partner violence by indicating lifetime prevalence of physical and/ or sexual partner violence among ever-partnered women in the fifteen sites in ten countries (Bangladesh, Brazil, Ethiopia, Japan, Namibia, Peru, Samoa, Serbia and Montenegro, Thailand and the United Republic of Tanzania) surveyed. They found lifetime prevalence of physical partner violence ranged from 13 per cent (Japan city) to 61 per cent (Peru province), with most sites falling between 23 per cent and 49 per cent. The range of lifetime prevalence of sexual partner violence ranged from 6 per cent (city sites in Japan and Serbia and Montenegro) to 59 per cent (Ethiopia province), with most sites falling between 10 per cent and 50 per cent. The proportion of women reporting either sexual or physical partner violence, or both, ranged from 15 per cent (Japan city) to 71 per cent (Ethiopia province), with most sites falling between 29 per cent and 62 per cent. Japan city consistently reported the lowest prevalence of all forms of violence, whereas the provinces of Bangladesh, Ethiopia, Peru and the United Republic of Tanzania reported the highest figures. Garcia-Moreno et al. (2006) point out that these results add to the existing body of research, which is mainly from industrialised countries, and confirms that violence by an intimate partner is a common experience worldwide. Furthermore, in all settings except one, women were more at risk of violence by an intimate partner than from any other perpetrator. It has been recognised that domestic violence is a significant problem that women share around the world.

Similarly, Alhabib, Nur and Jones (2010) conducted a systematic review to summarise the worldwide evidence on the prevalence of domestic violence against women. They found the highest levels of physical violence were seen in Japanese immigrants to North America (about 47 per cent), who also had high levels of emotional violence (about 78 per cent) along with respondents studied in South America, Europe and Asia (37–50 per cent). The mean lifetime prevalence of physical and sexual violence was found to be highest (30–50 per cent) in studies conducted in psychiatric and obstetrics/gynaecology clinics, and for emotional violence the highest rates were found in accident and emergency and psychiatric departments (65–87 per cent). Again, this systematic review is recognition that domestic violence has significant impacts on women across the world.

Some countries have conducted their own studies of the prevalence of domestic violence, which have again showed that domestic violence is a significant issue for women. In the United States, women were significantly more likely than men to report being victimised by an intimate partner, whether the time period covered was the individual's lifetime or the previous twelve months, and whether the type of victimisation considered was rape, physical assault or stalking (Tjaden

& Thoennes, 2000). Tjaden and Thoennes (2000) indicate that 7.7 per cent of surveyed women and 0.3 per cent of surveyed men were raped by a current or former intimate partner at some time in their life, and the most frequently reported intimate partner violence by far was physical assault. 22.1 per cent of surveyed women and 7.4 per cent of surveyed men said they were physically assaulted by an intimate partner at some time in their lifetime (Tjaden & Thoennes, 2000). In Australia, the Personal Safety Survey conducted by the Australian Bureau of Statistics (ABS) (2006) found that women were more likely than men to be victims of physical, sexual and other forms of violence by a partner, and men make up a significant proportion of reported abusers. For example, it was found that 10.1 per cent (*n* = 780,500) of all women and 4.4 per cent (*n* = 325,700) of all men reported physical assault since the age of fifteen. It was estimated that 1,293,100 women had experienced sexual assault since the age of fifteen, of whom 23.2 per cent (*n* = 299 700) reported being assaulted by a current or ex-partner in the most recent incident. By comparison, 362,400 men had experienced sexual assault, of whom none reported being assaulted by a current partner and 5.7 per cent (*n* = 20,700) reported being assaulted by a previous partner in the most recent incident. It was also found that women were more likely than men to report repeated violence, especially where the violence was perpetrated by a current partner.

We are focusing on women in this book because the prevalence studies show that domestic violence is a significant social and health problem for women and is found all over the world and in all cultures (Akyüz et al., 2012). It violates a woman's physical body, sense of self and trust, regardless of age, race, ethnicity or country. It is a major problem and a significant cause of death and incapacity among women worldwide (Alhabib, Nur & Jones, 2010). Research has predominantly shown that domestic violence can lead to a wide range of short- and long-term physical, mental and sexual health problems for women (Heise & Garcia-Moreno, 2002 and Jewkes, Sen & Garcia-Moreno, 2002, both cited in WHO/LSHTM, 2010). For example, Akyüz et al. (2012) reviewed the research literature on the effects of violence on women's reproductive health and reported that violence against women may cause physical problems such as cuts, fractures, internal organ injuries and permanent defects. They also reported that women exposed to violence are more likely to take part in self-harming behaviours such as alcohol and drug abuse or unprotected sex, and experience emotional imbalance, depression, fear, anxiety, decreased self-respect, sexual function defects, eating disorders, post-traumatic stress disorders and even suicide. Furthermore, women exposed to domestic violence often experience feelings of panic, have an expectation that something bad will happen and have sleep-related problems including sleeping and resting troubles and waking up with violent nightmares. Akyüz et al. (2012) reported this chronic stress and anxiety can cause some somatic disorders in women exposed to violence, such as hypertension, irritability, gastrointestinal disorders, asthma and headaches. Lastly, Akyüz et al. (2012) also concluded that women who experience domestic violence may have problems like unwanted pregnancies and serious pregnancy-related complications as a result of different kinds of abuse. In addition to having effects on reproductive health care, they also determined that women exposed to violence have less prenatal care. Similarly, Montero et al. (2011) aimed to compare the health of women in Spain with no history of violence with that of women with a history of intimate partner violence, non-intimate partner violence only, and both types of violence. The results showed that women with a history of violence reported significantly poorer physical and mental health than women with no such history. Women who reported intimate partner violence only were three times more likely to suffer from psychological distress and co-occurring somatic symptoms and twice as likely to use medication (e.g. antidepressants or tranquilisers). Compared to women who reported no history of violence, women who reported both intimate partner violence and non-intimate partner violence were almost five times more likely to suffer from psychological distress and co-occurring somatic symptoms, more than six times more likely to use tranquilisers or antidepressants, and more likely to perceive their health as poor.

We focus on women in the book because research across the world has shown convincingly that victims of domestic violence are primarily women, that large numbers of women across the world are affected by it, and that it invades almost all aspects of women's lives with far-reaching implications for families in terms of emotional and social wellbeing and educational and employment outcomes (Anda et al., 2001 and Dube et al., 2002, cited in WHO/LSHTM, 2010). In acknowledging the large-scale and extensive consequences of the problem, many countries around the world have passed laws to criminalise intimate partner and sexual violence, and many countries are increasingly providing legal, health and social services to abused women (see Walby, 2011, pp. 40–5). Domestic violence curtails women's ability to act as citizens because it stops women from moving and acting freely in their communities and homes (Lister, 2003).

## Gender in the lives of diverse communities of women

Bradley (2013) argues at the beginning of her book titled *Gender* that academic feminism has hit something of an impasse; that debate has stalled in the stalemate between modernity and postmodernist approaches and discussions on gender reflect this.

Influenced by modernity, 'gender' and 'patriarchy' were the key tools developed by second-wave feminists to explore the relations between women and men, encompassing the organisation of reproduction, the sexual divisions of labour, and cultural definitions of femininity and masculinity. In short, influenced by modernity, gender is seen as a set of social arrangements determining how women and men live, or a way of thinking that divides people up into two social categories; hence patriarchy is the social system of male dominance in this gender analysis (Bradley, 2013, p. 16). This understanding of gender has dominated domestic violence explanations; that is, gender is a set of relations between men and women embedded into social structures and institutions (Bradley, 2013, p. 48).

The creation of these binary opposites has been questioned by feminists influenced by post-structuralism. In post-structuralist analyses, the binary classifications that have structured and ordered social life in the modern era –

man–woman, masculine–feminine, nature–culture, public–private, heterosexual–homosexual, black–white, and so on – have been shown to be permeable, or less than absolute opposites. These binaries are not equal polarities but hierarchies that reproduce inequalities that support prevailing social arrangements of oppression (Burman, 1998). The distinction between sex and gender, for example, implies that sex is intrinsic to the body and that the body or sex exists independently of and prior to gender (Butler, 1990). Judith Butler and others argue that to accept the notion of sex as a biological given is to continue to be caught up in notions of biological determinism. Those influenced by the writings of Judith Butler argue that sex and gender should be collapsed into one because 'gender/sex' is performative; that is, we play out gender, we do gender repeatedly in our lives through the clothes we wear, words we use, activities we carry out, the way we relate to each other, and so on. This acting out of being a woman or man gives the illusion of stability and fixity and promotes the assumption that different behaviours between men and women flow from their biological differences. Born from this critique of gender as immutable and biologically determined is the argument that gender is socially constructed, variable and fluctuating; hence gender is unstable and not a consistent base of identity. Gender becomes a discursive phenomenon and so the object of study is the competing discourses and counter-discourses of femininity and masculinity (Bradley, 2013, pp. 75–6). Post-structuralist theorists are uncomfortable with the view that gender is embedded in social structures and institutions, which we see in domestic violence theorisation, because this is essentialist and views gender as fixed. Instead, post-structuralism emphasises difference and specificity, and researchers influenced by this theory look at particular groups of women (disabled women, lesbians, ethnic minority groups, and so forth) to explore their differentiated experiences of gender relations in specific contexts. Taking these ideas, theorists of domestic violence examine very specific contexts to explore local narratives of domestic violence. Theories of domestic violence then sit in local understandings and examine how gender is experienced within these contexts, emphasising the different nuances of gender relations, not only between men and women, but also among women themselves (Bradley, 2013, p. 77).

We believe that this sensitivity to gender relations in specific contexts provides an opportunity to advance feminist understandings and explanations of domestic violence because it moves beyond binary opposites and taken-for-granted propositions about the commonalities of gender or assumptions of an 'all-woman' experience. However, feminists have raised questions and tensions about this epistemological shift to valuing the local experiences and understandings of domestic violence and the gendered relations and identities that inhere in such experiences. Furthermore, at the beginning of this book we argued a case to focus on women's experiences as victims of domestic violence because empirical research has highlighted patterned tendencies surrounding gender and domestic violence for decades. To deny the gendered nature of and the commonalities in women's experiences of domestic violence therefore is to refute the evidence before us, which clearly suggests that domestic violence, along with rape and sexual assault, is a space in which it is permissible, if not necessary, to talk about gender in more universal terms. This book attempts to investigate these tensions through analysing how women understand, experience and 'do' gender in the context of domestic violence. In this way, we address questions such as: do post-structuralist accounts de-politicise women's collective experiences of domestic violence? And, is gender still relevant as a central category of analysis in domestic violence?

In our attempt to move beyond the stalemate, the impasse or any other descriptions of a feminist approach being 'stuck' in its focus on gender, we view these debates as operating on a continuum of theory rather than in opposition. We believe that such a position has far greater potential to both transform and enrich feminist theory. We concur with Bradley when she states: 'it is to suggest that a balance is needed between focus on specificity and identity and a consideration of patterned regularities and common tendencies' (2013, p. 78).

Bradley (2013, p. 78) argues that the sensitivity of difference is a great contribution to feminism and understanding gender. However, at the same time, she points out that if this exploration of 'difference' is sited too much at the level of individuals and identities there is a danger of neglecting the broader implications of gender and the patterns of gender disadvantage that extend across different social groupings. In fact, Bradley (2013, p. 78) raised the example that '*all* women of every class, ethnicity, age, nationality and religion are vulnerable to rape and domestic violence' to demonstrate her point (original emphasis).

In the context of domestic violence, understanding the patterned regularities and common tendencies is vital because they form legal, policy and practice responses to keep women and children safe and to enable healing from violence by intimate partners. Furthermore, like Bradley (2013, p. 23), we argue that gender is different from sex, and this distinction is vital in understandings of domestic violence. In other words, the collapse of the sex–gender dichotomy argued for by some post-structuralist theorists does not make sense to us in the context of domestic violence. Women experience pregnancy, birth, lactation, menstruation and mothering, which are distinct from male experiences, and this distinction is bound up in and played out in domestic violence, as outlined in the studies on the impacts of domestic violence on physical and mental health. For example, a 64-year-old woman who discussed her experiences of abuse in her early twenties recalled:

> He did not want me to have the baby, he wanted me to have an abortion but I resisted and had her anyway but I was not allowed to breastfeed the baby in front of him and he would not tolerate her crying. I would have to go out to the car to feed her.

> (2013)

O'Reilly (2007) reviewed the literature on domestic violence against childbearing women and identified that unintended or mistimed pregnancies have four times the odds of resulting in domestic violence towards women by their partners than those with planned pregnancies. Jasinski (2004) found that persistent violence is more likely to occur where the male partner perceived the pregnancy had occurred sooner than intended, and found that conflict between parents can be aggravated or intensified once a newborn baby arrives home. Furthermore, the prevalent threat of sexual and physical violence puts constraints on women's actions. The threat of physical or sexual violence is rarely an issue that men face in an intimate heterosexual relationship. Physical and anatomical power differences between men and women cannot be ignored, as the statistics demonstrate: women experience rape and sexual assault and homicide by an intimate partner at much higher rates than men (Bradley, 2013, p. 23). Women's fear of violence by men is enough to control the behaviour and limit the movement of all women in society (Yodanis, 2004).

We argue gender is a social construct and we learn femininity and masculinity throughout social interactions, but these are persistently bound up with power relations between women and men (Bradley, 2013, p. 4). Furthermore, we agree with Bradley (2013, p. 5) when she argues that gender must be seen as lived experience because gender refers to aspects of our lives that are all too real. Gender is both a material and a cultural phenomenon. Post-structuralism enables us to examine how individual women and men are actively involved in 'doing gender'; that is, creating and recreating our identities as gendered and sexual beings. But at the same time, feminism, born from modernity, reminds us to keep examining how gender is constrained by the structures and cultures that are our contexts (Bradley, 2013, p. 26). We will use these two understandings of gender to explore the specific contexts and local narratives of domestic violence within diverse communities of women, but at the same time look for the patterns of gender relations and disadvantage that consistently occur across the different social groupings. We argue that domestic violence both derives from and perpetuates gender differences and inequality, and that it represents lived experience where one can see the ubiquity and reproduction of particular gender relations as well as its variations.

There is an effort to move beyond the debates between modernist and postmodernist theories in feminism and gender discussions, towards a framework that builds on the strengths of each perspective. McCann and Kim (2013) point out that these new frameworks renew discussion of the grounds for feminist solidarity and they reassert the social group 'women', however unstable, as the agent of feminist politics. We write this book to contribute to feminist solidarity and recognise that a common gender identity can only be a political one (Bradley, 2013, p. 97). Gender affects every aspect of our lives and domestic violence is highly gendered (Walby, 2009, pp. 195–6). The recognition of diverse lives of women who experience domestic violence is not a block for gender justice or the universal rights of women (Bradley, 2013, p. 97); rather, it potentially demonstrates how gender is both differently and similarly played out in diversity.

## The authors and this research

Amongst its ambiguity, contestations and richness, feminist researchers have agreed that feminism is politically for women, should make sense of women's situations and should point to effective strategies for change (Kelly, Burton & Regan, 1994; Ramazanoglu with Holland, 2002; McCann & Kim, 2013). We write this book for women, to make sense of domestic violence, and to advance such understandings by grounding explanations in women's experiences of living in unjust and unsafe intimate relationships.

From being social workers and now academics, we have listened and spoken to many women about their experiences of domestic violence. This book is based on the more formal ways we have engaged with women through the research process, and hence draws heavily on our own experiences as researchers who have adopted interviewing as a research method. These face-to-face interactions with women have contributed much to our writings, research and advocacy in the area of domestic violence. Over the past fifteen years, between us, we have interviewed approximately one hundred women for the purposes of research because, like other feminist academics, we see interviews as providing the path through which intersubjectivity and non-hierarchical relationships between women researchers and women participants can be developed (Kelly, Burton & Regan, 1994). Specifically, semi-structured interviews have featured in our research, allowing us to talk with women about a wide range of topics including those reflected in the chapters of this book. Semi-structured interviews have allowed us to explore particular topics with women but also encouraged women to speak beyond the prompts of our interview guides. Our motivations for such an approach have been embedded in our broader aim to give voice to personal, experiential and emotional aspects of existence (Ramazanoglu with Holland, 2002, p. 155).

Kelly, Burton and Regan (1994) have reminded us for a long time that conducting and participating in research is an interactive process, and what women get or take from it should concern us. We have interviewed women about highly sensitive experiences and accounts of physical, sexual, emotional, financial, social and spiritual abuse by intimate partners, and are always mindful of their strength and willingness to share their time and stories with us. We are aware of the positive and negative outcomes that might arise for women who consent to talk about their experiences in the research interview setting; therefore ethics approval for our research and safety and care after the interview have always been paramount considerations in our research processes. We also recognise that participating in an interview has little direct impact on the lives of women who participate; however, we often hear from women that they decided to come forward and be interviewed as part of our research to make a difference in the lives of other women. This giving is an act we see time and time again as researchers in this field. For example, a Korean woman aged in her mid-twenties who was interviewed about spiritual abuse as a form of domestic violence said the following at the beginning of the interview:

> I moved out, the abuse was so extreme, I couldn't stand it. I mean actually the reason why I am participating in this research is because for the first time I am seeking professional help because the abuse was so abusive.

(2013)

At the end of the interview, she said something similar: 'I am participating because I have nothing to lose actually; I want to be a testimony for other people who experience this'.

Semi-structured interviews have kept us accountable to the women we interview and our audience by pushing us to be clear about the purpose of our research, what we are asking women and why, and to continually think about what we are arguing and concluding from their stories.

As feminist researchers, we also acknowledge that 'researcher' and 'researched' stand in some social relationship to each other, and these relationships are rarely balanced with fully shared meanings. We have the power to represent the lives and ideas of the women we have interviewed as similar or different across any divisions between them. A cursory inspection of the aims and contents of this book may elicit the question of why we have chosen to separate women into distinct groups or 'communities of women'. Some readers may even suggest that doing so ignores the intersectional nature of women's identities and circumstances, and that it creates an artificial separation between groups of women. Some readers may point out that there are numerous divisions between women who are socially constituted, for example, variations by language, sexual orientation, able-bodiedness, religion, class, ethnicity, regional orientation, and so on. Some readers may also recognise that those who are socially located in the same category can feel and think differently about their experiences and identify in different ways. People have differing experiences of what it feels like to be socially included or excluded, vocal or silenced (Ramazanoglu with Holland, 2002, p. 111).

We respect these valid viewpoints, but at the same time we want to be honest about our unease in using arguments about complicated interrelations of difference which, when taken to their extreme, mean that nothing can be known or communicated. Such a position, we argue, can potentially limit our understandings of women's collective experiences of domestic violence, without which there can be no way forward politically or otherwise. Hence, while we recognise that separating groups of women into distinct communities does not reflect the complexities of their lives, we saw it as the only way to draw out similarities within and across diverse groups of women, particularly in terms of how gender is implicated in their experiences of abuse. The central aim of the book is to identify and explore how women's different contexts and circumstances impact on their experiences of domestic violence and what this means in terms of understanding domestic violence as a gendered phenomenon. Hence, our aim is to draw attention to how women live and 'do' gender within and across their different communities. We believed that we could more successfully achieve this aim by focusing each chapter on a different community of women, and by exploring the unique factors impacting on domestic violence for women in each of these communities.

Ramazanoglu with Holland (2002, p. 112) argue that, in this shifting complexity of identities and the complex intersections of social divisions, it is difficult to confine emancipatory research to insider knowledge. What we can do as feminist researchers is to interpret our selections of data through our own ideas and values; hence why we have chosen particular groups of women and not others was also based on two other key factors. The first was the nature and extent of our own research in the area of domestic violence. As we have indicated, this book draws on a range of data collected and analysed by us over a number of years of researching women affected by domestic violence and, to a large extent, our choice of communities of women reflects the foci and intensity of this research. We have researched widely in the areas of rural and religious women, refugee and older women, for example, and we wanted the opportunity to develop this work further in the context of this book. The second factor was what we know anecdotally from practitioners and from the literature: that domestic violence in new and emerging communities, including refugee communities, and the role of religion in domestic violence are relatively new areas of research, and women with intellectual disabilities, older women and lesbians have often been neglected in domestic violence research and literature. Hence, we sought to include these communities of women in the book along with other communities of women who hold special significance in our society and cultures, such as mothers and Aboriginal women. We acknowledge that there are communities of women that we do not cover in the book and, given the complex nature of women's lives, it may not be possible to identify these communities, let alone include all of them.

Finally, in writing this book, we are also aware of the politics of representation. Ramazanoglu with Holland (2002, p. 123) state that, in representing others, feminists need to conceptualise relationships, social locations and boundaries in order to interpret meanings, and to make sense of experiences about which they have little or no personal knowledge or experience. Hence, we do not make claims about the authenticity of our accounts of these women's lives or regard the presentation of our discussion as evidence of truth or reality. In fact, we acknowledge that the sharing of our knowledge will always be limited because of the privileges and power inherent in our daily lives; that is, as academics we have the power to maintain and reproduce discourses and we benefit from institutionalised power relations in everyday practice. For example, we are white women, and are well paid because we work in universities. Yet we also have histories and other identities that have given us differing experiences, for example, growing up on a farm with a moderate income, growing up with the teachings and practices of Christianity, having migrant parents, being a single parent, and experiencing marriage and birthing and raising children.

We also bring to this book our semi-structured interviews and informal conversations with approximately one hundred human-service workers spanning over fifteen years of researching domestic violence. For example, in the context of research interviews, workers have provided anecdotal stories or examples of domestic violence experienced by the women they have worked alongside, which has been vital in our knowledge development for particular groups of women such as women living with intellectual disabilities and refugee women. Similarly, we have had the privilege of sitting and talking with Aboriginal women elders or Aboriginal human-service workers working in their own communities. Finally, we also bring with us our supervision of PhD and honours students, whom we have mentored and supported to conduct research in the field of violence against women, including ethnic women's experiences of child sexual abuse, women's experiences of receiving services related to female genital mutilation, young African people's experiences of violence in South Australia, working with men who use violence, and domestic violence experiences for lesbians and women living with intellectual disabilities.

Ramazanoglu with Holland (2002, p. 123) state that accounts of experience make a difference to what is known, and can change what counts as knowledge. This book comes from the experiences of women, who have lived domestic violence, workers, who have responded to domestic violence, and us, who have researched domestic violence for over a decade. Without experiential knowledge, there could be no general knowledge of what domestic violence is. We write this book to offer arguments and explanations for how and why gender must feature in our understandings of domestic violence.

## Outline of the book

The objectives of the book are: to examine different contexts of domestic violence; to interrogate the unique factors present in these different contexts that impact on women's experiences and understandings of abuse; and to demonstrate how gender is implicated in these unique factors that shape domestic violence. To bring gender to the forefront in each chapter we present the unique factors for particular groups of women, and use this background to identify discourses and subject positions that influence gender in contexts of domestic violence. Our argument for each chapter is grounded in the women's stories, that is, the women we have interviewed over time. We have included women's names and dates throughout the book to show the range and depth of interviews conducted. However, we have used pseudonyms to protect women's anonymity. The order of the chapters is based on the more common aspects of women's lives such as mothering and ageing and moves into more specific contexts in which women engage in gender, for example, religious, refugee and rural, and we conclude with those chapters that speak to gender in nuanced ways such as Aboriginal, lesbian and women with intellectual disabilities.

In Chapter 2 we examine feminist understandings of domestic violence by providing a brief chronological description of the main feminist ideas over the last five decades and the emergence of post-structuralist ideas in feminism broadly and in domestic violence specifically. We explore some of the tensions between feminism and post-structuralism and how some theorists have attempted to reconcile these tensions, in particular those tensions around the centrality of gender in domestic violence. We outline our theoretical framework for this book, which we use to illustrate the unique factors and complexities of domestic violence across a diversity of contexts. Such a framework enabled us to draw out gendered discourses and particular subject positions that women engage with in their everyday lives, and how they shape their experiences of domestic violence.

In Chapter 3 we explore the unique factors that impact on women as mothers in situations of domestic violence, including how women's understandings of and decisions about domestic violence are shaped by having children. We argue discourses of mothering have shifted focus to protection, that is, women being solely responsible for their children, their own safety and meeting the needs of their partners in contexts of domestic violence. Mothering discourses shape and reinforce gendered subject positions such as good wife, carer, nurturer and protector, and keep women trapped in relationships for long periods of time because women fear being constructed as the 'bad' mother. Mothering discourses provide women with a sense of self and identity. However, we argue that domestic violence is particularly hostile to mothers because they are forever navigating the contradictions of mothering discourses, that is, you are a bad mother if you stay but you are a bad mother if you break up the family.

In Chapter 4 we examine how the experience of domestic violence is influenced by women's age and position in the life span. In this chapter we explore the unique factors that impact on older women, including the accumulative effects of many years of abuse by an intimate partner, physical frailty of older women, different levels of resilience to the effects of abuse, differing levels of motivations to address abuse, and how long-term abusive relationships can become normalised and accepted in the lives of older women. We argue that older women have historically lived with discourses of traditional femininity, positioning women as inferior, passive, submissive and subservient, which have become entrenched across their life course because the passage of time has reinforced them. Together with ageing discourses we also show that gender discourses have positioned older women as sexually undesiring and undesirable as they age, creating subject positions that serve to make gender invisible in old age and thus invisible in domestic violence contexts.

In Chapter 5 we explore the unique factors that impact on the lives of women from various religious backgrounds, including how religious beliefs or practices can be used to force them into subordinate roles, as well as the denial or the misuse of religious or spiritual traditions to justify physical violence or other forms of abuse. We argue that religious women's experiences of domestic violence are grounded in the very constructions of gender whereby religious teachings, beliefs and rules are inscribed, felt and lived in relation to the divine. Gender is disciplined and done through behaviour and comportment that are shaped by these regulatory religious and spiritual contexts, which erases the ability to name domestic violence.

In Chapter 6 we discuss the ways that domestic violence manifests in culturally specific ways in refugee communities as well as how it is intensified by the context of war, displacement and resettlement. Specifically, we examine how pre-arrival experiences, such as rape as a weapon of war and persecution, have shaped refugee women's experiences of domestic violence. We also focus on how displacement and encampment can increase the incidence and intensity of domestic violence in refugee communities. We argue that gender and refugee discourses saturate women with restricted subject positions such as weak, passive, obedient and subservient to husbands and men, as well as grateful outsiders, 'other' and suspect in countries of resettlement, which come together to silence women in contexts of domestic violence.

In Chapter 7 we highlight the unique factors of living in a rural community that impact on women experiencing domestic violence. Rurality has been constructed or categorised as particularly patriarchal; that is, rural people are constructed as being more traditional and conservative than urban people or as being backward compared to urban people and such discourses can position domestic violence as part and parcel of backward rural culture. In this chapter, we explore the nuances and complexities of gender relations and subject positions in rural contexts, and argue that rural women construct themselves within the context of loyalty to family life or farming and property life. This loyalty shifts the gaze to women's responsibility in domestic violence and simultaneously makes men's behaviour invisible.

In Chapter 8 we explore the unique factors that impact on Aboriginal women in Australia when experiencing family violence. In this chapter we specifically focus on the Australian context because the history of colonisation, oppressive legislation, racism and stolen generations has shaped and influenced experiences of family violence in Aboriginal communities. We explore the tensions of writing about feminism, family violence and gender in the Australian context as non-Aboriginal women, and argue that post-structuralism has allowed for discussions of gender in the contexts of Aboriginal family violence. Through Aboriginal women's stories, we show how Aboriginal women have to balance their safety with their obligations to family and community.

In Chapter 9 we examine the unique factors and circumstances that impact on lesbians' experiences of domestic violence, particularly how heteronormativity influences understandings and responses to domestic violence. We argue that domestic violence for lesbians is saturated in the feminine, and while dominant gendered discourses position women as inherently nurturing, caring and indelibly connected to one another, they also position lesbians as 'bitchy' and intrinsically antagonistic towards each other. We show through women's stories that within such gendered discourses violence between women is constructed as a symptom or extension of women's 'bitchiness', and therefore it is less likely to be considered 'real' violence or anything 'out of the ordinary'.

In Chapter 10 we discuss the unique factors that impact on women with intellectual disabilities experiencing domestic violence, particularly being abused by multiple perpetrators over long periods of time. We show through women's and workers' stories that emotional manipulation, financial and sexual abuse frequently feature in domestic violence relationships for women with intellectual disabilities, and the backgrounds of trauma and the innocent emotional naivety of women with intellectual disabilities are often targeted by abusive men. We argue that the interactions between discourses of disability, functional capacity and abuse position this group of women as asinine or as asexual or promiscuous, which makes domestic violence in their lives seem non-existent or less serious than other women's experiences of violence and abuse.

In the final chapter we draw conclusions about the centrality of gender in the experience of domestic violence across the various groups of women that we have covered in the book. We review aspects of the previous chapters to illustrate our explanation of domestic violence being both an experience shaped by unique contextual factors as well as one in which gender is a central feature. We argue gender is different for different women but certain expectations and ways of doing gender, that is femininity for women, are similar for all women, and that men's and women's investment in and the doing of gender in everyday intimacy contributes to the continuance of domestic violence.

## References

Abramsky, T., Watts, C.H., Garcia-Moreno, C., Devries, K., Kiss, L., Ellsberg, M., Jansen, H.A.F.M. & Heise, L. (2011) What factors are associated with recent intimate partner violence? Findings from the WHO Multi-Country Study on Women's Health and Domestic Violence. *BMC Public Health*, 11, pp. 109–25.

Akyüz, A., Yavan, T., ahiner, G. & Kılıç, A. (2012) Domestic violence and woman's reproductive health: a review of the literature. *Aggression and Violent Behavior*, 17, pp. 514–18.

Alhabib, S., Nur, U. & Jones, R. (2010) Domestic violence against women: systematic review of prevalence studies. *Journal of Family Violence*, 25, pp. 369–82.

Australian Bureau of Statistics (2006) *Personal Safety Survey, Australia, 2005*, reissue, cat. no. 4906.0, Australian Bureau of Statistics, Canberra.

Bradley, H. (2013) *Gender*, 2nd edition, Polity, Cambridge.

Burman, E. (Ed) (1998) *Deconstructing Feminist Psychology*, Sage, London.

Butler, J. (1990) *Gender Trouble: Feminism and the Subversion of Identity*, Routledge, London.

Ellsberg, M. and Heise, L. (2005) *Researching Violence Against Women: A Practical Guide for Researchers and Activists*, World Health Organization, PATH, Washington, DC.

Garcia-Moreno, C., Jansen, H.A., Ellsberg, M., Heise, L. & Watts, C.H. (2006) Prevalence of intimate partner violence: findings from the WHO Multi-Country Study on Women's Health and Domestic Violence. *Lancet*, 368, pp. 1260–9.

Jasinski, J. (2004) Pregnancy and domestic violence: a review of the literature, *Trauma, Violence & Abuse*, 5(1), pp.47–64.

Johnson, M. (2011) Gender and types of intimate partner violence: a response to an anti-feminist literature review. *Aggression and Violent Behavior*, 16, pp. 289–96.

Johnson, M. & Ferraro, K. (2000) Research on domestic violence in the 1990s: making distinctions. *Journal of Marriage and the Family*, 62, pp. 948–63.

Kelly, L., Burton, S. & Regan, L. (1994) Researching women's lives or studying women's oppression? Reflections on what constitutes feminist research. In M. Maynard & J. Purvis (Eds) *Researching Women's Lives from a Feminist Perspective*, Taylor & Francis, New York, pp. 10–26.

Lister, R. (2003) *Citizenship: Feminist Perspectives*, Palgrave Macmillan, Basingstoke.

McCann, C. & Kim, S. (Eds) (2013) *Feminist Theory Reader: Local and Global Perspectives*, 3rd edition, Routledge, New York.

Montero, I., Escriba, V., Ruiz-Perez, I., Vives-Cases, C., Martín-Baena, D., Talavera, M. & Plazaola, J. (2011) Interpersonal violence and women's psychological well-being. *Journal of Women's Health*, 20, pp. 295–301.

Mooney, J. (2000) Revealing the hidden figure of domestic violence. In J. Hanmer & C. Itzon (Eds) *Home Truths About Domestic Violence: Feminist Influences on Policy and Practice, a Reader*, Routledge, London, pp. 24–43.

O'Reilly, R. (2007) Domestic violence against women in their childbearing years: a review of the literature. *Contemporary Nurse: A Journal for the Australian Nursing Profession*, 25, pp. 13–21.

Ramazanoglu, C. with Holland, J. (2002) *Feminist Methodology: Challenges and Choices*, Sage, London.

Tjaden, P. & Thoennes, N. (2000) *Full Report of the Prevalence, Incidence, and Consequences of Violence against Women: Findings from the National Violence against Women Survey*, NIJ/CDC, Washington, DC.

United Nations (1993) United Nations Women: Virtual Knowledge Centre to End Violence against Women and Girls. Available at: http://www.endvawnow.org/en/articles/295-defining-violence-against-women-and-girls.html

Walby, S. (2009) *Globalisation and Inequalities: Complexity and Contested Modernities*, Sage, London.

Walby, S. (2011) *The Future of Feminism*, Polity, Cambridge.

World Health Organization/London School of Hygiene and Tropical Medicine (2010) *Preventing Intimate Partner and Sexual Violence against Women: Taking Action and Generating Evidence*, World Health Organization, Geneva.

Yodanis, C. (2004) Gender inequality, violence against women, and fear: a cross-national test of the feminist theory of violence against women. *Journal of Interpersonal Violence*, 19(6), pp. 655–75.

# 2 Feminist understandings of domestic violence

## Introduction

Feminist explanations of domestic violence emerged and grew from trying to understand why men beat their wives, and so focused initial attention on heterosexual relationships within the institution of marriage or partnership. Feminist theorists used the concepts of patriarchy, gender, family and power to understand why men, as a group, use violence against their partners and to explain what function this serves for a given society in a specific historical context (Bograd, 1988). These concepts have also been used to examine the nature and consequences of domestic violence, different forms of abuse and to expose how institutions of marriage and family may promote, maintain and even support men's use of violence in the home (Bograd, 1988). This concentration built scholarship that argued that broader structural and cultural forces, such as patriarchy, allow for so many women to be victimised by their male partners. Hence, when structural factors within the institutions of marriage and family and those institutions such as law, religion and media that influence them are examined the question of why domestic violence occurs becomes answerable (DeKeseredy, 2011; Winstok, 2011). Feminist theorists defined domestic violence as fundamental to the social control of women (Hanmer & Itzin, 2000), and hence one of feminism's major contributions to domestic violence policy and practice has been to identify men as the primary perpetrators of domestic violence (Itzin, 2000). In this chapter, we provide a brief outline of the above concepts as they are an important foundation in understanding the emergence of post-structuralist ideas in feminism broadly and in domestic violence theory specifically. This brief chronology also enables a foundation for the particular theoretical tools we propose and use in the book to argue why gender must continue to feature in understandings and explanations of domestic violence.

## Patriarchy

The groundbreaking work of Dobash and Dobash (1980) named domestic violence as not only the means by which men control and oppress women but as the most brutal and explicit expression of patriarchal domination. They argued there are economic and social processes that operate directly or indirectly to support patriarchal domination and the use of violence against wives. Patriarchy has been understood as a 'system of social structures and practices in which men dominate, oppress, and exploit women' (Walby, 1990, p. 20) including the patriarchal mode of production, patriarchal relations in paid work, patriarchal relations in the state, male violence, patriarchal relations in sexuality, and patriarchal relations in cultural institutions. In understanding domestic violence, it has been argued that patriarchy is central and domestic violence needs to be considered as part of patriarchy and its associated economic and social processes, the history of the family and the status of women. In using patriarchy to explain domestic violence feminists, particularly radical feminists, have argued that male violence is the basis of men's control over women; it is a form of social control of women and, furthermore, the refusal of the state to intervene effectively in terms of welfare provision and criminal justice responses to support women is part of the problem. For example, if a woman cannot obtain the resources she needs to remain independent from a violent partner or the police do not support her allegations, she is pushed into returning to her violent partner (Walby, 1990). Feminists explain that there are patriarchal prejudices in structures of society such as the labour market, tax system, legal system and welfare system, and men are privileged or advantaged from and by these structures, which ultimately support male violence. In other words, men have traditionally received material/financial, emotional, social and judicial leverage due to the rights they have been afforded over time, history and culture, and hence power differences between men and women within a family can benefit the perpetrator of domestic violence who takes advantage of this infrastructure. Patriarchal power differentials contribute to both the likelihood of domestic violence and significant advantages for the man should he resort to violence (Horsfall, 1991). Feminist theorists have named gendered power relations as the essence of patriarchy and use this understanding to explain men who are violent towards women in the home.

Domestic violence did not even exist as a concept or phenomenon before feminist activism and theory. Feminists have pointed out that domestic violence is widespread and embedded as part of patriarchal domination; women modify their behaviour to survive it (Walby, 1990). This happens because patriarchy gives men the power to abrogate responsibility for themselves and their violence, and because violence is institutionalised and legitimised in many spheres of society (news, entertainment, war). Or, as Kelly and Radford (1996) argue, women are systematically encouraged to minimise the violence they experience from men, and this silence influences women's perceptions about the severity of violence they experience. Women find themselves caught between dominant 'male stream' definitions and their own experiential knowledge. Differential power relations between women and men are an intrinsic structural aspect of a patriarchal society and feminists argue that men benefit from such structural arrangements without necessarily being consciously aware of them (Bograd, 1988). Domestic violence is therefore explained as an act or phenomenon in which a man's violence towards his female partner provides him with a sense of security when he deems his world view or privilege to be under threat (Horsfall, 1991).

Feminist explanations of domestic violence in terms of patriarchal belief systems differ from most other explanations in that they avoid blaming or implicating the victim in any way; that is, feminist explanations do not focus on how women may inadvertently trigger or intentionally provoke men's violence, a notion that may be evident in some psychological theories of domestic violence. Instead, they see the violence as flowing from a choice made by the perpetrator and insist that this choice is structured by the wider social context, not by the behaviour of the victim (Hopkins & McGregor, 1991, p. 124). Most feminists agree that, structurally, patriarchy is a hierarchical organisation in which males have more power and privilege than women, and the ideology of patriarchy provides a political and social rationale for its own existence. Consequently, both men and women come to believe that it is natural and right that women be in inferior positions, which explains domestic violence (DeKeseredy, 2011).

## Gender and patriarchal ideology

Gender is one of the most fundamental concepts of feminist theorising; hence feminists argue that domestic violence needs to be understood in terms of gendered power relations (Bograd, 1988). In the past, feminists have argued that society devalues women as secondary and inferior as a result of patriarchy, and that men as a group benefit from how women's lives are restricted and limited because of their fear of violence by men. Bograd stated it succinctly when she wrote 'the reality of domination at the social level is the most crucial factor contributing to and maintaining wife abuse at the personal level' (1988, p. 14). Feminists name male entitlement as an explanation for domestic violence and often attribute male socialisation to it. For example, they have examined and named social beliefs and attitudes that support domestic violence including assumptions about women being men's property, women being responsible for keeping family and relationships together because they are good at emotional nurturing and caring, and men being the head of the household because they are rational, strong and provide (Wendt, 2009). Hence, feminist scholarship has argued that male violence is an outcome of the social processes by which masculinity is constructed and it stems from traditions, habits and beliefs about what it means to be a man. For example, two dominant beliefs that have been examined to explain domestic violence have included the belief that men have a right to exercise authority over their partners, or a right to deference and obedience from the women they live with; and that violence is a legitimate form of punishment that may be used in the exercise of authority (Hopkins & McGregor, 1991). Even though the law no longer sees wife assault as a legitimate exercise of male authority, feminists argue that these belief systems are so widespread and so well entrenched throughout society because they are part of patriarchal ideology. Patriarchal ideology is inculcated into men by the media, by peer group and family socialisation, and by other institutions (Hopkins & McGregor, 1991). Examination of this social context is vital in feminist analysis and theorising of gendered power relations because women and men are bound by familial, cultural and societal expectations of 'appropriate' behaviour (Hanmer, 2000).

Feminists argue that many of the problems women face, including domestic violence, are caused by such social, cultural and political forces, hence the feminist mantra 'the personal is political' (McPhail et al., 2009). This phrase was used to explain and challenge the separation between the public (male) sphere of work and the private (female) sphere of home, and feminists used it to focus attention on the politics of power differentials between men and women that are inherent in everyday life (Swigonski & Raheim, 2011). Feminists argue that domestic violence demonstrates the problem of gender inequality and discrimination at its utmost severity, and it is 'especially abhorrent in a relationship that should be, or allegedly is, intimate' because intimate relationships are the most significant social context in a person's life. Building on the 'personal is political' explanation of domestic violence, feminist theory has highlighted how gender inequality in this environment penetrates and threatens the deepest fabric of society, because accepting or not challenging violence against women in the family perpetuates the problem for generations to come (Winstok, 2011, p. 306). To be head of a nuclear family, or married within an extended family, carries considerable power and status for the male in the wider community (Hanmer, 2000).

### Family and patriarchy

Feminist scholars have named the family and heterosexuality as central institutions in patriarchal society. The family is where the private struggles around patriarchal power relations are enacted, and hence where violence frequently features as a form of control of the powerless by the powerful (Radford & Stanko, 1996). The family embodies ideologies and practices that derive from patriarchy. Power and gender relations are built into the family and the marital relationship. For example, Horsfall (1991, p. 123) argues it is within the family in the first instance that the promise of masculinity is perceived by the boy, and parents live out power differentials between boys and girls. Feminist theorists have strongly argued that domestic violence is closely related to the historical development of the isolated nuclear family in a capitalist society, to division of the public–private domains, to constructions of 'appropriate' male and female family roles, and to positions of wives as legally and morally bound to husbands (Bograd, 1988). The public–private split has been a specific focus for feminist explanations of domestic violence because it emphasises gender difference (Horsfall, 1991, p. 18).

In the private sphere of the family, the role of women has been of wife, to help and serve the head of the house, the husband, and of mother to rear children; hence the patriarchal role expectations for women in the family have been explicit and historically and politically embedded. Feminist theorists have shown that men and women live in a web of relationships bound by family and culture in which expectations of correct behaviour for women and men differ substantially (Hanmer, 2000), and ultimately this has ramifications for the potential for violence by husbands towards their wives. For example, the division between private and public spheres separates women from men, increasing the likelihood of male unity and female disunity, which exacerbates tendencies for male violence and inhibits tendencies for female support for female victims. The public–private split also contributes to the hidden nature of domestic violence and the invisibility of the perpetrators. In the public domain, with its patriarchal infrastructures, men wield economic, political, social and ideological power, which enables domestic violence to remain in the private realm. Feminists have argued that patriarchal ideology, values, beliefs and practices are manifest in the family, which is why the privacy of the family and domestic violence has been so strongly defended (Hopkins & McGregor, 1991; Horsfall 1991, p. 34).

To name domestic violence as a public issue, not a private matter, has met considerable resistance because it has profound implications for societies. Domestic violence is deeply threatening and it contradicts fundamental assumptions about the nature of intimate relations and the safety of the family. Naming domestic violence as a private issue exerts a powerful ideological pull because it affirms domestic violence as a problem that is 'individual' or that only involves particular male–female relationships; hence there is no social responsibility to remedy (Schneider, 1994). Feminists have highlighted that allowing domestic violence to be seen as a private issue has resulted in gender relations being ignored, focusing instead on the assaulted woman who is socially scrutinised, pathologised and blamed for the violence perpetrated against her. Feminists argue this focus refuses to confront issues of power and gender relations, and perpetuates the power of patriarchy, and hence have named the concept of privacy as a key aspect of this denial. Schneider (1994, p. 43) states that the concept of privacy, enshrined in patriarchal discourses of the family, encourages, reinforces and supports domestic violence. Privacy reinforces that domestic violence is immune from sanction, that it is acceptable, and an inevitable part of the basic fabric of family life.

### Woman-centred

Feminist explanations of patriarchy, gender and power theorise domestic violence as a systemic problem as opposed to explaining domestic violence as a private, individual matter, with individual explanations required for particular kinds of men and women. Feminist theoreticians do not deny that some wife abuse may be linked to psychopathology in either partner nor do they dismiss the validity or importance of psychological theories. Instead, they seek to connect psychological analyses with understandings of the patriarchal social context, of the unequal distribution of power and of the socially structured and culturally maintained patterns of male–female relations (Bograd, 1988, p. 17). Feminist theorising about domestic violence has therefore stood out as exemplary because it is dedicated to advocacy for women and aims to validate women's experiences (Bograd, 1988).

In challenging traditional views of what counts as knowledge, feminist scholars and researchers recorded women's experiences of violence. Naming and giving voice to women was a vital step in developing feminist theories of domestic violence. Feminists collected women's individual and personal experiences and stories as the basis from which to develop theoretical understandings (Radford, Kelly & Hester, 1996, p. 43). Feminist theorisation of domestic violence challenges traditional views of what counts as knowledge and raises complex discussions of epistemology; that is, feminists argue that male domination influences everything from brief interpersonal exchanges to the most abstract theories of human nature so that men's lives, values and attitudes are taken as the norm and women are rendered invisible. In contrast, feminist theorisation of domestic violence emerged from the experiences of women from their own frames of reference, arguing that women are survivors of violence and abuse and have many adaptive capacities and strengths (Bograd, 1988; Radford, Kelly & Hester, 1996; Swigonski & Raheim, 2011). The goal of feminist scholarship in the field of domestic violence is to more accurately reflect women's experiences to counteract the majority of theoretical frameworks that exclude, blame or devalue women. In summary, in understanding domestic violence, feminist theories have sought to analyse women's experiences, articulate the nature of social relations between women and men, and provide explanations that support efforts to transform these social relations (Bograd, 1988; Swigonski & Raheim, 2011).

### Developing feminist understandings of domestic violence: the emergence of post-structuralism

In reviewing feminist explanations of domestic violence of the past few decades, one can see recurring themes such as prioritising gender, agreeing that patriarchal structures and ideologies are a determinant of domestic violence, and viewing social institutions of marriage and family as special contexts that may promote and maintain men's use of violence against women in the home (DeKeseredy, 2011; Taylor & Jasinski, 2011). Domestic violence has been theorised as one manifestation of a system of male dominance that has existed historically and across cultures (Taylor & Jasinski, 2011). In summary, feminist explanations have provided a social structural analysis of domestic violence as a gendered phenomenon in a way that no other perspective has achieved. They have integrated and explained men's actions, women's responses and the reluctance of the state and society to intervene in domestic violence (Walby, 1990, p. 142).

There is little doubt that feminist scholars have produced abundant writings on domestic violence, and this literature has been driven by social/political action, consciousness-raising and the goal of influencing policy and practice. This is not surprising given that feminist perspectives challenge male entitlement and privilege as well as the traditional notion that domestic violence is a private family matter. Thus the literature reflects feminists' demands for public solutions, including the establishment of programs and services for women who experience domestic violence, treatment for their male partners and the involvement of the criminal justice system to hold men accountable for their abuse (McPhail et al., 2009). In addition to generating public awareness and solutions to domestic violence, feminists have also fought for women's suffrage and reproductive rights. They have challenged employment discrimination, promoted equitable wages and affirmative action initiatives, and sought rights to property ownership and university education (Gray & Boddy, 2010). In the academic realm, they have challenged the male-centred nature of theory and research and encouraged the recognition of women as serious contributors to academic knowledge both as actors in and subjects of research (Zajdow, 2007). The inclusion of women in the academe brought about not only a view of society from the position of women but a view of the world as fundamentally gendered (Abbott, Wallace & Tyler, 2005). From this position, feminist writers, theorists and academics were able to highlight the connections between the structural and social dimensions of women's lives and women's personal and private experiences of violence and abuse in the home.

Feminist theories of domestic violence that have focused on patriarchy, gender and family have an underlying assumption that it is legitimate to write of 'women' as a social category distinct from 'men' and hence discuss the collective interests of women and view women as uniform (Walby, 1990). In centring women's experiences, Radford et al. (1996, p. 5) acknowledged a decade ago that the question 'which women?' was asked from within feminism itself, and this has raised questions about essentialism in feminist theory and domestic violence theorisation. How violence was implicated in multiple structures of power relations and the effects these had on women's different experiences of oppression needed to be addressed. Differences in women's positions in relation to the power structures of race, ethnicity and culture (Sharma, 2001; Pan et al., 2006; Pease & Rees, 2008; Zannettino, 2012), class (Evans, 2005; Goodman et al., 2009; Nelson et al., 2012), sexuality (Mason, 2002; McClennen, 2005; Seelau, 2005), disability (Glover-Graf & Reed, 2006; Nixon, 2009; Hague, Thiara & Mullender, 2011) and age (Zink et al., 2003; Taft, Watson & Lee, 2004; Martino, Collins & Ellickson, 2005; Fisher & Zink, 2007) emerged and became vital to understanding feminist theory in the context of domestic violence (McPhail et al., 2009).

However, some feminist writers have highlighted the paucity of theory development or stagnation of theory development pertaining to domestic violence (McPhail et al., 2009; Hunnicutt, 2009). Feminists have also raised the question of whether or not feminists have advanced theoretical understandings of gender and domestic violence. Explaining domestic violence in relation to marital roles or gender roles has been viewed as limiting because this gender paradigm assumes gender is dichotomous or essential, and so ignores complex ways in which gender operates in social interactions between people (McHugh, 2005). Are gender relations changing, and what does this mean for understanding domestic violence are questions that come to mind. Some feminists have argued to advance understandings of domestic violence requires further development of gender. For example, Hunnicutt (2009, p. 556) argues that, given feminist scholars see gender as the primary mechanism of difference and that violence is patterned along gender lines, theorising should begin by examining the gender social order. She states that a gender-centred theory would expose how violence plays out in a gendered social context, the complexities and nuances of gendered positioning, and would permit understanding of the complex ways that gender interacts with other social conditions and processes. Similarly, Anderson (2005) argues an adequate understanding of gender and domestic violence must consider the ways in which gender is used to organise social life, hence feminism is the theoretical lens to push for questions of how gender matters in understanding domestic violence (Anderson, 2005).

These questions about or limitations of feminist theoretical understandings of domestic violence have also emerged from and in response to feminists' engagement with post-structuralism (Walby, 1990; Radford et al., 1996). Concepts such as patriarchy, woman and gender have been criticised by post-structuralist feminists for their assumed coherence and stability over time and culture instead of being viewed as shifting, variable social constructs (Walby, 1990). Furthermore, post-structuralism does not see material power residing primarily in structures of society such as gender, class and race but views power as diffuse, infusing all social and personal relationships (Radford et al., 1996).

Feminist writers have questioned whether domestic violence can adequately be explained by a single cause or addressed by a one-size-fits-all solution (McPhail et al., 2009, p. 838) and have looked for ways to integrate other perspectives that account for inequality based on gender, race, class, sexual orientation, age, disability and so on (Phillips, 2008). However, with this attempt to integrate, feminist writers have often expressed the concern of moving away from a single feminist explanation of domestic violence because this may render a gendered power analysis irrelevant (McPhail et al., 2009, p. 839). Phillips (2008) points out that for feminists there is a tension between theorising patriarchy and generalised oppression by men and postmodernism's focus on diversity and difference of women's experiences. This tension exists particularly for domestic violence theory because feminists have respected the need to move away from generalisation or homogenisation of women's experiences, but at the same time they have witnessed little or no shift in statistics that reflect domestic violence against women, or, as Phillips reports, are 'often struck by the relentless repetition of many aspects of women's lives' and a 'relentless repetition of men's many forms of violent acts against women' (2008, p. 58). The question remains, how can the ideas of post-structuralist thinking with its complexities of oppression or disadvantage situated in subjectivity and discourse sit alongside ideas of structural oppression? In order to address some of these questions, it is important to examine in some depth the relationships and tensions between feminism and post-structuralist theorising, including how feminist scholars have responded to and attempted to reconcile these tensions in the context of domestic violence.

### *The post-structuralist evolution in feminist theorising*

In the 1980s and 90s, feminism began to experience a rift from within. Feminists started to challenge the notion that women are a unified and uniform group in which all women are similarly affected by patriarchy. The basis of this claim was the notion that, while most women experience the effects of a patriarchal system, they do so in different ways and to various degrees; that gender oppression is mediated by class position, poverty, race, disability, and so forth. Susan Bordo succinctly conveys the essence of this point:

In 1987, I heard a feminist historian claim that there were absolutely no common areas of experience between the wife of a plantation owner in the pre-Civil War South and the female slaves her husband owned. Gender, she argued, is so thoroughly fragmented by race, class, historical particularity, and individual difference as to be useless as an analytical category. The 'bonds of womanhood,' she insisted, are a feminist fantasy, born out of the ethnocentrism of white, middle-class academics.

(1993, p. 215)

Black and lesbian feminists were dominant in this debate, claiming that they had been excluded and misrepresented by mainstream – white, middle-class and heterosexual – feminist accounts of women (see for example the work of bell hooks 1981, 1984, and Adrienne Rich 1980). As well as raising questions about women as a homogenous group, the interrogation and critique of the notion of 'women's oppression' as an experience shared by all women was being questioned within feminism. The fact that some women gain from the exploitation of other women illustrates this point. It was also argued that the term 'women's oppression' can function in a *totalising* way to efface the many different and specific forms of women's oppression brought about not only by gender but by race, class, sexuality, disability and so on.

Likewise, patriarchy as a totalising and all-encompassing source of women's oppression was also exposed and debunked, or at the very least viewed as involving qualitatively different relations within different societies and subject to historical changes (Stabile, 1995). Some feminists also argued that continual reference to patriarchy reinforces the divisions between women and men, affirming the essentialist view that women are by nature biologically and inherently different to men; a position that feminists have long rejected and fought against.

It was against this backdrop that postmodernism began to make its way into feminist theorising. The term postmodernism is commonly used to identify a historical epoch, the condition of post-industrial, post-Fordist or post-capitalist society. Central to the postmodernist understanding of society is the belief that the 'grand' or totalising principles of modernity, such as rationality, progress, humanity and justice, have no organic or singular reality. Hence, systems such as patriarchy are viewed as having little or no relevance to theorising the oppression of women (Stabile, 1995). Even feminist theory itself is characterised as having no universal basis or claim to reality and at best can produce only partial, local and historically specific insights (Bellwoar, 2005). In fact, the only invocation to reality permitted in postmodernism is that which is constructed within and by language. This is where post-structuralist critiques of language, subjectivity and representation have consolidated the postmodern rejection of a universal truth or a common experience of oppression (Stabile, 1995). As Stabile points out, 'where post-structuralism refers to theory, postmodernism is the practice. In other words, where poststructuralists criticized the foundations of modernism, postmodernists read these critiques as mandates for rejecting foundations altogether' (1995, p. 89). As Waugh states:

Post-modernism situates itself epistemologically at the point where the epistemic subject characterized in terms of historical experience, interiority, and consciousness has given way to the 'decentred' subject identified through the public, impersonal signifying practices of other similarly 'decentred' subjects ... There is only a system of linguistic structures, a textual construction, a play of differences in the Derridean sense.

(1989, p. 7)

The postmodern rejection of totalising realities and structures of oppression in favour of multiple realities constituted within language has been heavily criticised by some feminist theorists, particularly Marxist and radical feminists. Much of this criticism has stemmed from debates about the origins and purpose of feminist theorising. Unlike post-structuralism, the origins of contemporary feminist theorising were predicated on embracing rather than rejecting the notion of a system of oppression, in particular the system of male domination or 'patriarchy'. Feminist theory was, and arguably still is, considerably invested in emphasising the ways that patriarchy as a totalising reality affects the lives of all women. Hence, the purpose of feminism has been avowedly intellectual and political: to raise women's consciousness of their oppression and to promote social change along the lines of gender through the collective actions of women as a unified and distinct group (Stabile, 1995). According to Gray and Boddy (2010), postmodern feminism's abstract theorising about difference and diversity, identity and recognition, even if always a part of feminist discourse, has brought about the ascendance of academic feminism and the disappearance of feminist political action. For the most part, they suggest, 'feminism has lost its political edge in the quagmire of postmodern identity politics' (Gray & Boddy, 2010, p. 385).

Despite these concerns and criticisms of the postmodern turn in feminist theorising in recent decades, many feminists have embraced postmodernism and have integrated post-structuralist insights into their work. For example, some feminists have argued that post-structuralism contributes to basic feminist insights such as 'the personal is political' by providing the tools to deconstruct the public–private dichotomy, which supports women's oppression (Rabine, 1988; Flax, 1990). Foucault's theory about localised relations of power edifies the feminist view that the ostensibly personal and private relationships between women and men are relations of power (Flax, 1990), and some feminists are also of the view that post-structuralism has significant continuities with feminism in its discussion of dominant and subjugated discourses (Foucault, 1980). Post-structuralism has also extended earlier criticisms made by black and lesbian feminists that not all women share a common identity or experience through its argument that no 'reality' exists outside of language that represents women's common experience (Flax, 1990).

The post-structuralist turn in feminist theorising has also progressed feminism's fight against biological determinism by deconstructing the notion of biological sex itself. The sex–gender distinction, originally identified by Simone de Beauvoir in her landmark work *The Second Sex* (1973), was a breakthrough in feminism's fight against the view that women are biologically different to men. For de Beauvoir, sex may be a biological fact – that is, the invariant, anatomically distinct aspects of the female body – but gender is a social construct; that is, the cultural meanings given to the female body (Butler, 1986). Hence, according to de Beauvoir, 'one is not born, but rather becomes a woman' (1973, p. 267). However, post-structuralist feminists argue that the sex–gender distinction implies that sex is intrinsic to the body, and that the body or sex exists independently of and prior to gender (Butler, 1990). The sex–gender distinction, therefore, is the last stronghold of patriarchy because to accept the notion of sex and all the assumptions that it entails as a biological given is to continue to be caught up in notions of biological determinism. According to post-structuralist feminists like Judith Butler, there is no such thing as a purely biological 'body' or 'sex' as these constructs are already culturally shaped and interpreted. This means that the sexed body is not a fixed biological or natural given (as suggested in the work of de Beauvoir), but is as culturally constructed as gender.

Hence, while post-structuralism has produced a number of tensions in feminist theorising over the last thirty years or so, there is little doubt that it has revolutionised feminist thinking in relation to questions of gender, subjectivity, agency, universalism and biological determinism. This broader evolution in feminist theory has also been reflected in how feminists view violence against women in the home and this has led some feminists to challenge more traditional understandings of patriarchy, women's experience, gender and oppression in theorising domestic violence.

## Feminism and post-structuralism in theorising domestic violence: areas of contention and convergence

As we outlined at the beginning of this chapter, the most significant contribution of feminism to domestic violence theory has been to 'conceptualise it as a problem of men's violence in the context of gendered social power relations in terms of male dominance and female subordination' (Itzin, 2000, p. 360). Historically, feminists have argued that domestic and other forms of violence against women are the outcome of patriarchal structures that act to subordinate and oppress women. These include structural barriers to education and economic independence as well as a variety of subtle methods of controlling women, transmitted through cultural practices and forms such as sexist media representations of women and girls.

Hence, feminist theorising in domestic violence has been hitherto dominated by structuralist and gender-based theories highlighting patriarchy and male power over women. Post-structuralist ideas, on the other hand, have been and remain far less prevalent or well-developed in feminist explanations of domestic violence. That is, very few feminists have developed and/or applied post-structuralist theories in the context of domestic violence. Where this has occurred, analyses have tended to focus on the nexus between post-structuralism and feminism in research and practice contexts such as social work, where domestic violence is only one of many social concerns being addressed (e.g. Featherstone & Fawcett, 1995; Wendt & Boylan, 2008; Morley & Macfarlane, 2012).

The development of intersectional theory is, arguably, another area in which feminists have drawn on postmodern theory in the context of domestic violence (Sokoloff & Dupont, 2005). As Morley and Macfarlane state: 'Intersectionality theory, developed largely by black feminist social scientists, provides an instructive example of how postmodern thinking can be used to extend the emancipatory goals of feminism' (2012, p. 692). Feminist intersectional scholarship, they suggest, conceptualises social inequalities as power relationships constructed in specific historical and geographical contexts, creating fluid, shifting group relations that continue through time and space, but that are constructed differently in diverse contexts and communities (Morley & Macfarlane, 2012). In the context of domestic violence, intersectional theory has emphasised the need to move away from a generalisation or homogenisation of women's experiences of violence and oppression, to an understanding of how the diversity amongst women as a group will engender different experiences, contexts and responses to violence. For example, Richie makes the point that poor women and women from non-dominant cultural backgrounds are 'most likely to be in both dangerous intimate relationships and dangerous social positions' (2000, cited in Sokoloff & Dupont, 2005, p. 41). In theorising men's violence towards women in refugee communities, Pease and Rees (2008) are concerned with how domestic violence is shaped by other forms of oppression that cut across gender divisions, particularly during settlement for newly arrived refugees. They propose that an intersectional analysis will assist in identifying both similarities and differences in men's violence against women in diverse cultures and communities. In a similar vein, Bograd (1999) states that, while all women are vulnerable to abuse, an abused woman may judge herself and be judged by others differently if she is white or black, poor or wealthy, heterosexual or lesbian.

In this way, intersectionality has illuminated the ways that racism, poverty and heterosexual dominance present particular barriers for women and their children, which result in them living in unsafe situations. Such barriers have their own cultural specificity, including loyalty to one's partner, family and culture. What such loyalty means in each individual context will also be different. As Bograd suggests: 'Individuals may have internalized ideologies antithetical to disclosure of violence' (1999, p. 281). For example, our own research found that Liberian women in South Australia were fearful about engaging the police in situations of domestic violence as they were concerned that this would undermine their partners' opportunities for education and employment, which may have a negative impact on their capacity to provide for their families. Women's fears were also framed by their experiences of war and persecution in Liberia where men were suddenly taken from their families and imprisoned for prolonged periods of time, leaving women and children to fend for themselves (Zannettino, 2012).

While it has been suggested that the theory of intersectionality is an example of postmodern theorising in the context of domestic violence, we contend that this theory is epistemologically different to post-structuralist theorising. That is, intersectional theory still invokes structuralist analyses and the power and oppression ideologies of traditional feminist accounts of domestic violence but with attention to how 'gender inequality ... is modified by its intersection with other systems of power and oppression' (Bograd, 1999, p. 277). Laing and Humphreys (2013, p. 21) state that an intersectional approach to domestic violence enables consideration of the complex ways in which women's multiple social (dis)locations intersect to shape their experiences of victimisation and their opportunities to achieve safety and autonomy. Post-structuralist theorising, on the other hand, views gender relations between men and women as being constituted in language and discourse rather than multiple systems of domination such as patriarchy and other systems of power and oppression. Hence, gender inequalities are seen as the product of dominant discourses that construct hegemonic masculinities and submissive femininities. In this way, gender is contested, fluid, unstable and open to change.

If we view intersectional analyses as epistemologically different to post-structuralist analyses, we are left with very few examples of feminist appropriations of post-structuralist theory in the context of domestic violence. One explanation for this deficit is that feminists writing and working in the area of domestic violence have been blocked by the difficulties presented for feminism by post-structuralist theory (Weedon, 1997). While feminists have successfully applied post-structuralist insights in a range of contexts such as education (Yates, 1994; St Pierre, 2000), youth and popular culture (McRobbie, 1994; Walkerdine, 1997) and sport (Azzarito, Solmon & Harrison, 2006), this has been more difficult in domestic violence, which has had such a heavy investment in the structural and gendered power arguments of modernist feminism.

The epistemological shift from universal, macro analyses of structures and metanarratives such as patriarchy to a postmodern emphasis on language, discourse and difference is particularly problematic for feminists working in the area of domestic violence (Damant et al., 2008). The idea that power is inscribed within discourse, rather than exclusively residing in social structure, has been viewed by some feminists as undermining the very core of feminist responses to domestic violence, which have clearly advocated the need for a fundamental change in the patriarchal structure of society in order to reduce violence against women in the home. In this way, feminism has emphasised the importance of changes in the social relations of dominance and subordination 'as necessary preconditions for any change in the incidences of wife abuse' (Warters, 1992, p. 9). However, in post-structuralist analyses, because power is constituted through discourse, patriarchy itself is seen as changeable, fluid and multi-faceted. At the same time, dominant discourses and homogenous categories of 'woman' and 'victim' have also been challenged (Wendt & Boylan, 2008). For example, in applying post-structuralist ideas to her study of rural women experiencing domestic violence, Wendt suggests that she was provided with the opportunity to explore women's identities as not fixed but open, shifting and fluid, according to available discourses. And recognising the power relations constituted within discourses encouraged the opening up of multiple and diverse ways of knowing that shape rural women's ways of understanding their experiences (Wendt & Boylan, 2008). Similarly, Featherstone and Trinder (1997) argue that feminist post-structuralist understandings of domestic violence help us understand the complexities of family situations and family processes. They argue this complexity can be understood by exploring the range of subject positions that women engage with and which shift in different contexts, and this investment in some discourses and not in others allows for rich explanations of domestic violence.

The problems that post-structuralist theory poses for feminism and the concomitant lack of post-structuralist analyses in feminist accounts of domestic violence beg the question: *why use post-structuralist theory to inform and develop our feminist analyses of domestic violence?* There are two core reasons why we draw on post-structuralist theory in this book. The first relates to the central aim of the book, which is to re-examine gender in diverse contexts of domestic violence. Structural accounts of domestic violence, which focus on patriarchy in maintaining oppressive power relations between men and women, view gender as static and unchangeable and therefore beyond contestation. Intersectional theory, while demonstrating the ways that gender is changed by its intersection with race, class, sexual orientation and so forth, does not put gender at the forefront of its analyses. As Bograd notes, 'intersectionality suggests that no dimension, such as gender inequality, is privileged as an explanatory construct of domestic violence' (1999, p. 277). Post-structuralist theory, on the other hand, offers a way forward in disrupting the very integrity and concept of gender itself. We contend that a greater understanding of how gender is discursively constructed across different communities of women and the particular subject positions that are offered and taken up will advance feminist understandings of domestic violence.

The second reason for drawing on post-structuralist theory in this book pertains to the growing contestation in recent years between post-structuralist perspectives and a renewed interest in modernist or structuralist understandings of patriarchy and gender oppression in theorising about domestic violence (Pease, 2012). What is clear is that a post-structuralist feminist understanding of domestic violence is still largely underdeveloped, and as a consequence current contestations between modernist and postmodernist understandings of the problem are built on very thin and shaky ground indeed. Moreover, little has been done to show how feminism and post-structuralist insights, while in tension with each other, can still be synthesised to improve theoretical conceptualisations of gender and patriarchy – constructs that continue to preoccupy feminists in developing knowledge about domestic violence. Hence, we view this book as filling the current void in the development of post-structuralist feminist understandings of domestic violence. In demonstrating the application of feminist post-structuralist theory to specific communities and contexts of domestic violence, we hope to strengthen the foundations upon which current debates about feminist theory, gender and domestic violence are being waged.

## Feminist theory and re-examining the role of gender in domestic violence: our intention and method

The diversity of feminist theorising, particularly in relation to its post-structuralist renderings, has meant that feminism itself has often been splintered by the opposing positions of its own proponents. While some feminists view feminism's diversity and contention as weakening the feminist movement (see e.g. Gray & Boddy, 2010), we view it as providing the rigour necessary for continued reflexivity and development. As we stated in Chapter 1, we attempt to move beyond the stalemate created by the tensions between modernist and postmodern feminism by viewing these tensions as operating on a continuum of theory rather than as 'either/or' propositions. We believe that such a position has far greater potential to both transform and enrich feminist theory and keep gender at the forefront in explanations of domestic violence.

Furthermore, we argue that it is the antagonism at the edges of feminism rather than within that poses the greatest threat to its power to address women's abuse and oppression. Much of this antagonism stems from the question of whether domestic violence is a gendered issue, with women as the primary targets of male violence. According to DeKeseredy and Dragiewicz (2007), we still live in a climate characterised by vitriolic attacks on feminist scholarship, practice and activism intended to secure women's basic human rights. Much of this attack, they suggest, comes from the work of Donald Dutton (2006) and other proponents of 'gender symmetry' (see for example Straus, 2006), which propounds that women are just as violent as men. It is not our intention in this book to engage in this debate – many scholars have already successfully argued against 'gender symmetry' in domestic violence (see for example, DeKeseredy & Schwartz, 2003; Dobash & Dobash, 2004; DeKeseredy & Dragiewicz, 2007) – and both feminist and other research has verified that domestic violence is a gendered issue in which women are primarily victims and men primarily perpetrators.

Our intention in this book is to re-examine the role of gender in domestic violence by exposing the complexities and nuances of gender positioning, and how gender interacts with multiple social conditions, processes and discourses in the lives of diverse communities of women. In re-examining gender in the context of domestic violence we take a post-structuralist approach. We do this because post-structuralist theory offers a way forward in disrupting and interrogating the very integrity and concept of gender itself. As Weedon states:

> We can use categories such as 'gender', 'race' and 'class' in social and cultural analysis but on the assumption that their meaning is plural, historically and socially specific. The effects of using such categories will depend on both how they are defined and on the social context in which they are used.
>
> (1997, p. 178)

Our re-examination of gender in the context of domestic violence therefore is situated in the belief that gender is a social construct that is used to organise social life, but this organisation is contested terrain and this contestation is intensified by differences between women as well as the dynamics and effects of abuse.

However, we use a post-structuralist approach with caution for two main reasons. First, as we asserted in Chapter 1, we reject the purist post-structuralist notion that biological sex is as socially constructed as gender in the context of domestic violence because we view the anatomical and biological differences between men and women as inevitably and unavoidably bound up in various acts of violence. For example, the gravity of a man's threat of physical abuse or rape stems from his inherent physical and anatomical capacity to carry out such a threat, and women experience particular health problems resulting from domestic violence. Second, as we said in Chapter 1, while we believe that post-structuralism has much to offer feminist analyses in its exploration of different groups of women and their differentiated experiences of gender relations in specific contexts, the focus on 'difference' must never come at the expense of understanding the broader implications of gender and the patterns of gender disadvantage that extend across different social groups.

To re-examine gender in the context of domestic violence, we aim to identify, examine and understand how women from diverse backgrounds speak of and do gender in their experiences of domestic violence. We draw on two concepts central to post-structuralist theory in our attempts to expose the complexities and nuances of gender positioning in domestic violence: discourse and subjectivity. These tools enable us to interpret how meanings of gender are generated through different local contexts, constituted by criss-crossing discourses through which gender and gender practices acquire significance. Discourse is a broad concept referring to a way of constituting meaning that is specific to particular groups, cultures and historical periods and is always changing. Discourses are multiple and offer competing ways of giving meaning to the world (Gavey, 1989). Post-structuralist theorists argue that discourses offer subject positions for individuals to take up and in this way they constitute subjectivity.

Subjectivity refers to the conscious and unconscious thoughts and emotions of the individual, her sense of self and how she understands her relationship to the world (Weedon, 1997). Using the concept of positioning, feminists examine how women position themselves in relation to various discourses (Gavey, 1989; St Pierre, 2000). For example, we can examine how women can identify with and conform to a range of discursive constructions of gender in the context of domestic violence, and how they take up particular subject positions of femininity. Or similarly, we can interpret through the women's stories how men may identify with and take up particular subject positions of masculinity. Hence, subjectivity is a matrix of subject positions, which may have dominance, or be inconsistent or contradictory. We use this understanding of subjectivity as constituted in discourse to inform our analyses of how different communities of women live, think and 'do' gender in the context of domestic violence.

At the same time, however, we also consider how the adoption of particular subject positions has material and lived consequences for women. For example, a mother may be discursively positioned to stay in an abusive relationship for the sake of her children but such a 'subject position' has real and tangible consequences for her and her children and these consequences need to be acknowledged and articulated. In addition, we also recognise that certain discourses can gain or lose power in positioning women in domestic violence because of women's various social and cultural circumstances. For example, a refugee woman may not have access to human rights discourses pertaining to rape in marriage and therefore may be positioned in ways that compel her to view sex as her duty to her husband whether or not she desires or consents to this act.

Throughout the book, we use these post-structuralist tools to analyse women's stories of domestic violence to illuminate what gender means in a variety of contexts. We will use these tools to push ourselves as feminist scholars to expose how the complexities and nuances of gendered positioning help explain domestic violence. Post-structuralism enables us as feminists to advance our theoretical arguments of gender mattering in domestic violence (Anderson, 2005).

## References

Abbott, P., Wallace, C. & Tyler, M. (2005) *An Introduction to Sociology: Feminist Perspectives*, Routledge, London.

Anderson, K. (2005) Theorising gender in intimate partner violence research. *Sex Roles*, 52(11/12), pp. 853–65.

Azzarito, L., Solmon, M.A. & Harrison, L. (2006) '… If I had a choice, I would …': a feminist poststructuralist perspective on girls in physical education. *Research Quarterly for Exercise and Sport*, 77(2), pp. 222–39.

de Beauvoir, S. (1973) *The Second Sex*, Vintage, New York.

Bellwoar, H. (2005) Orienting, disorienting, and reorienting: multiple perspectives on poststructuralist feminist pedagogies. *NWSA Journal*, 17(3), pp. 189–94.

Bograd, M. (1988) Feminist perspectives on wife abuse: an introduction. In K. Yllo & M. Bograd (Eds) *Feminist Perspectives on Wife Abuse*, Sage, London, pp. 11–26.

Bograd, M. (1999) Strengthening domestic violence theories: intersections of race, class, sexual orientation and gender. *Journal of Marital and Family Therapy*, 25(3), pp. 275–89.

Bordo, S. (1993) *Unbearable Weight: Feminism, Western Culture, and the Body*, University of California Press, Berkeley, CA.

Butler, J. (1986) Sex and gender in Beauvoir's *Second Sex*. *Yale French Studies*, 72, p. 35.

Butler, J. (1990) *Gender Trouble: Feminism and the Subversion of Identity*, Routledge, London.

Damant, D., Lapierre, S., Kouraga, A., Fortin, A., Hamelin-Brabant, L., Lavergne, C. & Lessard, G. (2008) Taking child abuse and mothering into account: intersection feminism as an alternative for the study of domestic violence. *Affilia: Journal of Women and Social Work*, 23(2), pp. 123–33.

DeKeseredy, W. (2011) Feminist contributions to understanding woman abuse: myths, controversies, and realities. *Aggression and Violent Behavior*, 16, pp. 297–302.

DeKeseredy, W.S. & Dragiewicz, M. (2007) Understanding the complexities of feminist perspectives on woman abuse: a commentary on Donald G. Dutton's *Rethinking Domestic Violence*. *Violence Against Women*, 13(8), pp. 874–84.

DeKeseredy, W.S. & Schwartz, M.D. (2003) Backlash and whiplash: a critique of Statistics Canada's 1999 General Social Survey on victimization. *Online Journal of Justice Studies*, http://ojjs.icaap.org/ (accessed August 2013).

Dobash, R. & Dobash, R. (1980) *Violence Against Wives: A Case Against the Patriarchy*, Open Books, London.

Dobash, R.P. & Dobash, R.E. (2004) Women's violence to men in intimate relationships: working on a puzzle. *British Journal of Criminology*, 44, pp. 324–49.

Dutton, D.G. (2006) *Rethinking Domestic Violence*, University of British Columbia Press, Vancouver, Canada.

Evans, S. (2005) Beyond gender: class, poverty and domestic violence. *Australian Social Work*, 58(1), pp. 36–43.

Featherstone, B. & Fawcett, B. (1995) Oh no! Not more 'isms': feminism, postmodernism, poststructuralism and social work education. *Social Work Education*, 14(3), pp. 25–43.

Featherstone, B. & Trinder, L. (1997) Familiar subjects? Domestic violence and child welfare. *Child and Family Social Work*, 2, pp. 147–59.

Fisher, B.S. & Zink, T. (2007) Older women living with intimate partner violence. *Ageing Health*, 3(2), pp. 257–69.

Flax, J. (1990) *Thinking Fragments: Psychoanalysis, Feminism and Postmodernism in the Contemporary West*, University of California Press, Berkeley, CA.

Foucault, M. (1980) *Power/Knowledge: Selected Interviews and Other Writings, 1972–1977*, Pantheon, New York.

Gavey, N. (1989) Feminist poststructuralism and discourse analysis: contributions to feminist psychology. *Psychology of Women Quarterly*, 13, pp. 459–75.

Glover-Graf, N.M. & Reed, B.J. (2006) Abuse against women with disabilities. *Rehabilitation Research, Policy, and Education*, pp. 43–56.

Goodman, L., Smyth, K., Borges, A., & Singer, R. (2009) When crises collide: how intimate partner violence and poverty intersect to shape women's mental health and coping? *Trauma, Violence & Abuse*, 10, pp. 306–29.

Gray, M. & Boddy, J. (2010) Making sense of the waves: wipeout or still riding high? *Affilia: Journal of Women and Social Work*, 25(4), pp. 368–89.

Hague, G., Thiara, R. & Mullender, A. (2011) Disabled women and domestic violence: making the links, a national UK study. *Psychiatry, Psychology and Law*, 18(1), pp. 117–36.

Hanmer, J. (2000) Domestic violence and gender relations: contexts and connections. In J. Hanmer & C. Itzin (Eds) *Home Truths about Domestic Violence: Feminist Influences on Policy and Practice, a Reader*, Routledge, London, pp. 9–23.

Hanmer, J. & Itzin, C. (Eds) (2000) *Home Truths about Domestic Violence: Feminist Influences on Policy and Practice, a Reader*, Routledge, London.

hooks, b. (1981) *Ain't I a Woman: Black Women and Feminism*, South End Press, Boston, MA.

hooks, b. (1984) *Feminist Theory: From Margin to Center*, South End Press, Boston, MA.

Hopkins, A. & McGregor, H. (1991) *Working for Change: The Movement against Domestic Violence*, Allen & Unwin, North Sydney.

Horsfall, J. (1991) *The Presence of the Past: Male Violence in the Family*, Allen & Unwin, North Sydney.

Hunnicutt, G. (2009) Varieties of patriarchy and violence against women: resurrecting 'patriarchy' as a theoretical tool. *Violence Against Women*, 15(5), pp. 553–73.

Itzin, C. (2000) Gendering domestic violence: the influence of feminism on policy and practice. In J. Hanmer & C. Itzin (Eds) *Home Truths about Domestic Violence: Feminist Influences on Policy and Practice, a Reader*, Routledge, London, pp. 356–80.

Kelly, L. & Radford, J. (1996) 'Nothing really happened': the invalidation of women's experiences of sexual violence. In M. Hester, L. Kelly & J. Radford (Eds) *Women, Violence and Male Power: Feminist Activism, Research and Practice*, Open University Press, Buckingham, pp. 19–33.

Laing, L. & Humphreys, C. with Cavanagh, K. (2013) *Social Work & Domestic Violence: Developing Critical and Reflective Practice*, Sage, London.

Martino, S.C., Collins, R.L., & Ellickson, P. (2005) Cross-lagged relationships between substance use and intimate partner violence among a sample of young adult women. *Journal of Studies on Alcohol*, pp. 139–48.

Mason, G. (2002) *The Spectacle of Violence: Homophobia, gender and knowledge*, Routledge, London.

McClennen, J. (2005) Domestic violence between same gender partners: recent findings and future research. *Journal of Interpersonal Violence*, 20(2), pp. 149–54.

McHugh, M. (2005) Understanding gender and intimate partner abuse. *Sex Roles*, 52(11/12), pp. 717–24.

McPhail, B., Busch, N., Kulkarni, S. & Rice, G. (2009) An integrative feminist model: the evolving feminist perspective on intimate partner violence. *Violence Against Women*, 13(8), pp. 817–41.

McRobbie, A. (1994) *Postmodernism and Popular Culture*, Routledge, London.

Morley, C. & Macfarlane, S. (2012) The nexus between feminism and postmodernism: still a central concern for critical social work. *British Journal of Social Work*, 42, pp. 687–705.

Nelson, G., Heise, L., Kiss, L., Schraiber, L.B., Watts, C., & Zimmerman, C. (2012) Gender-based violence and socioeconomic inequalities: Does living in more deprived neighbourhoods increase women's risk of intimate partner violence? *Social Science & Medicine*, 74(8), pp. 1172–94.

Nixon, J. (2009) Defining the issue: the intersection of domestic abuse and disability. *Social Policy & Society*, 8(4), pp. 475–85.

Pan, A., Daley, S., Rivera, L.M., Williams, K., Lingle, D. & Reznik, V. (2006) Understanding the role of culture in domestic violence: The Ahimsa project for safe families. *Journal of Immigrant and Minority Health*, 8(1), pp. 35–43.

Pease, B. (2012) Gender and masculinity in violence prevention policies and intervention programs. Paper presented at the Preventing and Responding to Violence Against Women: Issues, Challenges and Best Practice Symposium, Adelaide, 15 June.

Pease, B. & Rees, S. (2008) Theorising men's violence towards women in refugee families: towards an intersectional feminist framework. *Just Policy*, 47, pp. 39–45.

Phillips, R. (2008) Feminism, policy and women's safety during Australia's 'war on terror'. *Feminist Review*, 89, pp. 57–72.

Rabine, L.W. (1988) A feminist politics of non-identity. *Feminist Studies*, 14(1), pp. 11–31.

Radford, J., Kelly, L. & Hester, M. (1996) Introduction. In M. Hester, L. Kelly & J. Radford (Eds) *Women, Violence and Male Power: Feminist Activism, Research and Practice*, Open University Press, Buckingham, pp. 1–16.

Radford, J. & Stanko, E. (1996) Violence against women and children: the contradictions of crime control under patriarchy. In M. Hester, L. Kelly & J. Radford (Eds) *Women, Violence and Male Power: Feminist Activism, Research and Practice*, Open University Press, Buckingham, pp. 65–80.

Rich, A. (1980) Compulsory heterosexualilty and lesbian existence. In *Blood, Bread, and Poetry*, Norton Paperback, New York.

Schneider, E. (1994) The violence of privacy. In M. Albertson Fineman & R. Mykitiuk (Eds) *The Public Nature of Private Violence: The Discovery of Domestic Abuse*, Routledge, New York, pp. 36–58.

Seelau, S. (2005) Gender-role stereotypes and perceptions of heterosexual, gay and lesbian domestic violence. *Journal of Family Violence*, 20(6), pp. 363–71.

Sharma, A. (2001) Healing the wounds of domestic abuse: Improving the effectiveness of feminist therapeutic interventions with immigrant and racially visible women who have been abused. *Violence Against Women*, 7(12), pp. 1405–28.

Sokoloff, N.J. & Dupont, I. (2005) Domestic violence at the intersections of race, class, and gender: challenges and contributions to understanding violence against marginalized women in diverse communities. *Violence Against Women*, 11(1), pp. 38–64.

Stabile, C.A. (1995) Postmodernism, feminism, and Marx: notes from the abyss. *Monthly Review*, 47(3), p. 89–107.

St Pierre, E.A. (2000) Poststructural feminism in education: an overview. *Qualitative Studies in Education*, 13(5), pp. 477–515.

Straus, M.A. (2006) Future research on gender symmetry in physical assaults on partners. *Violence Against Women*, 12, pp. 1086–97.

Swigonski, M. & Raheim, S. (2011) Feminist contributions to understanding women's lives and the social environment. *Affilia: Journal of Women and Social Work*, 26(1), pp. 10–21.

Taft, A.J., Watson, L.F. & Lee, C. (2004) Violence against young Australian women and associated reproductive events: a cross-sectional analysis. *Australian and New Zealand Journal of Public Health*, 28(4), pp. 324–9.

Taylor, R. & Jasinski, J. (2011) Femicide and the feminist perspective. *Homicide Studies*, 15(4), pp. 341–62.

Walby, S. (1990) *Theorizing Patriarchy*, Blackwell, Oxford.

Walkerdine, V. (1997) *Daddy's Girl: Young Girls and Popular Culture*, Macmillan, London.

Warters, W. (1992) The social construction of domestic violence and the implications for 'treatment' for men who batter. *Men's Studies Review*, 8(2), pp. 7–16.

Waugh, P. (1989) *Feminine Fictions: Revisiting the Postmodern*, Routledge, London.

Weedon, C. (1997) *Feminist Practice and Poststructuralist Theory*, 2nd edition, Blackwell, Malden, MA.

Wendt, S. (2009) *Domestic Violence in Rural Australia*, Federation Press, Sydney.

Wendt, S. & Boylan, J. (2008) Feminist social work research engaging with poststructural ideas. *International Social Work*, 51(5), pp. 599–609.

Winstok, Z. (2011) The paradigmatic cleavage on gender differences in partner violence perpetration and victimization. *Aggression and Violent Behavior*, 16, pp. 303–11.

Yates, L. (1994) Feminist pedagogy meets critical pedagogy meets poststructuralism. *British Journal of Sociology of Education*, 15(3), pp. 429–37.

Zajdow, G. (2007) The gender order. In J. Germov & M. Poole (Eds) *Public Sociology*, Allen & Unwin, NSW, Australia, pp. 239–58.

Zannettino, L. (2012) '… There is no war here; it is only the relationship that makes us scared': factors having an impact on domestic violence in Liberian refugee communities in South Australia. *Violence Against Women*, 18(7), pp. 807–28.

Zink, T., Regan, S., Jacobson, C.J. & Pabst, S. (2003) Cohort, period, and aging effects. *Violence Against Women*, 9(12), pp. 1429–41.

# 3    Mothers

I told my husband, I say you kill your wife for a long time already, I die already, but you still see me. It's not me, it might look like a spirit but that's come from my kids, it made me alive to look after the kids. I am alive because of my kids, not alive because of you.

(Mia, Cambodian woman, 3 children, 2013)

## Introduction

In this chapter we explore the unique factors that impact on women as mothers in situations of domestic violence. Women with children are three times more likely to be subjected to domestic violence than childless women, and the risk of domestic violence is higher for women during pregnancy and following birth (Buchanan, Power & Verity, 2013). Indirect costs of pain, fear and suffering incurred by women and their children can be long-lasting and devastating including physical, developmental, psychological and behavioural effects, and the impact of trauma and developmental regression (Bromfield et al., 2010).

We recognise that not all women are mothers and women without children do experience domestic violence. However, we could not ignore discourses of motherhood in a book that celebrates women's diversity and aims to examine how gender is constructed in experiences of domestic violence. Discourses define what it means to be a woman or a man and provide a range of gender-appropriate subject positions (Weedon, 1999), and discourses of motherhood are particularly powerful. They can be found in societies across the world, whereby cultural messages construct women as designed to be mothers, and women who are not mothers as unhappy and unfulfilled (Bradley, 2013; Miller, 2007). Within discourses of motherhood, the mother–child dynamic is set up as the ultimate paradigm of natural caring relationships and so notions of woman and mother overlap in a way that leads to dominant constructions of woman that are dependent on the concept of mother (McNay, 1992). Discourses of motherhood are so gendered and deeply embedded in everyday life that they can become invisible through the arrangements of work and family life. Or, as Lorber (2010, p. 245) states, motherhood is a gendered dance and through the dance we are gendered.

We argue that discourses of motherhood are so universally pervasive in women's lives that we needed a chapter on mothers' unique experiences of domestic violence because these discourses shape gendered subject positions and power relations in such contexts. Throughout our years of interviewing women about their experiences of domestic violence, we have found conversations about children's wellbeing and being a mother do not sit outside of domestic violence but are very much intertwined within it. Women are active meaning makers, and so will and do express their meanings through their personal and social realities of being a mum (Buchbinder, 2004). In addition, for women who are not mothers, discourses of motherhood do not disappear; they surround all women and influence subjectivities:

> My outlet was my children. I tried to fulfil my roles as wife and mother and did my house duties the best I could. I was happy to help the kids and be involved with them because that was all I had.
>
> (Cate, 2 children, 1999)

> I felt that pressure of being in a relationship … it is that whole generational thing where your grandmother wants you to get married and your mother is wondering whether you were going to get married. It felt like I was going to be left on the shelf. I wanted to do the right thing and get married and have kids because if you have kids and marriage there are networks for that.
>
> (Donna, no children, 2002)

> Somebody said to me once, 'you're so blessed, your sons are blah, blah, blah'. And then they said 'Nothing to do with being blessed, you've worked hard'. And I thought, that's true, it has been hard at times, but very rewarding … I've said to my sons, 'You make decisions as a parent, at the time, you have to make a decision, what is right at the time.' I always say, despite my personal relationships, I was dedicated and committed to making sure my sons had what they needed, to have good lives.
>
> (Lyn, 4 children, 2013)

Mothering can be defined as a socially constructed set of activities and relationships involved in nurturing and caring for people (Arendell, 2000, p. 1192). It is women who do the work of mothering and motherhood is entwined with notions of femininity, all symbolically laden with relational devotion. Even though not all women are mothers, womanhood and motherhood are so often treated as synonymous identities; mothering is universally associated with women (Arendell, 2000). Arendell (2000) points out that most political and social debates like abortion, women's employment, welfare reform and reproductive technologies, have mothering at their core. Debates such as these show societal expectations of women and womanhood and position childhood and arguments about what children's needs are and whether or not they are being met with mothering. We argue that domestic violence does the same. In this chapter we explore discourses of mothering and the associated subject positions and how they shape women's experiences of domestic violence.

Even though mothering discourses will feature throughout the book, we felt we needed a chapter on mothering because not only do women experience the oppressive large-scale social relations that come from discourses around mothering, but experience oppressive micro-relations with intimate partners (mostly men) in their lives whereby their role of mother can be targeted and abused (Semaan, Jasinski & Bubriski-McKenzie, 2013).

## Domestic violence and mothering

Despite feminist practitioners, academics and writers pointing out that domestic violence is an everyday reality that affects many women's experiences of mothering; that is, domestic violence has profound and far-reaching effects on women's feelings and behaviour towards their children, as well as on their sense of identity as mothers and as women, the literature on the issue of mothering in the context of domestic violence has been limited (Lapierre, 2010a). Some studies have focused on the strengths and capabilities of women parenting in domestic violence, arguing that we should not assume that being a victim automatically diminishes parenting ability, whereas other studies report mother–child relationships are characterised by insecurity, disturbed bonding, negative emotions, and lack of caring and emotional responsiveness (Buchbinder, 2004; Casanueva et al., 2008). The research into women's mothering in domestic violence raises many questions regarding the extent to which women as victims have a duty and responsibility as parents to protect their children and the consequences of failing to do so (Buchbinder, 2004).

The quality of maternal parenting has been raised as an important factor in studies about how children are affected by domestic violence and debate has fallen into arguments about 'adequate or not' mothering (Lapierre, 2010a). This debate is quite visible in child protection sectors. For example, Humphreys and Absler's (2011) study found striking commonalities in how domestic violence was constructed across child protection services and sectors whereby domestic violence was often not regarded as part of the remit for state intervention, but a private problem to be resolved by the couple. They found when intervention does occur the focus is often on the woman but not her specific needs in relation to domestic violence but on her role as a mother, particularly in relation to her responsibility to protect her children. Humphreys and Absler (2011) argue that in child protection contexts women are often considered primarily responsible for providing a safe environment for children and for ending the violence for the sake of the children, regardless of the man's responsibility in perpetrating the abuse.

With this question raised regarding 'adequate or not', feminist researchers have interrogated the idea of 'good' mother and how that impacts on and shapes women's experiences of domestic violence. They often argue that these debates do not recognise the burden of responsibility that is placed upon women whereby they are expected to reach a higher standard of parenting than women in non-violent environments. It is argued these questions of 'adequate or not' shift the focus away from men's violence on to women, so that the problem becomes defined in terms of women's failures as mothers rather than in terms of fathers' actions (Lapierre, 2010a). Furthermore, feminist researchers have pointed out these debates create an illusion that women are passive, when in reality women often attempt multiple ways to manage or end the abuse and these attempts can be subtle such as compliance to decrease conflict and aggression (Radford & Hester, 2001); hence studies have been conducted to bring the complexity of mothering to the forefront in domestic violence.

The research of Lapierre (2010a), in which he interviewed women in the UK, has been central in investigating women's experiences of mothering in the context of domestic violence, and explores the challenges and difficulties that abused women face in regard to their mothering. Lapierre (2010a, p. 1442) reported from his interviews that women consistently aimed for what constitutes good mothering; that is, putting children first, and trying to protect, provide and care for them, and he argues domestic violence seems to amplify women's sense of responsibility to their children. Lapierre's (2010a, p. 1443) study provides examples of women trying to protect their children from domestic violence such as preventing them from being exposed to violence, trying to respond to their emotional needs after witnessing violence, and not leaving children alone with partners. Lapierre (2010a, p. 1444) also found that, even though women reported an increased sense of responsibility in regard to their children, they also reported a significant loss of control over their mothering. This is due to the fact that violence impacts on their physical and mental health, making it more difficult for them to perform the hard and time-consuming work involved in caring for their children. Furthermore, mothering was made more difficult when men intentionally and specifically targeted mothering. Lapierre (2010b) argues that women mother under difficult circumstances because domestic violence creates a context that complicates mothering because men target their partner's mothering and mother–child relationship as part of their violent strategies.

In the context of domestic violence, feminist researchers have argued it is important not to forget the mother's capacity to maintain her parenting abilities under adverse conditions. Indeed, researchers have exposed that women can create protective factors that ensure children affected by domestic violence can grow up and do well (Humphreys, Thiara & Skamballis, 2011). Such recognitions have the potential to not stereotype all mother–child relationships as damaged in the aftermath of domestic violence. For example, Humphreys et al.'s (2006, p. 57) studies have shown that mothers are the single most important source of help and support reported by children, even where their relationship had not survived unscathed. Mothers and children draw enormous support from each other, they develop strategies of protection, and children can draw positively from their mother's ability to parent even in the face of adversity.

With this recognition, studies have focused on the concept of protection in domestic violence contexts. Haight et al. (2007) interviewed seventeen women involved in the child welfare system to explore their strategies for protecting and supporting their children. They reported mothers protected children's physical wellbeing during episodes of domestic violence by physically separating their children from the violence, calling a third party for assistance, signalling with their children to warn them away from impending violence, and trying to calm the partner or restraining themselves from arguing. They also found that mothers protected children's psychological recovery from domestic violence by using reassuring and supportive strategies such as expressing love and reassurance. Mothers also provided the children with limited truth-telling so that the facts of abuse would not traumatise children further or cause distress. Instilling hope was another strategy that mothers used such as encouraging their children not to dwell on the abuse and trying to socialise their children to avoid violence by naming the violence as wrong. Haight et al.'s (2007) findings also showed that women often tried to separate spousal and parental roles, that is, they avoided speaking ill of the children's father and tried to normalise the children's father such as 'he is tired', 'not mad at you', which positioned the domestic violence as adult problems.

Peled and Gil (2011) found through interviews with ten women that their perceptions of mothering in domestic violence centred on 'good', 'intensive' mothering; that is, the women positioned themselves as mothers first and foremost, by stressing their children come above all else, they would do everything for the sake of the children and they were primarily, if not exclusively, responsible for raising their children. Peled and Gil (2011) reported examples of women trying to fulfil these perceptions of good, intensive mothering by: striving to maintain an absolute separation between the violent 'external world' and the 'children's world'; trying to create a violence-free reality for their children; attempting to prevent the abuse from adversely impacting on their mothering; trying to preserve their partner's image as a father in the eyes of their children; and shielding children from any exposure to violence. Peled and Gil (2011) found that women tried to be mothers as if they were not abused; that is, not living in domestic violence; and hence tried to separate the worlds of mothering and domestic violence.

More recently, Buchanan, Power and Verity (2013) aimed to explore women's emotional experiences of forming relationships with their babies while being subjected to domestic violence. They argued that domestic violence not only creates acute fear but also generates a climate of fear and this impacts on how mothers protect their children. For example, they found women can become compliant with the abusive partner's demands or try to reason with him until his aggression lessens as a way to establish safety so they can comfort their baby.

By asking women about their experiences of mothering in the context of domestic violence, these studies have found that women do recognise protection and have strong desires to be a 'good mother'. In fact, these studies show that women do engage with and support notions that children are women's responsibility; that is, they are responsible for keeping them safe and for putting them first. Hearing the accounts of women shows firsthand that women aim to do their best in order to protect and care for children in very difficult circumstances.

However, feminist researchers have also argued that this social construct or ideal of the 'good mother' sets women up to fail, particularly in domestic violence situations. Mullender et al. (2002) argue the 'good mother' positions all women as being solely responsible for the wellbeing and safety of their children and for mediating relationships between children and fathers; however, such a positioning is dangerous in domestic violence situations in which women are unsafe and powerless in terms of adult familial relationships. The domestic violence environment is deeply unconducive to achieving even 'good enough' mothering, yet women are still expected to achieve the ideals of mothering, that is, being the emotional sponge in the family, managing and mopping up conflicts and distress, in hostile and unsafe contexts. These tasks become impossible when women are being abused, yet these expectations prevail in family and service systems whereby this sense of failure becomes even more pronounced in the lives of women experiencing domestic violence (Mullender et al., 2002).

Within this field of research into mothering and domestic violence, feminists have also called for the recognition that the perpetrator's abusive tactics undermine the mother–child relationship. Specifically, Humphreys, Thiara and Skamballis (2011) have argued that domestic violence is an attack on the mother–child relationship, that the tactics of abuse undermine the relationship and are part of a continuum of direct and indirect attacks. Examples of direct attacks are seen through extreme examples such as child homicides, attacks during pregnancy and child abductions, through to other direct attacks such as the abuser insulting and criticising mothers in front of their children, sexual insults, accusations of sexual infidelity, criticising the woman's mothering and punishing her if she cannot control the children to meet the partner's unrealistic expectations, and undermining quality parenting like sabotaging reading, playing and constant surveillance (Humphreys, 2010; Humphreys, Thiara & Skamballis, 2011, p. 168). Examples of indirect attacks include ensuring that women are unavailable for their children through disabling them physically or mentally (Humphreys, Thiara & Skamballis, 2011, p. 169). Lapierre (2010a) found similar abusive tactics and identified men using mothering as a target in their violence, such as pressure to have an abortion, controlling contraception, exploiting women's vulnerability when pregnant, threatening or using violence towards children to torment the mother, and using violence towards the mother in front of children to send messages of who is boss. Domestic violence also creates silence between mothers and children, that is, Humphreys et al.'s (2006) research showed that mothers often do not talk to their children because they are trying to protect them from the full knowledge of what has gone on. Mothers worry about children and try to shield them from domestic violence. Similarly, children do not talk to mothers because they have picked up the message that these things are not to be mentioned and because they see their mums as having enough to cope with.

The research by Mullender et al. (2002), Lapierre (2010a) and Humphreys, Thiara and Skamballis (2011) has also shown that mother blame is another tactic used by male partners to routinely criticise women; that is, verbalise and call them bad mothers in front of children, reprimand them for children's behaviour and threaten their mothering by reporting women to authorities. Morris (2010, p. 223) names these tactics as maternal alienation; that is, deliberate tactics used by some perpetrators in families to alienate women and children from one another. She argues that maternal alienation includes perpetrators' messages to children that they cannot trust their mother because she does not love them, she lies and tricks, she is lazy, selfish, crazy, and stupid, a slut, monstrous, and so on. She is to blame for everything negative in the family, including his violence and sometimes his sexual abuse of his children.

Research has shown that mother blame does not stay in the confines of an intimate partner relationship in domestic violence. Humphreys, Thiara and Skamballis (2011) warn that mothering in the context of domestic violence is a difficult terrain to explore because it is an area in which mother blaming is rife; that is, because of domestic violence and the associated vulnerability, there is a fine line between drawing out strengths and resilience of mothers and highlighting problems. As Humphreys and Absler (2011) point out, in domestic violence contexts perceptions of 'failure to protect' fall on women and ignore the impact of men's violence or do not hold men responsible. This scrutiny of women fosters mother-blaming discourses. Feminist researchers have named mother blaming not to say that women should not hold any responsibility in relation to their children in domestic violence contexts but to highlight the gendered processes by which women are unfairly defined as bad mothers in such circumstances (Humphreys & Absler, 2011). Similarly, Morris (2010) argues that maternal alienation is remarkably successful in turning the gaze of everyone away from the man's violence and towards the women's supposed moral failures and complete responsibly for the disasters in her family. This includes the breakdown of her relationship with her children, the ultimate sign of a so-called 'bad mother'.

Mother blaming has been found to be particularly strong in domestic violence contexts because it occurs within the micro worlds of families and households, and has resonance within the macro social order and discourses (Weisz & Wiersma, 2011). For example, mothering discourses position women with guilt and the overwhelming burden of blame for problems in relationships and families. Women experience this personally; they are inscribed with the responsibility for actions that are not theirs and over which they have no control. Studies have shown that a sense of failure and guilt is extremely common in mothers' experiences of domestic violence. For example, Mullender et al. (2002) found women are often able to reflect from the outside on the damage children have sustained; that is, to see what outsiders may have seen at the time, particularly statutory professionals. Women are often aware, at some level, that all is not well with the children despite their best efforts to protect them in domestic violence situations. Women are often reflective and aware that their children's needs for reassurance, attention and support are accentuated because of the domestic violence, but at the same time their resources as mother are often taxed to the limit and invariably depleted as a result of the abuse they are personally experiencing. Women encounter a high number of misconceptions concerning the dynamics of domestic violence and, when combined with societal expectations of mothers, these all work against women who then have to face 'failure to protect' accusations (Terrance, Plumm & Little, 2008). In comparison, father blame is virtually non-existent in discussions about parenting and domestic violence. Douglas and Walsh (2010) found in their study on mothers, domestic violence and child protection that women experience a higher level of scrutiny than male perpetrators, and while women are burdened with responsibility to remove children from abusive situations, male perpetrators of violence were sometimes judged to be satisfactory fathers, just not 'good husbands'. What mother-blaming discourses do in domestic violence is shift responsibility for parenting primarily to women and, despite the increasing recognition of gendered features of violence in adult intimate relationships, fatherhood is still overwhelming constructed as essentially non-violent (Eriksson & Hester, 2001) as shown in the positions of 'bad husband'/'good father'. Such subject positions treat violence against women as separate to violence against children, even when the evidence shows that violence against women can have a deleterious impact on the wellbeing of children both in the short and long term.

In addition to the studies that have interviewed women about their experiences of mothering and domestic violence, a small number of studies have examined adult children's experiences and memories of growing up in domestic violence. These studies have found that, despite fathers being severely violent, the disappointment and bitterness experienced by children and others is often directed towards the mother. This again shows the positioning of mother and father roles and expectations – with mothers bearing the brunt of responsibility for all that is intimate, social and familial (Buchbinder 2004). For example, O'Brien et al. (2013) utilised a mixed case study and consensual qualitative research design to present exemplar study documents detailing the recollected memories of six non-clinical female former child witnesses of domestic violence in Australia. They found that participants remembered their mothers had provided them with the physical necessities of life but they were unable to provide them with the emotional support they needed to make sense of their home situation. While many participants stated over the course of the abuse they had come to side with their mothers, this had not stopped them in their adult years for feeling angry and resentful towards their mothers. O'Brien et al. (2013, p. 102) reported that if anger, resentment and frustration were the emotional experiences germane to the women's recollections of their relationships with their mothers, their recollections of their fathers were more mixed and conflicting. They described them in terms of sadness, fear, hatred and love. Similarly, Kiraly and Humphreys (2012) found children in kinship care arrangements expressed much hurt and sometimes anger in relation to their mothers whereas they often felt let down by but less emotional about their fathers.

Krane and Davies (2002) point out the essentialist notion of 'woman' is no longer adequate, and other facets of social location are important in understanding experiences of domestic violence such as age, religion, race, ethnicity, sexuality, disability, place, and so on. We argue that mothering must also feature in understandings about domestic violence because mothering discourses offer discursive practices and subjectivities that are lived out and engaged with daily. For example, mothers operate under intense strain daily, knowing that if anything goes wrong with their children they will be held to account, and this pressure intensifies when domestic violence is present, making women feel even more anxious and fearful. We argue that mothering needs to feature in understanding gendered power relations in domestic violence because women's understandings, responses and help-seeking behaviours are often shaped by children's needs and desires. Mothering is another layer that creates unique experiences in the diversity of women's lives when experiencing domestic violence. We know there is a history or lineage of the discourse of mother blaming in domestic violence but we cannot underestimate the extent to which the practices of these discourses are gendered and directed at women in their gendered role as mothers (Humphreys & Absler, 2011).

## Domestic violence, mothering and gender

Cultural messages such as trying to be a good wife, striving to keep the family intact, and the belief that children need a father, regardless of the costs to women and children, are common in women's experiences of domestic violence (Kelly, 2009; Humphreys & Absler, 2011). The influence of these messages is shown when women return to the abuser because of pressures from their own or the abuser's family, or when women tolerate high levels of emotional or physical maltreatment without considering it abuse. These interpretations come from dominant constructions of what wives and mothers should be. Discourses of mothering saturate domestic violence contexts; that is, motherhood is tied to cultural messages of keeping the peace, keeping life private and nurturing all in the family as wife and mother. These cultural messages keep women in relationships for protracted periods of time (Kelly, 2009), and shape and expose gender power relations in domestic violence. Men do not experience these same cultural and social messages to endure, to tolerate, to protect and to keep the family intact. Mothering discourses shape and reinforce gender patterns and expectations in families and offer particular subject positions to women (Humphreys, 2010) such as devoted, instinctive, caring, sacrificing and provider of all physical and emotional support (Semaan, Jasinski & Bubriski-McKenzie, 2013). On the other hand, discourses of mothering also offer women the opposite subject positions, such as selfish, unnatural, uncommitted and non-caring. These positions construct the bad mother who fails to protect her children by staying with the man who abuses her, that is, the demonised mother (Semaan, Jasinski & Bubriski-McKenzie, 2013). These are all positions women can and do take up but they are particularly stark in domestic violence contexts. The cultural tensions and contradictions of what is expected of 'mother' are exposed and reinforced in this environment.

Keeping the family intact and ensuring children have a mother and father are messages we have heard repeatedly from women themselves in their attempts to explain why they remained in domestic violence for prolonged periods of time. This repeated story or answer shows the contradictions women experience when navigating discourses of mothering because you are a bad mother if you stay but you are a bad mother if you break up the family. Discourses of mothering are very much entwined with idealised notions of the family, offering subject positions that both assume and reinforce the traditional gender-based division of labour, and idealised images of white, middle-class, heterosexual couples with children in a self-contained family unit (Weedon, 1999; Arendell, 2000). For example:

> It is a complex thing, because you want that happy marriage, so you want to keep your husband happy. You really want your children to be happy, so you do whatever it takes. And also, you don't want to be seen as a failure in the outside world – her marriage didn't last, again – she's failed again.
>
> (Lyn, 2013)

> My family was so screwed up when I was a child, and he was like 'at least my parents are still together' … I just felt really obligated and I was Catholic and you don't get divorced when you are Catholic, you don't raise children as a single mother and you certainly don't become a single mother.
>
> (Daisy, 2013)[1]

Discourses of mothering are reinforced in institutions such as the family, church, media and medicine, which position women as responsible for expending time, energy and emotion in raising their children. Women, as mothers, are expected to meet their child's needs single-handed, to care for and stimulate the child's physical, emotional and mental development and to feel fulfilled in doing so (Hays, 1996; Weedon, 1997). We found that these subject positions – provider, nurturer and carer – dominated women's stories of domestic violence:

> I had to basically save my own money so that I could leave. I had to leave the family home, with the kids, so I had nothing to go to. I had a business but everything had to be stopped because I had to be there for my kids. I had nowhere to live, so I had to start from scratch. But after I was settled and I started renting a place, it was like a big fog cloud lifted. Obviously feeling the kids feeling sad and them going through their stuff, I couldn't be there 100 per cent for them so I made sure they had counselling for themselves because I wanted to be clear in my mind for them … because I've got two boys, I didn't want them to grow up and be like that, because it's just wrong. So I was just like, I have to get out of there and just get them sorted.
>
> (Julie, 2013)

> The only reason I stayed in the marriage was that my daughter was in a TAFE course that was going to dovetail her into university. I thought I would just get them through high school, get them to uni and settled and then I will leave.
>
> (Alison, 2002)

> Mum put up with it longer than she should. In one way you can call it quite shallow but in another way it is so vital. We would never have had a decent roof over our head, computers to give us that decent start. It would have been a lot harder to make a new start.
>
> (Alison's daughter, 2002)

In domestic violence contexts we also found that the subject position of nurturer extended to expectations around the position of wife; that is, discourses of mothering not only position women as responsible for children's needs but also responsible for meeting all of her husband's needs. The nurturer position fosters messages of the need to care for him, understand him and support him so he can succeed at achieving what he wants to do. Nurturing others remains central within discourses of femininity and mothering (Choi et al., 2005), and nurturing a partner to keep him happy and to keep the peace was one of the ways that women managed domestic violence. For example, after seven years of marriage and four years of separation, and extreme physical violence during these times, Mia applied for divorce. However, she spoke about her obligation to look after her husband and the difficulties she has in letting that go:

> I still let him come to my house and see the kids and sometimes I let him stay overnight here, but we sleep like separate room, I still cook for him sometimes … But actually inside I still love him, I still worry about him. I worry like who can look after him, because he can't do anything, even cook, no, he can't cook. I always take care of my husband when he's not well, I have to take care of him. I look after my husband, look after my kids. That's why sometime I feel like I love him more than myself.
>
> (Mia, 2013)

For other women, nurturing their partners was hard work and a source of resentment. For example, Dee was married for thirty years and had been separated for two years:

> Gee, I used to love it about 7.30 at night when he used to go to bed that was my free time. I could actually relax finally at that time. I mean you still had to keep the kids quiet but you knew that he was at least in bed and sleeping and that was a break. But nine times out of ten you were just busy making sure the house was all clean and sorted out before you went to bed because you knew damn well if he got up early in the morning and things weren't right he would start shouting and waking up the whole household.
>
> (Dee, 2013)

> When you've got a husband who is extremely lazy and believes that it is all about him and his needs, but you still continue to do those things for him. In the end I got frustrated and I did say 'I'm not your mother'.
>
> (Lyn, 2013)

Women can and do provide for their children in domestic violence. However, the domestic violence context and the balancing of children's and partners' needs often create a quandary for women. On the one hand, discourses of mothering reinforce notions of family unity and mothers' roles being vital in building and maintaining the relationships between children and their fathers. On the other hand, building father–child relationships clashes with the subject positions of nurturer, protector and carer when violence is present (Mullender et al., 2002). These clashing subject positions create doubt, confusion and contradiction for women experiencing domestic violence. For example, Kylie was with her partner for ten years and spoke about balancing her relationship with her son and her partner (he was not the biological father of her son):

> It's sort of like you're torn, like because I really wanted to keep him safe but I also knew that by excluding [names her partner] from him [her son] would actually … and that's a tricky balance to sort of, yeah I don't know how else to explain it other than that. I just feel like I was always on guard, always going, okay is it going to be okay today? Because he was never consistent, so some days he'd be really lovely with [names her son] and cuddle and kiss and play, and then other days 'Get away from me you little shit'. So for me it was about trying to protect him in going, 'Alright, well, [names her partner] is not in a great mood so maybe you and mummy will go to the playground' … I find those ones hard to get words around because it's, you know there's anguish, there's anxiety, there's sadness, there's vigilance, all that kind of stuff around it.
>
> (Kylie, 2013)

In the context of domestic violence, men are more likely to be positioned as a 'bad husband' but 'good father' and hence are not subjected to the high level of scrutiny that women experience as mothers; however, as Humphreys (2010, p. 512) points out, this is an oxymoron in domestic violence contexts. Bad husband/good father is a much simpler, friendlier subject position in domestic violence contexts than positions offered to women who are judged as failing to protect, oppressed, responsible – all positions that sit uneasily together (Terrance, Plumm & Little, 2008). In domestic violence contexts, mothering discourses place women under constant scrutiny particularly in how they protect their children, whereas men are offered 'good enough' fathering, that is, fathers are deemed to offer children something that can benefit them. Women are required to navigate contradictory messages that come from mothering discourses in domestic violence such as mothers need to protect children but children need a father, and these are always at odds with each other in domestic violence (Eriksson & Hester, 2001). Women told many stories of battling this contradiction and, despite the violence, abuse and fear they experienced, they still attempted to enable relationships between children and fathers:

> After we separated he would feed my boys bad things about me, I was a slut, whore and all of these; he spoke about me in extremely filthy ways. I on the other hand if he didn't turn up for access visits would say 'oh well, he must have forgotten or he is sick or had to work' and I would make excuses for him – as mothers we want to protect our children and see them happy and when we know they are disappointed or hurt, we make excuses for the other party and that was my downfall. I didn't let them see him as he was.
>
> (Lyn, 2013)

I feel torn on what is the right thing not only for me, him, but for the children. It's happened to me, where I have these child psychologists or whatever they are, family assessors, telling me 'leave your kids with the father whom is the perpetrator'. But when she's at his place she goes to her room and that's it. She's not eating right. She's not cleaned properly. Just little basic things that you notice as a mother; it has affected her. She's not who she is, but when she's like showing signs of separation anxiety from me, wringing of her hands, psoriasis around her hairline, not eating. It's difficult for her.

(Lesley, 2013)

Discourses of motherhood also position women as morally superior, sensitive and emotionally more sophisticated than men. It is women that create a home that is sweet and safe for both children and husbands coming home from work and daily activities (Hays, 1996). We found this was a common expectation that women had of themselves, and an expectation often expressed by partners in the context of domestic violence; that is, it was her job to manage and control the children, particularly from 'annoying' their father.

Because I wanted that lovely, peaceful, happy life for my children, about half an hour before he'd come home, I'd say 'He's going to be home soon, when he comes in, don't say anything, don't pounce on him and ask him to do this or the other, just leave him for a while and then I'll ask or you can ask him.' So I wanted them to be protected from his anger.

(Lyn, 2013)

Yeah, so if he did tend to start drinking and yelling, I'd make sure she's out of the room. And she always, I always made sure her bedtime was when she was little, it was pretty early, 7:30pm and then 8:30pm when she was in high school.

(Hannah, 2013)

As soon as my son got up, it wasn't a big house and when he came from his room and started making noise, you know it would be 'shut that fuckin' kid up', yelling and screaming, 'you're not a good mother, you're not looking after that kid'. I was able to be calm, keep calmness with the children. I let them sleep with me. I felt intuitive to them.

(Rose, 2013)[2]

Furthermore, these discourses create an expectation or illusion that women can navigate and meet both husbands' and children's needs all the time, even in dangerous contexts. The many stories we have heard of women trying to please both her partner and meet her children's needs at the same time have shown us the pressure women feel within domestic violence contexts to get this right. The expectation set up in discourses of mothering such as keeping the peace, smoothing over and being ready emotionally as a wife/partner and mother at all times is an impossible ask for all women generally, but is an expectation that is insufferable in situations of domestic violence. Ameena, an Iranian woman, spoke about her Australian partner and how their relationship changed once they had a baby:

> And I'm sick … And then I go to the doctor, sick, sick, sick, and baby again is in the middle. Lucky we had a good baby, when he was baby he wasn't that bad screaming and crying. He was a good baby but again when we go and sit in GP for say two hours because you want to see the doctor. And [names partner] comes in and says 'You've been here for two hours!' And next thing we have to go because it's really a problem and [partner's name] yells and the doctor he can see. Oh my god that was one point and then I come home and this baby he wants milk … I just can't do it, not because I don't want to … I prefer to put something in [partner's name] mouth and shut him out and then okay baby can have milk, just because he was good baby and he could wait maybe.
>
> (Ameena, 2013)

Discourses of mothering and the subject positions they offer are also available to partners, who can draw on them and use them to abuse in domestic violence contexts. These tactics are highly gendered because they specifically target mothering. There have been numerous examples in the literature and elsewhere of perpetrators targeting mothering by undermining women's relationships with their children and/or hurting women's children to inflict further abuse on women. Not only do perpetrators of abuse target mothering but they also use mothering discourses to position women with guilt, doubt and blame in domestic violence. Exploiting discourses of mothering is powerful and often 'successful' in domestic violence because mothering is located in a societal context organised by gender and prevailing gender belief systems, which position women as responsible for their children and impose particular expectations upon them (Krane & Davies, 2002; Lapierre, 2010a). Through interviewing women, we have heard many specific examples of partners using mothering to create guilt, doubt and blame in domestic violence contexts. For example:

> I went to read a book to my daughter because I always read to her at night. And 'What are you doing? You're not going in and reading to her, she's bloody four, she can read to herself.' She couldn't read but he is yelling, 'She doesn't need you sitting there reading.' So I'd come out and I'd do the right thing to keep the peace. So now I live with that guilt of 'if only I'd have just stuck up for her.' I also remember a time she'd eaten half a watermelon, she didn't wet the bed before, but because I went in there he starts yelling 'She can change her own sheets.' And I wasn't even allowed to go in there and change the sheets for her; she had to do it herself.
>
> (Hannah, 2013)

I guess more around me as a parent and then also him as a kid, because he's a really full-on little boy and he's like 'Well you just need to give him a smack' and I'm going 'Yeah no, don't touch my child'. Like I think if you've got someone telling you often enough you're really bad at something, you'll believe it. And I think because he did say, and not all the time but at the right time 'You're a really shit mum' … he was smart enough to know when and how to say those things to me.

(Kylie, 2013)

Some women actually spoke about how partners would deliberately target their mothering because they were jealous of the mother–child relationship and hence tried to sabotage it. For example, Jodie had two children and was married for thirty-one years. Her husband was a prominent drug dealer. She described how she was expected to serve him every night before he went out such as laying his clothes out on the bed, being in the bathroom while he showered and making sure his possessions were ready for him:

He never laid a finger on me or anything until later and it was after we got married and his excuse to all of it was because once the kids came along that he meant nothing to me so it was like a jealousy sort of thing. We've got children you have to put them first. You have to devote a lot of time to them … The violence got more and more. Yeah, so it was constant 'cause children when they're little they need you all the time and I believe he became jealous of the kids 'cause they were getting a lot more attention.

(Jodie, 2013)

Domestic violence complicates women's mothering yet places high expectations on women in such contexts, and hence does not offer women in domestic violence very many alternative subject positions except 'bad' mother or 'unnatural' mother. Discourses of mothering as a social and moral construct will mostly position women experiencing domestic violence in the 'bad' mothering camp; that is, they are mothers that require surveillance and intervention because of their 'bad' mothering (Malacrida & Boulton, 2012). We recognise that in interviewing women about their mothering we may only get representations of particular subject positions because women may be keen to show themselves in a positive light in such contexts that are tainted as 'bad'. Discourses of mothering elevate the status of women through motherhood and so it is possible that this leads women in domestic violence to overemphasise the importance of motherhood in their thinking and actions (Semaan, Jasinski & Bubriski-McKenzie, 2013). We understand that mothering may be the only source of women's identity and power in domestic violence contexts and hence they are keen to showcase the many and varied strengths they have in such contexts, and we do not question or deny these strengths. However, domestic violence is a hostile context and one that has potentially long-term impacts on women's and children's wellbeing. This context makes it extremely difficult for women to uphold and fulfil the requirements of mothering discourses, which some have argued have become more 'intensive' over time (Hays, 1996). Listening to women's stories of domestic violence, we recognised that women are aware of being positioned as a 'bad' mother because domestic violence exists in their lives, but we also found they are generally aware of their own limitations in such contexts:

> Like my son used to sleep in my room but when [names partner] came along I didn't let that happen anymore because [names partner] didn't like it. I also didn't want him taking it out on my son by yelling and screaming and carrying on … I think emotionally I wasn't as available either. I can't think of anything specific but I just know that I was always, in the back of my head going 'Okay what kind of mood is he going to be in when he gets home, how's he going to react' all that kind of stuff so I couldn't be 100 per cent emotionally available for [names her son].
>
> (Kylie, 2013)

> And instead of following my instincts and not going into that relationship, I don't want to bring children up in that situation and so I was angry at myself, that I made those choices, that I knew what he was like. I was angry at myself, very angry and it is hard to admit that you made a mistake … admitting you made that mistake, you haven't done the right thing by your children.
>
> (Rose, 2013)

> I feel like a hopeless mother because I couldn't protect them, because I was living in such absolute terror all the time and desperation all the time, we never had enough to eat, we weren't well, we were unhealthy, I was massively depressed and if I showed the slightest frustration or anxiety that would trigger an enormous conflict or event and he was hitting the children. It was just awful.
>
> (Daisy, 2013)

> I know I used to constantly beg the children just to do as they're told and stay in their rooms and unfortunately when I knew he was sort of worked up 'cause he would abuse me constantly over the phone and whatnot and you knew that if everything was not as it should be and in its right place when he gets home you know it was going to go crazy. I had to beg the kids to tidy things up and put things back and be hidden in their bedrooms and not dare be out of their rooms when he came home. I suppose I used to suffer anxiety and I used to get pretty worked up … But unfortunately you do start taking it out on the kids. I used to yell and scream at them because I knew what was about to happen the minute he pulled in that driveway … I used to be on edge constantly.
>
> (Jodie, 2013)

Featherstone (1999) explores feminist writings on mothering and makes the point that we need a fuller discussion about the complexities of mothering, particularly in contexts where children are in danger. Mothering discourses stress instinctual love and self-abnegation and women's superiority over men, and because these discourses have such power and influence, we know little about maternal ambivalence; that is, the experience shared by mothers in which feelings of love and hate for their children exist side by side. Featherstone (1999) argues that ambivalence itself is not the problem but rather the societal taboo on the expression of ambivalence in Western culture. Much guilt felt by mothers can stem from the difficulties they experience in weathering these complicated feelings. Trying to understand and express this ambivalence in contexts of domestic violence becomes highly problematic for women who are already positioned as bad mothers by discourses of mothering. Partners who are violent provide no space for mothers to express ambivalence or frustrations that come with parenting. In our interviews with women over time about their experiences of domestic violence, we have found expressions of ambivalence to be rare. This is most likely because the two topics, admitting ambivalence in mothering and admitting domestic violence, each carry such stigma that confessing to both simultaneously becomes almost unbearable for women who are trying to protect what little remains of their identities as women and as mothers. Ameena spoke about how sad she felt about her relationship experience. She came from Iran to Australia to be with her partner and described how she felt stuck in Australia. She felt stuck because she believed her son needed a relationship with his father:

> I sometimes think, it's not good to say, I made the mistake and this son I sometimes don't like him because to be honest I don't like it. Because I used to buy everything for my nieces or I do everything I wanted. But for this one I can't do anything, I just stuck here you know. The only thing I can do just take him to playground; okay go play with kids, that's all.
>
> (Ameena, 2013)

As Featherstone and Trinder (1997, pp. 152–3) point out, discourses and subjectivities enable an interrogation of how masculinities and femininities are constructed and operate in relation to each other. Mothering discourses show particular insight into how women and men are located within systems where expectations around roles and responsibilities are sites of struggle and definition. Mothering discourses and their subject positions allow us to appreciate the contradictions and dilemmas women experience in domestic violence contexts. Women gain affirmation and strength through their positions as mothers; that is, gendered power relations create women's ability to act as mothers. It is often where power can be exercised by women in domestic violence; hence mothering may take on greater meaning in this context than it does in others. Domestic violence in actual fact exacerbates the burden of responsibility to protect and care for children and this responsibility is mostly placed on women despite the violence being perpetrated by partners and fathers. This expectation complicates the work involved in mothering. As Peled and Gil (2011) suggest, women who experience domestic violence are inclined to idealise motherhood because they are already positioned as outside dominant discourses of devotion and intensive mothering; hence mothers are reluctant to admit to a mothering experience that is not ideal or to any negative feelings that it may entail.

# Conclusion

Motherhood and mothering are dynamic social interactions and relationships, located in a societal context organised by gender and prevailing gender belief systems (Krane & Davies, 2002; Arendell, 2000). The mother–child dynamic is set up as the ultimate paradigm and so notions of woman and mother overlap in such a way that dominant constructions of woman are inevitably dependent on the concept of mother (McNay, 1992; Kilty & Dej, 2012). All women are exposed to discourses of mothering throughout history and in most societies; that is, women are seen as responsible for raising children and for providing for all their needs. But women are agentic (Choi et al., 2005), which means that they engage with and embrace culturally available discourses of mothering as a resource offering positive subject positions. Hence, mothering subject positions are particularly comforting and vital for women and their children surviving domestic violence. Women can and do take up subject positions emanating from discourses of mothering and can be and are 'good' mothers in very difficult circumstances. However, we argue that in contexts of domestic violence these cultural messages and expectations can further exacerbate feelings of anxiety, frustration, guilt, low self-esteem and inadequacy that women share because the social and personal perceptions of good mothering and the reality of the mothering experience in domestic violence are very different. Furthermore, within this context, discourses of mothering can also be used as weapons by perpetrators of abuse, compounding the guilt and doubt women normally experience as mothers (Lapierre, 2010a). The danger, hostility and fear embedded within domestic violence position women outside discourses of good mothering. We argue this is perhaps why it is important for women to draw on good mothering discourses because not doing so threatens their sense of self and identity as women. Such an investment perhaps can be argued as a vital defence in surviving domestic violence and one that contradicts perceptions of failure but, at the same time, such discourses can hide the difficulties and tensions women experience in domestic violence contexts (Choi et al., 2005).

# Notes

1  We thank and acknowledge Dr Fiona Buchanan who conducted the interview with Daisy.
2  We thank and acknowledge Dr Fiona Buchanan who conducted the interview with Rose.

# References

Arendell, T. (2000) Conceiving and investigating motherhood: the decades of scholarship. *Journal of Marriage and Family*, 62(4), pp. 1192–1207.

Bradley, H. (2013) *Gender*, 2nd edition, Polity, Cambridge.

Buchanan, F., Power, C. & Verity, F. (2013) Domestic violence and the place of fear in mother/baby relationships: 'What was I afraid of? Of making it worse'. *Journal of Interpersonal Violence*, 28(9), pp. 1817–38.

Bromfield, L., Lamont, A., Parker, R. & Horsfall, B. (2010) Parenting and child abuse and neglect in families with multiple and complex problems. *Child Abuse Prevention*, Issues, 33.

Buchbinder, E. (2004) Motherhood of battered women: the struggle for repairing the past. *Clinical Social Work Journal*, 32(3), pp. 307–26.

Casanueva, C., Martin, S., Runyan, D., Barth, R. & Bradley, R. (2008) Quality of maternal parenting among intimate-partner violence victims involved with the child welfare system. *Journal of Family Violence*, 23, pp. 413–27.

Choi, P., Henshaw, C., Baker, S. & Tree, J. (2005) Supermum, superwife, supereverything: performing femininity in the transition to motherhood. *Journal of Reproductive and Infant Psychology*, 23(2), pp. 167–80.

Douglas, H. & Walsh, T. (2010) Mothers, domestic violence, and child protection. *Violence Against Women*, 16(5), pp. 489–508.

Eriksson, M. & Hester, M. (2001) Violent men as good enough fathers? A look at England and Sweden. *Violence Against Women*, 7(7), pp. 779–98.

Featherstone, B. (1999) Taking mothering seriously: the implications for child protection. *Child and Family Social Work*, 4, pp. 43–53.

Featherstone, B. & Trinder, L. (1997) Familiar subjects? Domestic violence and child welfare. *Child and Family Social Work*, 2, pp. 147–59.

Haight, W., Shim, W., Linn, L. & Swinford, L. (2007) Mother's strategies for protecting children from batterers: the perspectives of battered women involved in child protection services. *Child Welfare*, 86, pp. 41–62.

Hays, S. (1996) *The Cultural Contradictions of Motherhood*, Yale University Press, New Haven, CT.

Humphreys, C. (2010) Crossing the great divide: response to Douglas and Walsh. *Violence Against Women*, 16(5), pp. 509–15.

Humphreys, C. & Absler, D. (2011) History repeating: child protection responses to domestic violence. *Child and Family Social Work*, 16, pp. 464–73.

Humphreys, C., Mullender, A., Thiara, R. & Skamballis, A. (2006) 'Talking to my mum': developing communication between mothers and children in the aftermath of domestic violence. *Journal of Social Work*, 6(1), pp. 53–63.

Humphreys, C., Thiara, R. & Skamballis, A. (2011) Readiness to change: mother–child relationship and domestic violence intervention. *British Journal of Social Work*, 41, pp. 166–84.

Kelly, U. (2009) 'I'm a mother first': the influence of mothering in the decision-making processes of battered immigrant Latino women. *Research in Nursing & Health*, 32, pp. 286–97.

Kilty, J. & Dej, E. (2012) Anchoring amongst the waves: discursive constructions of motherhood and addiction. *Qualitative Sociology Review*, 8(3), pp. 6–23.

Kiraly, M. & Humphreys, C. (2012) Perspectives from young people about family contact in kinship care: 'don't push us – listen more'. *Australian Social Work*, 66(3), pp. 314–27.

Krane, J. & Davies, L. (2002) Sisterhood is not enough: the invisibility of mothering in shelter practice with battered women. *Affilia*, 17(2), pp. 167–90.

Lapierre, S. (2010a) More responsibilities, less control: understanding the challenges and difficulties involved in mothering in the context of domestic violence. *British Journal of Social Work*, 40, pp. 1434–51.

Lapierre, S. (2010b) Striving to be 'good' mothers: abused women's experiences of mothering. *Child Abuse Review*, 19, pp. 342–57.

Lorber, J. (2010), *Gender Inequality: Feminist Theory and Politics*, 4th edition, Oxford University Press, Oxford.

Malacrida, C. & Boulton, T. (2012) Women's perceptions of childbirth 'choices': competing discourses of motherhood, sexuality and selflessness. *Gender & Society*, 26(5), pp. 748–72.

McNay, L. (1992) *Foucault and Feminism*, Polity Press, Cambridge.

Miller, T. (2007) Is this what motherhood is all about? Weaving experiences and discourse through transition to first-time motherhood. *Gender & Society*, 21(3), pp. 337–58.

Morris, A. (2010) Seeking congruence: bring language to experiences of maternal alienation and gender violence. *Australian Feminist Studies*, 25(64), pp. 223–34.

Mullender, A., Hague, G., Imam, U., Kelly, L., Malos, E. & Regan, L (2002) *Children's Perspectives on Domestic Violence*, Sage, London.

O'Brien, K., Cohen, L., Pooley, J. & Taylor, M. (2013) Lifting the domestic violence cloak of silence: resilient Australian women's reflected memories of their childhood experiences of witnessing domestic violence. *Journal of Family Violence*, 28, pp. 95–108.

Peled, E. & Gil, I.B. (2011) The mothering perceptions of women abused by their partner. *Violence Against Women*, 17(4), pp. 457–79.

Radford, L. & Hester, M. (2001) Overcoming mother blaming? Future directions for research on mothering and domestic violence. In S.A. Graham-Berman & J.L. Edleson (Eds) *Domestic Violence in the Lives of Children*, American Psychological Association, Washington, DC, pp. 135–56.

Semaan, I., Jasinski, J. & Bubriski-McKenzie, A. (2013) Subjection, subjectivity, and agency: the power, meaning and practice of mothering among women experiencing intimate partner violence. *Violence Against Women*, 19(1), pp. 69–88.

Terrance, C., Plumm, K. & Little, B. (2008) Maternal blame: battered women and abused children. *Violence Against Women*, 14(8), pp. 870–85.

Weedon, C. (1997) *Feminist Practice and Poststructuralist Theory*, 2nd edition, Blackwell, Malden, MA.

Weedon, C. (1999) *Feminism, Theory and the Politics of Difference*, Blackwell, Oxford.

Weisz, A. & Wiersma, R. (2011) Does the public hold abused women responsible for protecting children? *Affilia: Journal of Women and Social Work*, 26(4), pp. 419–30.

# 4  Older women

I was a very unconfident person. I always felt ugly. So what actually happened was the first person that asked me to marry them I did. I didn't even know the person. I just thought 'oh my God, this is ...' This was in 1968. It was quite a while ago. I guess things just went from there.

(Jeanne, 2013)

## Introduction

In this chapter we explore how the experience of domestic violence is influenced by women's age and position in the life span. While we focus on older women's experiences of abuse, that is, women who are fifty-five years of age or older, we also invoke the experiences of younger women and women in mid-life. We explore how women's varying positions across the life span afford and accommodate different experiences of abuse. In other words, we argue that women's experiences of abuse are very different when refracted through the lens of age and position in the life span. These differences stem from how women are discursively positioned by dominant discourses of gender. For example, what it means to be an older woman in society is mediated by a range of discursive repertoires to which younger women and women in mid-life are less exposed. These discourses, we contend, shape the ways that older women understand themselves as gendered subjects, which in turn influences their experiences and responses to domestic violence. Adding a further layer to our considerations of how domestic violence is shaped by women's position in the life span is how older women's experiences of abuse have changed across time. Many older women were victims of domestic violence in their youth or have been victims of abuse throughout their life course, which means that they have also experienced abuse as young women and in mid-life. An examination of how older women remember and understand their experiences of abuse in their younger years provides a window into how gender and domestic violence were constructed and experienced in particular historical contexts. For example, women who are currently aged in their sixties were young women at a time that was socially and culturally different to the one experienced by young women today. These older women were on the cusp of womanhood in the 1960s and 1970s, a period marked by rapid change in the social and cultural fabric of society, particularly in relation to the rights of women. Taking into account women's experiences of abuse in a historical context demonstrates how dominant discourses of gender, which have shifted and changed over the last thirty to forty years, have impacted on older women's experiences of abuse over the life course.

In this chapter we draw on data collected during a small qualitative study conducted in 2013 that examined the impact of age on women's experiences of domestic violence. Many of the older women interviewed during the study experienced abuse in their younger years and were no longer living with the abuser. Others were victims of longstanding abuse, beginning in their youth and continuing into their older years, and some of these women were still living with the abuser. Older women who were still living with the abuser clearly articulated their abuse experiences as domestic violence, not elder abuse. For several of these women, the abuse was longstanding, occurring throughout the many years of their marriage. Older women who were no longer living with the abuser also described their abuse experiences as domestic violence but suggested that, at the time the abuse was occurring, they did not realise that what they were experiencing was domestic violence. This was particularly the case for older women who experienced abuse in their youth and reflects the social and cultural environment at particular historical junctures (e.g. the 1960s, 70s and 80s). As one woman noted, 'Like I say, in those days, I did not ever really think that it was domestic abuse. I knew that it was an uncomfortable situation to live in. I knew that mum and dad's relationship wasn't like that' (Veronica, 2013).

## Domestic violence and age

Domestic violence has been viewed as primarily a problem of women in their teens to thirties, with the highest levels of violence being found to occur in younger women (Bachman & Saltzman, 1995). While it is acknowledged that domestic violence occurs across the life span, empirical evidence has suggested that the risk and occurrence of violence decreases with age and is therefore a diminishing problem for older women (Wilke & Vinton, 2003). However, in more recent times, researchers and advocates from a range of disciplines have found that domestic violence continues to be a problem for adult women in all stages of life (Mouton, 2003), and that older women experience domestic violence well into old age (Grossman & Lundy, 2003; Rennison & Rand, 2003; Teaster & Roberto, 2004). Given the rapidly ageing population in many countries across the globe, the problem of domestic violence in later life is likely to increase (Hightower, Smith & Hightower, 2001; Brandl & Cook-Daniels, 2002; Fisher & Regan, 2006). National studies in the United States have found that women over the age of sixty-five do experience both physical violence and verbal aggression (Pillemer & Finkelhor, 1988). For example, 76.3 per cent of surveyed women aged sixty years and older had experienced emotional/psychological abuse and 71.4 per cent were victims of physical abuse (National Center on Elder Abuse, 1998), and the National Crime Victimization Survey estimated that 118,000 incidents of intimate partner violence were committed against women aged fifty-five years and older during a nine-year period between 1993 and 2001 (Rennison & Rand, 2003). A more recent study by Fisher and Regan (2006) found that the type of abuse most frequently experienced by older women was psychological and emotional abuse. In addition, active and intentional neglect is a form of abuse that is much more likely to occur in relationships between older people due to increasing frailty, illness or ageing (Straka & Montminy, 2006).

For older women, domestic violence may involve the continuation of longstanding abuse, commonly referred to as domestic violence grown old, violence that starts only in old age or violence that begins with a new relationship in later years (Seaver, 1996). It has been found that the same power and control tactics (i.e. threats and intimidation) are used by perpetrators of domestic violence across the life span (Wisconsin Coalition Against Domestic Violence, 1997, cited in Wilke & Vinton, 2003). Although it is clear that domestic violence occurs throughout the life course, older women have been largely unrecognised in research, and the characteristics and circumstances of their experiences with violent partners remains under-examined (McGarry & Simpson, 2011; Lazenbatt, Devaney & Gildea, 2013).

The invisibility of older women in domestic violence research may be explained in part by domestic violence being conflated with or categorised as elder abuse (Pillemer & Finkelhor, 1988; Straka & Montminy, 2006). Older women experiencing domestic violence are more likely to be viewed by service providers, in both ageing and domestic violence services, as victims of elder abuse rather than as victims of domestic violence (Vinton, Altholz & Lobell-Boesch, 1997; Regan et al., 2004; Fisher & Zink, 2007). The invisibility of older women in discourses of domestic violence may also be compounded by the fact that older women do not report or seek assistance for domestic violence in the same ways as younger women (Zink & Fisher, 2007). For example, it is unusual for women over sixty to seek services through domestic violence programs or shelters (Lundy & Grossman, 2004), and older women are less likely than younger women to access and receive individual or group counselling services (Lundy & Grossman, 2009). Alternatively, older women's under-utilisation of services may be due to the fact that many domestic violence services, such as shelters, are not appropriately set up to meet the needs of older women (Beaulaurier et al., 2007). Another likely explanation is that long-term abusive relationships may become normalised and accepted in the lives of older women, making these women less likely to view their problem as domestic violence for which they need to seek help (Zink et al., 2003; Lundy & Grossman, 2009).

It is clear that the way society constructs the problem of domestic violence influences how individuals label and act on the problem (Vinton, Altholz & Lobell-Boesch, 1997). Discourses of ageing shift violence and abuse in women's lives into the realm of elder abuse and away from domestic violence, thus hiding the dynamics of power and control (Spangler & Brandl, 2007). While the broad and diverse concept of elder abuse includes situations of domestic violence such as that occurring against an older woman by her partner, the field of elder abuse has not generally included a gendered analysis of violence and, until recently, domestic violence has not been established as a theoretical category of its own within elder abuse (Straka & Montminy, 2006). The problem of domestic violence against older women, therefore, falls into the gap between these two fields, and this may be one reason for its relative invisibility (Straka & Montminy, 2006). This gap does not allow for ageing and gender discourses to be explored and exposed in older women's experiences of domestic violence (Wilke & Vinton, 2003).

## Domestic violence and older women

While there are similarities in the dynamics and effects of domestic violence across the life span (Vinton, 1998), there are unique factors that impact on older women. First, generational differences in relation to gender role socialisation and even the ageing process itself impact on how older women understand domestic violence and what actions they are willing to take (Vinton, 1998). Older women have been socialised with more traditional attitudes and values, particularly those relating to traditional gender roles, marriage and the nuclear family (Zink et al., 2003). Subservience and submitting to a partner's will, even when the partner is abusive, is consistent with the traditional socialisation of women (Beaulaurier et al., 2007). As older women are more likely to have been socialised to be submissive in the context of relationships and family, these discourses are particularly powerful in the experiences of domestic violence for older women (Beaulaurier et al., 2007). Older women may be more vulnerable to abuse from a violent partner because of adherence to traditional discourses of gender that establish and normalise power differentials between men and women in intimate heterosexual relationships.

Older women have also been socialised with an ardent sense of privacy about family matters and a strong commitment to family loyalty and unity (Seaver, 1996; Hightower et al., 1999). Such values can prevent older women from discussing family problems with others, particularly at a time when domestic violence was only viewed as a private family matter. For example, a study by Beaulaurier et al. (2005) identified key factors that prevented older abused women from seeking help for abuse: self-blame, powerlessness, hopelessness, the need to protect the family and the need to keep the abuse a secret from others. Nearly all these factors have continuities with how older women have been socialised. Moreover, for many older women, the processes of gender role socialisation have been reinforced by traditional religious values (Zink et al., 2003). For example, Beaulaurier et al. (2007) also found that there were strong indications that if older women were inclined to talk with anyone about domestic violence their 'first stop' would be a member of the clergy. This response, they suggested, may be due to the connection between religious beliefs and marriage in the minds of many older women. Clergy responses were most often characterised as maintaining the status quo by reinforcing the message that domestic violence was a private problem (Beaulaurier et al., 2007).

Second, in drawing out unique factors that impact on older women, we can also look to more historically material explanations, arguing older women are often trapped in violent relationships because of their lack of education and resources. Even though other groups of women also experience restrictions in access to education and resources, these issues are worsened by the passage of time. Many older women did not have paid employment when they were younger, so even women who are not at retirement age may be unemployable because of both ageism and lack of work experience (Hightower, Smith & Hightower, 2001). Older women who have had minimal or no employment are less likely to have savings or to own their own homes. These factors, along with increasing age, and in some cases poor physical and emotional health, can prevent older women from leaving abusive relationships (Teaster, Roberto & Dugar, 2006). Older women who have diminished cognitive capacity and/or physical disabilities resulting from a range of age-related conditions and illnesses face additional challenges in dealing with domestic violence, particularly if their condition means that they are dependent on the abuser for care and support. The abuse perpetrated by her partner may be viewed as being associated with the stress of caring for her and so the seriousness of domestic violence is lessened, which leads to responses that do not appropriately address domestic violence (Spangler & Brandl, 2007). Alternatively, although some older women are receiving care from their abusive partners, others may be providing care. Due to the strong care ethic that may have been instilled in older women from a young age, it may be extremely difficult for an older woman to leave a dependant, abusive husband (Seaver, 1996). This is particularly the case when responses are situated within an elder abuse approach, which tends to ignore gender-specific forms of abuse (Hightower, Smith & Hightower, 2001).

Third, older women are much more likely than younger women to have endured abuse over many years. Women are often victims of domestic violence throughout the life course rather than at a specific age (Reinharz, 1986). A recent study by Bonomi et al. (2007) found that older women reported a lifetime partner violence prevalence of 26.5 per cent, with 18.4 per cent of women experiencing physical or sexual abuse, or both, and 21.9 per cent experiencing non-physical abuse (i.e. psychological abuse defined as threats or controlling behaviour). As well, the intimate partner violence experienced by older women may intensify as she and her partner grow older (Finkelhor & Pillemer, 1988). For example, research has indicated that increasing age of both women and their partners is correlated with physical and sexual violence (Coker et al., 2000b). The protracted nature of abuse in the lives of older women has implications for their physical and mental health as well as how they respond to such abuse. For example, it has been found that the physical impacts of violence are 'dose-dependent' (Coker et al., 2000a, p. 1020), which means that the length of the relationship as well as the severity of the abuse and the frequency of incidents play a role in determining the extent of the injury and/or illness resulting from violence (Sutherland, Bybee & Sullivan, 2002). The effects of long-term trauma, alongside mental health problems such as depression and anxiety, were found to increase morbidly and mortality (Scott et al., 2004). Furthermore, older women may have become resigned to living in situations of longstanding abuse and may be unable to see that there are other choices available to them (Wolf, 2000, cited in Straka & Montminy, 2006).

Fourth, domestic violence may compound or exacerbate the already poor or deteriorating health of many older women, even long after the abuse has ceased (Anetzberger, 1997; Campbell et al., 2002; Bonomi et al., 2006). A study by Regan et al. (2004) found that significantly larger percentages of older women experiencing domestic violence reported problems with chronic pain, depression and digestion. A later study by Fisher and Regan (2006) found that older women who experienced psychological/emotional abuse – alone, repeatedly, or with other types of abuse – had significantly increased odds of reporting bone or joint problems, digestive problems, depression or anxiety, chronic pain and high blood pressure or heart problems. While it has been found that younger women who experience domestic violence also report more health conditions than those who are not abused (Campbell et al., 2002), the experience of poor health as a consequence of domestic violence has greater implications for older women whose general health may also be deteriorating as a result of the ageing process. Given that many older women have been victims of longstanding domestic violence, the health consequences may be far more extensive than for younger women. Moreover, women are at greater risk of the harmful effects of domestic violence if their health deteriorates at the same time as they are experiencing emotional and physical abuse (Finkelhor & Pillemer, 1988). For example, domestic violence can often result in traumatic stress, and stressful life course events such as menopause, retirement, loss of loved ones, onset of illness and hospitalisation can exacerbate symptoms of post-traumatic stress (Graziano, 2003, cited in Sormanti & Shibusawa, 2008).

Fifth, while social isolation is a risk factor in domestic violence for women of any age, older women are more likely to experience social isolation due to the death or illness of their peers. In some cases, the abusive partner may be the only person with whom the older woman has social interaction (Straka & Montminy, 2006). It has been found that abused older people have significantly fewer social contacts than those who are not abused (Godkin, Wolf & Pillemer, 1989). While younger women report seeking help and support from friends and family, such resources may not exist for older women (Straka & Montminy, 2006).

Sixth, support services and resources for women experiencing domestic violence, such as shelters, crisis intervention counsellors and peer support groups, are either not offered to older women or are not set up appropriately to meet their specific health and social needs (Vinton, Altholz & Lobell-Boesch, 1997; Blood, 2004; Beaulaurier et al., 2007; Lundy & Grossman, 2009). Many older women are not aware of the existence of services (Beaulaurier et al., 2007). For older women living in rural communities, the problem of access to support services is compounded by geographic isolation, economic constraints and strong social and cultural pressures that emphasise keeping family matters private, taking responsibility for personal mistakes and upholding the covenant of marriage (Few, 2005; Wendt, 2009). For older women from culturally and linguistically diverse backgrounds, cultural misconceptions that normalise certain behaviours hinder recognition and access to services and support (Burman, Smailes & Chantler, 2004). While elder abuse services can assist older abused women with a range of complex health and social needs, they are not able to address the gender specificity of domestic violence, nor do they focus on the power and control dynamics in the relationship. Without such a perspective, it is difficult to appropriately assist older women in these situations (Straka & Montminy, 2006).

The domestic violence movement and the women's movement in general have been criticised for leaving the needs of older women unrecognised and unmet (Wilke & Vinton, 2003; Straka & Montminy, 2006). Straka and Montminy (2006), whose work is situated within a Canadian context, argue that there are two different intervention networks that can potentially help older women experiencing domestic violence: (a) the women's shelter network in the community, which uses a feminist domestic violence approach, and (b) ageing resources, including adult protective services, in the health and social services network, which use an elder abuse approach. The first of these is grounded in a gender perspective but does not account for age; the second is grounded in an ageing perspective but does not account for gender. Older women are located at the intersection of these two dimensions of age and gender. The problem lies in the fact that these approaches are embedded in two different paradigms, with two different types of intervention for the same presenting problem. Straka and Montminy suggest that neither the feminist nor the elder abuse paradigm have been able to provide an adequate response to domestic violence experienced by older women. The exploration of ageing and gender discourses that surround older women can provide much insight into how domestic violence is experienced by this group of women. The marginalisation of older women's voices in domestic violence explanations is a reflection of a double dose of invisibility; that is, ageing and gender discourses offer subject positions that marginalise on the grounds of not only being a woman but also of growing old. In our Western society, ageing and being aged are closely aligned with dependence, unproductiveness and being a burden (Bagshaw, Wendt & Zannettino, 2009).

## Domestic violence, age and gender

The historical socio-political climate cannot be overlooked in understanding women's circumstances and behaviours across different age cohorts, particularly in understanding older women's experiences of domestic violence (Lundy & Grossman, 2009). Older women have historically lived with discourses of traditional femininity, positioning women as inferior, passive, submissive and subservient. Traditional discourses of femininity have offered women restricted subject positions, which have become entrenched across their life course because the passage of time has reinforced them. Hence, many older women entered marriage and had children at a young age:

> I was married at an early age, not because I was pregnant but because we did in those days. I got married at 19. I turned 19 in September and got married in October and I had my first child a couple of years later. I had two children by the time I was 23.
>
> (Cheryl, 2013)

In our interviews with older women about their experiences of domestic violence, gender became visible through subject positions that were submissive, particularly in their younger years, and self-blaming and asexual, particularly in their older years. These subject positions are supported and sustained by gendered discourses that promote the sanctity of marriage, mother blaming and the polarisation of women's sexuality in relation to age. We examine these shifting gender constructions across time to show how ageing shapes gender relations and hence domestic violence experiences over time.

During the telling of their stories, older women very much positioned themselves as being submissive to their husbands and seeing marriage as their only real option in life. Our naming of the subject position of female submissiveness is not intended to present women as weak and therefore somehow responsible for domestic violence in their lives but rather it is to show the historical contexts of such a subject position. Given that many of these older women were experiencing domestic violence in historical contexts where violence in the home was still considered to be a private matter and in which women were expected to submit to the will of their husbands and accept their lot in life, it is likely that these women felt that they had little option but to accept their situations:

> I think I just went along with what I thought was my role at the time, like most women did. You got married, you had kids. You looked after your husband, you made sure his meal was on the table and you cleaned the house. So I never really questioned it until I started going to uni and seeing there was a whole other field of thought about a lot of things out there.
>
> (Vivian, 2013)

> In that period of time, Australian women – young women – were treated not very well by Australian men. That's how it was. If you've ever seen that movie *Puberty Blues*; that was very, very typical of how boys looked at girls. They were always treated as second-class citizens.
>
> (Veronica, 2013)

> Then would you believe I married and – at an early age of twenty, so went and married a man who stupidly promised me that he would always look after me and always provide for me. Within twelve months of that relationship, I was heading off to the local deli to get chocolate bars on a Sunday while my husband was off doing something else, because I felt he was more important than me. He was the worldly one. He'd been working since he was sixteen, so therefore he must know how the world works.
>
> (Glenda, 2013)

For many older women, engaging in a submissive femininity was part and parcel of women's lives at particular historical junctures, particularly the 1960s, 70s and 80s. The dominant discourses of femininity and masculinity in these historical contexts provided women with subject positions that produced passivity and submissiveness across all areas of their lives but which were extremely visible in contexts of domestic violence. A sixty-year-old woman who was married at eighteen for twenty-five years said that she catered to her husband's every need in the hope that he would be less abusive towards her and her children:

> He'd go and get in the shower and I'd lay his clothes out for him on the bed and then I'd go and make his breakfast for him. I'd do his lunch and then I'd make sure that he was all packed and ready to go off to work, yeah. When he was on night shift, he would get up at 11 o'clock. He'd try and have a sleep in the evening before he went to work. I'd stay up until 11 and then I'd have to go and wake him up, try and get him out. If he'd been drinking, it was a nightmare.
>
> (Veronica, 2013)

A sixty-four-year-old woman who was married at nineteen for eleven years spoke about how she would pander to her husband's ego so that he would feel less threatened by her studying to be a teacher:

> I eventually got accepted to do teaching, which was what I always wanted to do and so I was just so thrilled by that, but [names her partner] was totally against it and totally threatened by it. So for the three years that I studied for my teaching diploma, I could not bring out a book in front of him. I had to do all my study while he was at work or in between times ... So I just wasn't allowed to even talk about what I was doing in my life and then he'd say things like 'I know you're going to leave me. As soon as you do this, you'll leave me.' I'd say 'No, I'm not. No. I'm not thinking like that at all. Think about it. It will be good and we can do more things' and he said 'No. You'll be earning all this money. You won't want me.' He was a carpenter and he was a very good carpenter and I tried to say 'but you're trained in what you do and you're good at what you do'.
>
> (Vivian, 2013)

Hence, in the context of domestic violence, women were able to engage with the submissive subject position to cope with and attempt to stop domestic violence. Paradoxically, however, this subject position allowed and justified the perpetuation of abuse in their lives as all these women remained with their abusive partners over many years. While dominant discourses of gender in the 1970s and 1980s contributed to older women's subservience to the abuser in contexts of domestic violence, prevailing discourses that sanctified marriage and demonised divorce, particularly if there were children involved, also contributed to women's submissiveness in the context of domestic violence because it prevented women from speaking out about and/or leaving the abuser. These discourses were also inherently gendered as it was far less acceptable for a woman with children to be a divorcée than it was for a man at this particular historical juncture. The dominant discourses of divorce created extremely negative subject positions for women such as 'damaged goods', failure, immoral and sinful, while the discourse of the 'married woman' created subject positions aligned with dignity and respect. These subject positions were reinforced by the lack of opportunity for women with children to live independently of men:

> I went into marriage thinking it would be you stayed in a marriage. Then, especially when you have children, you stay in that marriage, you think, for the children … I tried to stay. I thought 'right, I don't want to be – I don't want to be a single mum. That's not why I got married. That's not why I had children.' But in the end, as far as I was concerned, it was the only option.
>
> (Jan, 2013)

> I mean, the other thing was that I didn't want to admit to a second marriage failure. I wanted to do my hardest to try and keep things going and keep things together because it was – it was just something that I was trying to avoid at all costs.
>
> (Jeanne, 2013)

> I had left a couple of times. I know my kids have said to me since then 'mum, the first time you left dad, we wished that you'd never, ever gone back to him'. But because the kids were so ratty as well, I had no control over the kids either, so it was just – I was in such a – you feel like a jellyfish. You've got no backbone. You just – it's just awful.
>
> (Veronica, 2013)

So powerful were the gendered discourses sanctifying marriage and demonising divorce that many older women tolerated horrific experiences of abuse for decades. The subject positions of the submissive female, the respectable married woman and the sinful divorcée were the dominant subject positions made available to women by the prevailing discourses of femininity and masculinity at this time. Often, the dominant discourses appear 'natural', claiming their own impartiality and gaining their authority by appealing to common sense (Weedon, 1997), making it difficult to challenge or abandon them. For older women, the discourse replicates and reinvents itself through other discursive repertoires such as the 'nuclear family', and these discourses also create memories and experiences for women across their life span, which are reinforced through the passage of time.

In many cases, the older women we interviewed would have most likely remained in the abusive relationship if significant events outside of their control had not intervened. A sixty-year-old woman who was married at eighteen years of age and lived with her abusive husband for twenty-five years discussed how her experience of abuse had finally led to her having a nervous breakdown. She viewed her nervous breakdown as the turning point in her life that finally allowed her to leave the abusive relationship:

> I had a complete breakdown in about 1995. I had a complete breakdown. I don't know how I managed to even keep going for the amount of years that

I had lived through it … because I had tried to make it work and stick with it for so long, something had to give in the end … but it was good. What came out of it was the fact that I was able to get away completely and never go back to him.

(Veronica, 2013)

A sixty-four-year-old woman who was married at nineteen for eleven years spoke about how she wanted to leave her abusive husband but doubted her ability to go through with it. It was her husband's eventual suicide that had ended her relationship with him but it also left her with tremendous guilt and self-blame:

I'm thinking, the whole idea was just overwhelming me completely. I thought 'am I going to actually even be able to do this?' I couldn't actually … Yeah. Looking back, I don't think I would ever actually have done it. But what happened was he suicided. He took an overdose of tablets on the belief that I was going to leave him. I was just filled completely with guilt and it took me over twenty years to come to terms with … that I didn't cause his death … I said a couple of times to my sister about it, I said 'people get twenty years for murder' and I said 'I've had twenty years. I've done my sentence of twenty years.' I just beat myself up so badly about the whole thing.

(Vivian, 2013)

All women are exposed to gendered discourses that offer subject positions saturated with different constructions of femininity, but older women – unlike younger women – lived much of their lives in a social and cultural context that only offered traditional, strict and rigid feminine subject positions, which at the time held such verisimilitude – for example, it is women's duty to serve men and cater to their needs. Consequently, older women may not have recognised more subtle forms of abuse such as social put-downs and emotional and financial abuse because these experiences were part and parcel of women's lives at this time. It was only when abuse became extreme and outside of the ordinary experience of women's generalised oppression at this time that older women began to view their situations as abusive:

But definitely his head set about women – I mean, he was – I should have picked this up earlier too – he was obnoxious towards his own mother. I was horrified with the way he used to speak to her. So there were all these signs that I should have noticed … So I was maintaining contact with him because of arrangements to do with our son … So [our son] would stay at his place sometimes – he was seventeen at that point. He got drunk one night and beat [our son] up … That was the incident that – where I decided 'no, this is it now'. Our son was old enough to be making his own decisions. I didn't have to do what I used to do before – like keep the waves smooth so that he didn't visit any of his wrath on our son.

(Jeanne, 2013)

Hence, the more nuanced complexities of gender power relations were invisible, and it was only when they became extreme that women came to identify them as domestic violence, resulting in older women remaining in abusive relationships for many years and only leaving them when the situations became extreme or unbearable. Unlike older women, younger women we interviewed seemed more able to recognise how subtle forms of abuse can lead to more serious violence, making them less likely to stay in an abusive relationship for many years and more likely to leave their abusers on their own volition. For example, a twenty-three-year-old woman who was in an abusive relationship for eighteen months at the age of seventeen spoke about how she learned how to behave in subservient ways in her relationship with her boyfriend who was both physically and emotionally abusive towards her. However, her fear that her boyfriend would become progressively more abusive over time led to her ending the relationship:

> He'd say you know 'get me a beer'. You'd get up and you'd get a beer. If you didn't you'd be yelled at in front of everyone. It was humiliating. So you just did it. I think that friendship group influenced me a lot in thinking that it was normal, whereas since I've been out of it I've got a new partner now, being around his friends I realise that's just not on … I got to a place where I was like, if he gets a hold of me and ends up doing something horrible and ends up killing me, you have to almost lose that fear and be like, if it's going to happen, it's going to happen whether I stay or go. I just need to lose that fear and just do it, and just deal with what happens. That's what happened with me. I just sort of snapped and thought I don't really care anymore. I just can't be in it.
>
> (Jasmine, 2013)

A twenty-six-year-old woman who had been in an emotionally abusive relationship with her boyfriend for seven years said that she would avoid raising topics of conversation that she thought might anger him but left her abuser when he became physically abusive towards her:

> I eventually stopped talking about personal things with him as he would start yelling at me and pushing me around … I knew what he was doing wasn't right, but when he did finally hit me I knew I had to leave.
>
> (Madeline, 2013)

For older women, traditional gendered discourses that have their power reinforced in the context of heterosexual marriage construct limited feminine subject positions. Older women lived these subject positions by virtue of their age and their experiences of everyday life as housewives to their husbands. In the context of domestic violence, these subject positions made subtle forms of violence invisible so that women endured in their relationships longer and only recognised abuse in its extreme form. They also blinded older women to alternative subject positions because the discourses they were exposed to had such verisimilitude in their lives.

However, we also recognise that discourses change over time, and time mediates how people interpret their experiences. Older women experienced abuse at a time when there was limited or no language to speak about and understand their experiences as domestic violence:

> I wasn't educated and I wasn't aware of my rights. Because he hadn't hit me, I didn't … I wasn't aware that it was abuse when he'd kicked the back door in and he was stalking. He'd watch when I left the house and he'd kick the back door in. I didn't consider it as abuse … he told me that he was allowed to do that because he owned the property.
>
> (Cheryl, 2013)

Older women who experienced domestic violence in their youth had tolerated abuse for many years because the strength of particular female subject positions embedded in discourses of marriage, divorce and children were so dominant that it was difficult to see an alternative. Moreover, alternative subject positions were unavailable or devalued, making gender for older women rigid and monolithic. For younger women today, gendered discourses are much more diverse and productive of alternate subject positions for women, particularly those pertaining to women's rights and domestic violence. However, for some older women, the exposure to domestic violence and women's rights discourses over time had created new subject positions previously not available or permitted. These more emancipated subject positions appeared to have greater power and traction in some older women's lives because they were perceived as 'hard won' and 'fought for', and were often framed in the context of their memories of how difficult their lives were in the past. Hence, women's constructions of their more emancipated selves appeared to gather strength and resonance through the prism of memory and the passage of time:

> I met up with some friends who I hadn't seen for fifteen of the seventeen years that I've been apart from the ex-husband … We met for coffee and they didn't recognise me – physically they recognised me, but they didn't recognise me as the person that I was in the marriage with him.
>
> (Dianne, 2013)

> If my current husband were to pass away first or was to meet another woman or something, I could – that wouldn't – I couldn't imagine having another relationship with a man and part of my decision to marry this husband was to give my children a father because my son used to cry and would say are you going to find us a new dad?
>
> (Vivian, 2013)

The availability of more emancipated feminine subject positions also impacted on older women who had suffered longstanding abuse and were still living with the abuser. A sixty-year-old woman who had been living with domestic violence for forty years and was still living with the abuser spoke about how her experiences of emotional abuse in the early years of her marriage had made her think that there was something wrong with her:

> I just kept thinking, 'Well it's something wrong with me, there's something wrong with me. He keeps asking these strange things and doesn't do things how I think things should work, financially and emotionally and as a family, so it must be me.'

(Glenda, 2013)

However, in more recent years, her access to the internet had enabled her to become more educated about her husband's behaviour towards her, and this led to her changing her view of herself in the context of the abusive relationship:

> I thought, 'Oh my God, all this time that I've been re-channelled, re-directed, not giving right answers, lies, stretching the truth, non-negotiation, it's not all me.' It was a relief, but it was a trauma because then you had to go through 'Why didn't you get this before? Why didn't you realise or why didn't you do something about it? You're a professional person; you're supposed to be highly intelligent. Why didn't you get it?' So then I did some more research on my own, and found out that I was emotionally co-dependent. That I'd never been supported in my life, so he was the myth, my knight in shining armour. He didn't live up to expectations either, or promises or whatever.

(Glenda, 2013)

Despite alternative discourses of gender emerging over time, and some older women engaging with these constructions, the traditional feminine role still had a strong foothold in women's lives because such a role had been so readily performed in their everyday lives over an extended period of time. Moreover, material circumstances reinforced such a role because the traditional female subject position gets its strength from women's role in the home, serving her partner and children, caring for them and engaging in home duties. Hence, throughout our interviews with older women we found that they were more likely to look to themselves to explain what was going wrong in their households and relationships because relationships and the home were seen to be 'their business', while the dynamics of abuse breed the self-entitlement and power of men. Older women who had been victims of domestic violence in their youth or who had been victims of longstanding abuse blamed themselves for the abuse they had experienced. For example, Cheryl, who had been married for forty-four years and had recently left her partner, said:

> I had an understanding it wasn't right, but I didn't have an understanding that it was against the law, that you had some rights. I thought it was my own fault – personally I thought it was self-inflicted because I chose to stay there and be a part of it so ...

(Cheryl, 2013)

Similarly, Veronica, who had lived with her partner for twenty-five years, said:

> That's the thing that happens with women is that they – by not standing and doing something about it, by not seeking help, by not doing anything, just trying to ignore the situation and just thinking to themselves 'Look, it'll be better tomorrow, it'll be better tomorrow.' What they're actually doing is they are enabling that person, that man to keep the abuse going. They're actually equipping him to do that really, but that's what happens. You get into that mind frame.
>
> (Veronica, 2013)

For many older women, however, constructions of self-blame were clearly and firmly situated within and supported by discourses of exclusive mothering and mother blaming. We found older women appeared to bear tremendous levels of guilt and responsibility, especially for how domestic violence affected their now adult children. Many older women reflected and spoke about how domestic violence affected their capacity to parent their children appropriately:

> It was like walking on eggshells. You didn't ever know what would set him off. It's an awful thing to say, but I did … I took it out on the kids, because you're so unhappy and you're trying to keep them quiet and for them not to – and my son picked up on that. He said 'Mum, dad's mean to you and then you're mean to us'. He could see that happening.
>
> (Jan, 2013)

> I worried the whole time til – the kids were eight and six, when he died, so I worried right through til they were in their twenties of how that's going to affect them. Did all of these actions towards them to make up for it and all this sort of thing … even now, things will come up and I take things the wrong way, perhaps, if my kids are upset or something. I think 'They blame me for that'. I think women in particular do that. We just load ourselves with so much guilt about our kids.
>
> (Vivian, 2013)

> I have said to my sons 'You never heard me when I would go to him [the abuser] and say "You have to stop treating the boys like this. You've got to stop saying the things that you say to them. It's not right what you're saying to them. You can't treat them like that."' I would go to him and have it out with him when the kids weren't around, but I never actually stood for them. Shame on me really because I should have damn well done something to stop it. But I just didn't, because I was so fearful. I told the kids I was terrified of him.
>
> (Veronica, 2013)

In many cases, women constructed self-blame in the context of domestic violence by using the language of choice, for example, 'their choice of husband and father' as well as 'their choice to stay with the abuser':

I worked in the bank at that stage and eventually gave up work, had two children and, I guess, during that time, I just had very low self-esteem with choosing him as a partner and I was probably pretty naive as well.

(Vivian, 2013)

Basically I said to myself 'it's your choice, you've made the choice. You've decided to stay there and put up with it [the abuse] because you want to see your granddaughters.'

(Cheryl, 2013)

This was particularly the case for women whose adult children were experiencing mental health or substance abuse problems. Jan, who had three young children while living in a situation of domestic violence, questioned whether her now adult daughter's self-harming behaviour was directly related to her father not wanting her to be born, a situation she blamed herself for as she chose to proceed with the pregnancy despite her husband wanting her to have an abortion:

My daughter's got a real problem with alcohol ... and she occasionally self-harms as well. A couple of years ago – it may have even been last year – I got this call in the middle of the night, 'Mum, can you come and take me to hospital?', which I did. But, there was a lot of stuff that came up then and she is obviously – I don't know where she's got it from, but she did mention something that dad said she was a difficult child or something like this. I just thought I wonder what he said to her. I wonder if he's told her that he didn't want another child.

(Jan, 2013)

Similarly, Jeanne blamed herself for the suicides of her three adult children, suggesting that her choice to stay with her violent partner had made her children extremely unhappy while they were growing up:

The worst thing for me about that entire experience was the impact on my children. That was the hardest thing and it's still the hardest thing for me to come to terms with. I still feel very guilty about that. I have a lot of guilt about that. I mean, there's nothing I can do about it ... It's hard to explain to someone why you persevered for so many years in a situation that was abusive to you and your kids. But you just – you know, as an intelligent woman, you just – there's just something about it that just keeps you there. It holds you there. It's horrible ... So they lived in an environment like that, where the minute he was out of the house they would come to me to pour out their miseries. But really it was more the psychological and emotional stuff with them – with all of us – like calling my daughter a little bitch and – just that sort of – the way he used to stand over people. I just think that had to have an impact on them.

(Jeanne, 2013)

Constructions of self-blame in the context of domestic violence were clearly and firmly constituted within and supported by discourses of mothering and mother blaming, which position women as the carer, nurturer, servant, and so on. These discourses positioned women in ways that emphasised their responsibility for exposing children to the abuse, particularly in relation to 'choosing the wrong partner and father' or 'choosing to stay with the abuser'. This self-blame does not dissipate easily because it is reinforced by the subject position of mother, a position so entwined with the feminine positions of carer, nurturer and protector that children's problems come to be seen as the mother's fault. So powerful are these discourses that there is little room for women to negotiate understandings that place responsibility for the abuse on the abuser, and which take into consideration the social and historical context within which decisions about choosing a mate or staying with the abuser were made. There was a lack of recognition by the older women that they had first experienced and endured abuse at a time when women were both legally and socially discouraged from seeking employment, pursuing a career or buying property, which not only made them extremely vulnerable to abuse but also prevented them from being able to support themselves and their children should they want to leave the relationship. These material realities uphold and support dominant discourses of gender that position women in the home as wife and mother. Women took up and embraced these subject positions because the alternative was materially, socially and culturally unacceptable. However, these historically produced subject positions are often lived out and understood by women and others as a personal failure or weakness for which they should take full responsibility and blame. In some cases, older women's sense of failure and blame was reinforced by their own adult children:

> I feel for my kids. I feel for the two boys, because they desperately would want a relationship with their father. All boys want a relationship with their father. It's taken me a long time to re-establish my relationship with them. It was very tenuous for a long time. They both had a real go at me and lashed out at me because of the situation that they were brought up in … They blamed me for not stopping him but you see, also in those days, we were always brought up to believe that you don't argue in front of your children. If the children are being disciplined, then you don't step in and stop it. That's what we were always brought up to do. That's how it was in a marriage. The wife, if she's got something to say to her husband, she waits till the children aren't there. She never defends them in front of the father.
>
> (Veronica, 2013)

> It's done so much damage to the family, like my mum and my son, he can't – he said, 'Mum, I helped you twelve years ago'. He said 'I didn't want to get involved this time, you went back and I was always frightened you were going to go back again. It's done so much damage; I've seen so much, mum.' He said, 'Why didn't you leave? Why didn't you?'
>
> (Cheryl, 2013)

Like we found during interviews with mothers, in some cases the discourses of mothering and mother blaming were consciously invoked by abusers in order to perpetuate abuse, particularly in cases where older women were no longer living in the abusive relationship. That is, women's positioning within a discourse of exclusive mothering and mother blaming was exploited by abusers who operated through women's adult children to emotionally manipulate and control older women. Hence, traditional discourses of gender offer women particular subject positions such as mother, nurturer and protector that can be used as a weapon by the perpetrator repeatedly and across the woman's life, even after her relationship with him has ended. A sixty-four-year-old woman who had recently separated from her abuser spoke about how she was emotionally manipulated to stay in her abusive relationship by her daughter who had been co-opted by her abusive husband (her daughter's father) to forbid her from seeing her grandchildren should she leave the relationship:

> And then my grandchildren … it was very – not just – I became almost a parent to my own granddaughters. So I was very heavily involved and children have meant a lot to me. So that was the way that they knew they could hurt me and control me, was by saying that 'You think of leaving' – because he wanted to stay in the marriage to collect another inheritance – 'so if you think of leaving before dad's ready to leave you, think again, you won't get to see your granddaughters.'
>
> (Cheryl, 2013)

A sixty-two-year-old woman who no longer lived with her abusive husband spoke about how he emotionally manipulated his children as a way of maintaining a menacing presence in her life and that, while she was aware of his tactic of abuse, she felt guilty about hurting her children by not allowing their father to be present at family events:

> When I had my sixtieth birthday, again my daughter said, 'I feel really bad because dad's not invited'. I said, 'No, he's not invited'. The day before, she said, 'Mum, I can't help it; I have to ask dad if he wants to come'. She said, 'he won't, so it's OK'. I looked at her and I said, 'Yes he will'. She said, 'But he didn't come to my twenty-first'. I said, 'No, but he'll come to this though'. I don't know what it is. It's this power he has over them. I couldn't believe it. I don't want to upset my kids though.
>
> (Jan, 2013)

Younger women and women in mid-life also engage in constructions of femininity that are self-blaming and constituted within discourses of mothering and mother blaming. The point of difference across age is how these discourses are taken up and the impact they have on women's meaning making around domestic violence. Older women have been exposed to these discourses across time, and time exposes them to blame across the life span, even when their children are adults. Older women are more likely to position themselves to blame because they did not fulfil their mothering role to the standard expected by their children, partners and society generally. This blame can be seen in examples of older women positioning themselves in paradigms of 'choice'; that is, 'choosing' to stay with him, often for decades. Instead, the stories of younger or mid-life women utilised discourses of mother blame to leave domestic violence, centralising their children as the main reasons. For example, a forty-six-year-old woman who had recently separated from her abusive partner suggested that her main reason for leaving the abuser was to protect her daughter:

> Sometimes she gets confused about what she is or who she is and I've had her sit and cry on a stool and say, 'I just want to be a kid'. That really hurts me because I feel guilty because I put her in that situation and it was just really hard ... My whole intention in leaving was to stay alive, just to stay sane, to protect my daughter, to have half responsibility of my daughter. It took a lot for me to forgive myself for what I had done to my daughter. I still don't forgive myself completely ... I've got to be strong for my daughter. That's who I've got to be strong for and that has been, that is really my main object for leaving.
>
> (Lesley, 2013)

Similarly, a thirty-eight-year-old woman who had been with her partner for ten years left him within three years of having her son:

> I was with him for ten years. It was only the last three years because I think having [names her son] made me really just go 'I can't do this' and also because [names her son] is a boy I kind of thought 'he is going to look at this person as a role model and I don't want him to grow up like that'. And then I said 'well why am I with him ...?' All those bits come together in that I thought 'I don't want him to be like that so why should I be with him?'
>
> (Kylie, 2013)

Hence, for older women, self-blaming was a passive process in which women lamented their decision to stay with the abuser, while for younger and mid-life women it was an active process that catalysed them to take action to leave the abuser. The power of exclusive mothering and mother blaming discourses in women's lives across generational and age cohorts is significant, especially given that it is likely that younger women have been less exposed to discourses of mother blaming, particularly in situations of domestic violence, than older victims either as younger women or as older women. While it seems that younger women are just as likely to be affected by discourses of exclusive mothering and mother blaming as older women, younger women are more likely to be positioned in ways that compel them to leave the abuser to prevent further harm to their children. This positioning is supported by current material and social contexts that make it easier for women to live independently of men. Older women tend to stay with the abuser but blame themselves 'after the fact' for how their 'choices' affected their children. In this way, older women are caught in contradictory discourses in which traditional discourses of gender position them as 'bad mothers' for *leaving* their marriages while mother-blaming discourses position them as 'bad mothers' for *staying* with the abuser.

As women grow older, they are further swamped by discourses of ageing that tend to denigrate them by objectifying the bodies and sexuality of both older and younger women. For example, age can often position older and younger women against each other in the processes of measuring women's value and worth, particularly through sexuality, beauty and productivity. Ageing positions women as sexually undesiring, unproductive, burdensome and valueless. These representations of age suggest that much of women's power is vested in their capacity to attract men and to bear children. Hence, women's worth is wrapped up in their sexual attractiveness and reproductive capacity, both of which decline over time as women age. Discourses of femininity are tied around the desirable, sexual woman or the pure, caring, nurturing mother (Walker, 1998), all to serve and complement the masculine. Hence, these discourses and the subject positions they offer not only separate older and younger women but also slice across women of all ages. Sexualised and mothering subject positions that characterise gendered discourses for women across the life span have unique implications for older women experiencing domestic violence.

If older women are positioned as asexual, and no longer procreating, they are constructed as incapable of either desiring or being in an intimate relationship. Moreover, the occurrence and effects of sexually exploitative and abusive behaviours are likely to be minimised or missed altogether. For example Brossoie, Roberto and Barrow (2012, p. 797) sought to gauge public awareness of domestic violence in old age but found that some respondents struggled, particularly with connecting older adults with sex. Phrases they reported from their study, such as 'The thought of a 75 year old woman steppin' out to get her freak on is just a little too much for most of us to take!' and 'Seriously? I think Alzheimer's has set in' demonstrated that the public perceive violence and abuse in the lives of older people as the result of dementia. Domestic violence and gender disappear in dominant discourses of ageing, which push particular deficit subject positions.

Gendered discourses operate to polarise women's sexuality in relation to age. That is, older women are not expected to be sexual beings and, if they are, it is expected to be hidden and not discussed, whereas younger women are expected to be avowedly sexual and, if they are not, they are considered to be 'frigid' or 'unfeminine'. Sexualised subject positions that characterise gender for women across the life span have implications for older women experiencing domestic violence. For example, a human-service worker spoke about how the asexual subject position serves to hide both gender and domestic violence in the lives of older women, which can lead to their situations being ignored or misunderstood:

> Given the almost intractable view that women's sexuality declines with age, it is inevitable that, where age is a factor, women's sexuality will be overlooked

or ignored, even in situations where perpetrators engage in sexually specific forms of abuse such as husbands threatening to sexually assault their wives. When sexuality is ignored or made invisible, the situation is less likely to be seen as domestic violence because people automatically think that domestic violence has to involve people who are intimate with each other. I have been involved in cases where you can tell that the husband has always been abusive towards his wife but because of how old the couple is it is pushed into the background and it all becomes about what supports can be put in place to help them better manage their lives rather than challenging the husband's behaviour towards his wife.

(Abigail, 2013)

While abused older women are exposed to discourses that position them as asexual, younger women are positioned by discourses of romantic love, which tend to hyper-sexualise them in contexts of domestic violence. The discourse of romantic love and its conflation with sex operates in ways that can make younger women more tolerant of abuse, particularly sexual abuse. A human-service provider whose work involved helping young women to have safe and healthy relationships stated:

Young women tend to fall head over heels in love and they think that their boyfriend can do no wrong – he is perfect in their eyes and if the boyfriend gets nasty they look at themselves and say 'well that's obviously my fault'. Worse than that though, they feel that they have to make themselves sexually available to their boyfriend, even if they're not ready to or not mature enough. They also sometimes think that their boyfriend being rough or sexually demanding is a reflection of how much he desires or loves them rather than seeing it for what it really is, which is how little he respects where they are and how they feel in the relationship.

(Brenda, 2013)

An older woman's reflection on why she stayed in her abusive relationship during her twenties and thirties demonstrates the ways that discourses of romantic love can be consciously taken up by abusers to emotionally control women in contexts of domestic violence:

I think the thing that hooked me into staying with him longer than I should have, was that I absolutely loved him – I absolutely loved him. He professed to love me all the time and everything … When you're there you're just holding out all this hope. There's just so much hope that things will be different. You've got these promises. He used to write me notes of love and stuff. I just kept getting hooked back into it all the time. Then he would try and kill himself if I wanted to leave. So it was a whole range of things that kept you there.

(Jeanne, 2013)

However, some older women appeared to use the subject position of the 'sexless' older woman to break from the abuser or to better manage their relationship with him while living under the same roof. A sixty-four-year-old woman who had recently separated from her abusive husband of forty-four years spoke about how not having a sexual relationship with him for fifteen years had made it easier for her to finally end the relationship, despite the other difficulties involved in the separation such as losing contact with her grandchildren:

> We hadn't slept together for fifteen years, so there was no marriage, it was just an existence. Younger women obviously they have more needs – sexual needs – and that doesn't bother me, I'm not sexually active, so therefore I'm not needy in that way. Whereas I think younger women are and I think that's what they come to battle with too and I think – I see it so often that the younger women, they separate and go through domestic violence which is definitely domestic violence, they've got – they're black and blue. They go back, he says he's sorry, they sleep with them and then they think 'No, he's going to change'. I see that so often happen. Whereas I think you cloud the boundaries once you start – you're separated, you don't go back and sleep with them because you can't make a decision. That was never the case for me, and that was easier for me. I feel for the women because they're younger, they're more naïve in that area, and once they do go back and sleep with them, you can see the resolve is gone. A lot of them just go back and only to face the same thing. That was never an issue with me … I wasn't sexually active so therefore I didn't have that need, which made it easier for me in that respect. The hard aspect for me was that I had to say goodbye to my grandchildren. But I think once you start having sex with them and you're separated, well you just cloud the lines. You just cloud it. You can't make a sound judgement.
>
> (Cheryl, 2013)

A sixty-year-old woman who had been married to her abusive husband for forty years and had remained in the relationship for financial reasons spoke about how living 'sexually apart' from her husband while still maintaining the appearance of conjugal unity made it easier for her to deal with his emotionally abusive behaviour:

> See now, with the new house, which has taken me forty years to get, and with the job which I think I'm going to terminate, and probably at sixty I'm not going to get another job that – well I'll try, I'm stuck there. Now I have to learn through psychologists that he's there – he's still providing the income, which I think is – I feel a bit of a fraud taking that, but then I think well, I've provided it for so long. So I now have to – I have to live in the same house with him, but just try and live my own life … it's semi-working but sometimes when I drive in the driveway and into the garage, and I go 'Oh, he's home'. So you're still thinking those things, what might happen.
>
> (Glenda, 2013)

While some older women were able to take advantage of being discursively positioned in asexual ways, the corollary of this positioning is that abused older women may not be considered to be living in an intimate relationship, which may contribute to their situations being interpreted as elder abuse rather than as domestic violence. Hence, the subject position of the sexless older woman can both protect and harm older women experiencing domestic violence. It can protect by enabling older women who take on this subject position to break from or manage their abusive relationships. However, living out this subject position can harm older women by making gender and domestic violence invisible in their lives.

This invisibility of gender and domestic violence in the lives of older women is supported by elder abuse discourses that position abuse as only the result of age-related factors such as illness, cognitive capacity and the stress involved in providing care (Spangler & Brandl, 2007). The view that caregiver stress is the cause of abuse in later life, which is still widely held and promoted in the literature (Spangler & Brandl, 2007), also supports subject positions that obscure domestic violence and gender in the lives of older women. Older women have been and continue to be shaped by discourses that encourage women to serve men, to be dependent on and look after men. Hence, caregiving is a subject position brought about and galvanised by traditional discourses of femininity and masculinity – women have been primarily responsible for providing care, usually for the benefit of men, both in the private and public domains (Hochschild, 1983), and they have been expected to fulfil this role with stoicism, even in the most difficult of situations. Consequently, in situations of domestic violence in which the woman is the carer and is abused, her experiences of abuse are overshadowed by the expectation that it is her duty to provide care to her husband, even under the most challenging of circumstances, and the perpetrator's responsibility for his abuse is eclipsed by his frailty and the subject position of entitlement that his masculinity affords him. In this context, age in combination with dominant discourses of femininity and masculinity make domestic violence imperceptible.

An examination of the criss-crossing discourses surrounding gender and age shows how age can erase gender in domestic violence contexts. As gender becomes progressively invisible along the life span, domestic violence too disappears because explanations for abuse are situated as random and unintentional (Meyers, 1997). The underlying complexities of abuse that inhere in gendered subject positions, and therefore power relations within abusive relationships, disappear when ageing is equated with deficit such as impairment, illness and associated stress in later life (Penhale, 1999). The subject position of deficit overshadows gender because it also makes sexuality absent in the construction of older women's lives. To reject the sexuality of older women is to accept that gender-specific acts of violence, particularly those involving control of women's sexuality and sexual abuse, do not occur in the relationships of older couples. The denial of sexual and desirable subject positions in the lives of older women is reinforced by the contrasting discourses of hyper-sexuality to which women in their teens to thirties are exposed. Gender needs examination in the experiences of domestic violence for older women because gender is evident in many different forms across the life course. Ageing does not operate outside of the dominant discourses of gender that position women; instead, ageing and gender discourses cross and reinforce each other in the context of domestic violence.

## Conclusion

Older women have historically lived with discourses of traditional femininity, positioning women as inferior, passive, submissive and subservient. Such discourses of femininity have offered women restricted subject positions, which have become entrenched across their life course because the passage of time has reinforced them. These discourses have also positioned older women as sexually undesiring and undesirable as they age, creating subject positions that make gender invisible in old age and thus invisible in domestic violence contexts. We found that older women engaged with the submissive subject position to cope with and attempt to stop domestic violence. Paradoxically, however, this subject position allowed and justified the perpetuation of abuse in their lives as all these women remained with the abuser over many years. Gendered discourses sanctifying marriage and demonising divorce, particularly if there were children involved, also contributed to women's submissiveness in the context of domestic violence because they prevented women from speaking out about and/or leaving the abuser, resulting in their enduring in abusive relationships for decades. We found traditional, strict and rigid feminine subject positions dominated the older women's stories because they held such verisimilitude; consequently, the more nuanced complexities of gendered power relations were unrecognisable or invisible, and it was only when abuse became extreme that women came to identify domestic violence in their lives. Consequently, many older women remained in abusive relationships for many years, only leaving them when the situations became extreme or with the assistance of forces outside of their control. While exposure to domestic violence and women's rights discourses over time created new and more emancipated subject positions for older women, dominant discourses of mother-blaming and exclusive mothering meant that older women still blamed themselves, rather than the abuser, for the issues and problems of their adult children.

## References

Anetzberger, G.J. (1997) Elderly adult survivors of family violence. *Violence Against Women*, 3, pp. 499–514.

Bachman, R. & Saltzman, L.E. (1995) *Violence against Women: Estimates from the Redesigned National Crime Victimization Survey* (NCJ-154348), US Department of Justice, Washington, DC.

Bagshaw, D., Wendt, S. & Zannettino, L. (2009) *Preventing the Abuse of Older People by their Family Members*, a stakeholder paper for the Australian Domestic & Family Violence Clearinghouse, University of New South Wales, NSW.

Beaulaurier, R.L., Seff, L.R., Newman, F.L. & Dunlop, B.D. (2005) Internal barriers to help seeking for middle aged and older women who experience intimate partner violence. *Journal of Elder Abuse and Neglect*, 17(3), pp. 53–74.

Beaulaurier, R.L., Seff, L.R., Newman, F.L. & Dunlop, B. (2007) External barriers to help seeking for older women who experience intimate partner violence. *Journal of Family Violence*, 22, pp. 747–55.

Blood, I. (2004) *Older Women and Domestic Violence*, Help the Aged and HACT (Housing Association Charity), London.

Bonomi, A.E., Anderson, M.L., Reid, R.J., Carrell, D., Fishman, P.A., Rivara, F.P. & Thompson, R.S. (2007) Intimate partner violence in older women. *The Gerontologist*, 47(1), pp. 34–41.

Bonomi, A.E., Thompson, R.S., Anderson, M.L., Reid, R.J., Dimer, J.A. & Carrell, D. (2006) Intimate partner violence and women's physical, mental, and social functioning. *American Journal of Preventive Medicine*, 30, pp. 458–66.

Brandl, B. & Cook-Daniels, L. (2002) *Domestic Abuse in Later Life*, National Resource Center on Domestic Violence, Harrisburg, PA, http://www.vawnet.org/applied-research-papers/print-document.php?doc_id=376

Brossoie, N., Roberto, K.A. & Barrow, K.M. (2012) Making sense of intimate partner violence in late life: comments from online news readers. *The Gerontologist*, 52(6), pp. 792–801.

Burman, E., Smailes, S. & Chantler, K. (2004) Culture as a barrier to service provision and delivery: domestic abuse services for minoritized women. *Critical Social Policy*, 24(3), pp. 332–57.

Campbell, J., Jones, A.S., Dienemann, J., Kub, J., Schollenberger, J., O'Campo, P., Gielen, A.C. & Wynne, C. (2002) Intimate partner violence and physical health consequences. *Archives of Internal Medicine*, 162, pp. 1157–63.

Coker, A.L., Sanderson, M., Fadden, M.K. & Pirisi, L. (2000a) Intimate partner violence and cervical neoplasia. *Journal of Women's Health & Gender-Based Medicine*, 9(9), pp. 1015–23.

Coker, A.L., Smith, P.H., McKeown, R.E. & King, M.J (2000b) Frequency and correlates of intimate partner violence by type: physical, sexual, and psychological battering. *American Journal of Public Health*, 90(4), pp. 553–9.

Few, A.L. (2005) The voices of black and white rural battered women in domestic violence shelters. *Family Relations*, 54, pp. 488–500.

Finkelhor, D. & Pillemer, K. (1988) Elder abuse: its relationship to other forms of domestic violence. In G.T. Hotaling, D. Finkelhor, J.T. Kirkpatrick & M.A. Straus (Eds), *Family Abuse and its Consequences: New Directions in Research*, Sage, Thousand Oaks, CA, pp. 244–54.

Fisher, B. & Regan, S. (2006) The extent and frequency of abuse in the lives of older women and their relationship with health outcomes. *The Gerontologist*, 46(2), pp. 200–9.

Fisher, B.S. & Zink, T. (2007) Older women living with intimate partner violence. *Ageing Health*, 3(2), pp. 257–69.

Godkin, M., Wolf, R. & Pillemer, K. (1989) A case-comparison analysis of elder abuse and neglect. *International Journal of Aging and Human Development*, 28(3), pp. 207–25.

Grossman, S.F. & Lundy, M. (2003) Use of domestic violence services across race and ethnicity by women aged 55 and older: the Illinois experience. *Violence Against Women*, 9, pp. 1442–52.

Hightower, J., Smith, M.J. & Hightower, H. (2001) *Silent and Invisible: A Report on Abuse and Violence in the Lives of Older Women in British Columbia and Yukon*, BC/Yukon Society of Transition Houses, Vancouver, Canada.

Hightower, J., Smith, M.J., Ward-Hall, C.A. & Hightower, H.C. (1999) Meeting the needs of abused older women? A British Columbia and Yukon Transition House survey. *Journal of Elder Abuse & Neglect*, 11(4), pp. 39–57.

Hochschild, A.R. (1983) *The Managed Heart: The Commercialization of Human Feeling*, University of California Press, Berkeley, CA.

Lazenbatt, A., Devaney, J. & Gildea, A. (2013) Older women living and coping with domestic violence. *Community Practitioner*, 86(2), pp. 28–32.

Lundy, M. & Grossman, S.F. (2004) Elder abuse: spouse/intimate partner abuse and family violence among elders. *Journal of Elder Abuse & Neglect*, 16(1), pp. 85–102.

Lundy, M. & Grossman, S.F. (2009) Domestic violence service users: a comparison of older and younger women victims. *Journal of Family Violence*, 24, pp. 297–309.

McGarry, J. & Simpson, C. (2011) Domestic abuse and older women: exploring the opportunities for service development and care delivery. *Journal of Adult Protection*, 13(6), pp. 294–301.

Meyers, M. (1997) *News Coverage of Violence against Women: Engendering Blame*, Sage, Thousand Oaks, CA.

Mouton, C.P. (2003) Intimate partner violence and health status among older women. *Violence Against Women*, 9(12), pp. 1465–77.

National Center on Elder Abuse (1998) *The National Elder Abuse Incidence Study: Final Report*, NCEA, Orange, CA, http://www.aoa.gov/abuse/report/default.htm

Penhale, B. (1999) Bruises on the soul: older women, domestic violence, and elder abuse. *Journal of Elder Abuse & Neglect*, 11(1), pp. 1–22.

Pillemer, K. & Finkelhor, D. (1988) The prevalence of elder abuse: a random sample survey. *The Gerontologist*, 28, pp. 51–7.

Regan, S., Gothelf, E., Zink, T., Rinto, B., Fisher, B. & Pabst, S. (2004) The prevalence and incidence of domestic violence in older women in primary care practices: why it is important to screen. *The Gerontologist*, 44(1), p. 414.

Reinharz, S. (1986) Loving and hating one's elders: twin themes in legend and literature. In K.A. Pillemer & R. S. Wolf (Eds), *Elder Abuse: Conflict in the Family*, Auburn House, Dover, MA, pp. 25–48.

Rennison, C.M. & Rand, M.R. (2003) Nonlethal intimate partner violence against women: a comparison of three cohorts. *Violence Against Women*, 9, pp. 1417–28.

Scott, M., McKie, L., Morton, S., Seddon, E. and Wosoff, F. (2004) *Older Women and Domestic Violence in Scotland … and for 39 Years I got on With It*, NHS Health Scotland, Edinburgh.

Seaver, C. (1996) Muted lives: older battered women. *Journal of Elder Abuse & Neglect*, 8(2), pp. 3–21.

Sormanti, M. & Shibusawa, T. (2008) Intimate partner violence in midlife and older women: a descriptive analysis of women seeking medical services. *Health & Social Work*, 33(1), pp. 33–41.

Spangler, D. & Brandl, B. (2007) Abuse in later life: power and control dynamics and a victim-centred response. *Journal of the American Psychiatric Nurses Association*, 12(6), pp. 322–31.

Straka, S.M. & Montminy, L. (2006) Responding to the needs of older women experiencing domestic violence. *Violence Against Women*, 12(3), pp. 251–67.

Sutherland, C.A., Bybee, D.I. & Sullivan, C.M. (2002) Beyond bruises and broken bones: the joint effects of stress and injuries on battered women's health. *American Journal of Community Psychology*, 30(5), pp. 609–36.

Teaster, P.B. & Roberto, K.A. (2004) Sexual abuse of older adults. *The Gerontologist*, 44, pp. 788–96.

Teaster, P.B., Roberto, K.A. & Dugar, T.A. (2006) Intimate partner violence of rural aging women. *Family Relations*, 55, pp. 636–48.

Vinton, L. (1998) A nationwide survey of domestic violence shelters' programming for older women. *Violence Against Women*, 4(5), pp. 559–71.

Vinton, L., Altholz, J.A.S. & Lobell-Boesch, T. (1997) A five-year follow up study of domestic violence programming for older battered women. *Journal of Women & Aging*, 9(1–2), pp. 3–15.

Walker, M.B. (1998) *Philosophy and the Maternal Body: Reading Silence*, Routledge, London.

Weedon, C. (1997) *Feminist Practice and Poststructuralist Theory*, 2nd edition, Blackwell, Malden, MA.

Wendt, S. (2009) *Domestic Violence in Rural Australia*, Federation Press, Sydney.

Wilke, D.J. & Vinton, L. (2003) Domestic violence and aging: teaching about their intersection. *Journal of Social Work Education*, 39(2), pp. 225–35.

Zink, T. & Fisher, B. (2007) Intimate partner and interpersonal violence: abuse in women over 55 in primary care practices. *Journal of Elder Abuse & Neglect*, 18(1), pp. 83–105.

Zink, T., Regan, S., Jacobson, C.J. & Pabst, S. (2003) Cohort, period, and aging effects. *Violence Against Women*, 9(12), pp. 1429–41.

# 5  Religious women

I felt like there are no options. For a Christian woman it is still not enough. If you suffer, you suffer – that's not a good enough reason to get out. Not because you are unhappy; not because you are incompatible; or he's a dickhead – not because of any reason – you've got to work it out. I do this and I am in sin and I am in sin if I do that.

(Nina, 2013)

## Introduction

In this chapter we explore the complex role of religion in domestic violence by drawing out the unique factors that impact on the lives of women from various religious backgrounds. These factors centre on how religious beliefs or practices can be used to force women into subordinate roles, as well as the denial or the misuse of religious or spiritual traditions to justify physical and sexual violence or other forms of abuse. We highlight how religion can be a barrier for women seeking help in understanding and addressing domestic violence, and paradoxically how religious practice and beliefs can be a significant source of strength for achieving resilience in the face of domestic violence and for contributing towards women's healing after leaving a relationship.

We acknowledge that the terms 'spirituality' and 'religion' are often used interchangeably and definitions are complex. For the purposes of this chapter, religion is defined as a systematic body of beliefs and practices that are related to a spiritual search, such as organised practices and institutions for the expression of faith, and spirituality is defined as the search for meaning and purpose in life, that is, an understanding of one's place in the world (Bouma, 2006). Judaism, Christianity, Islam, Buddhism and Hinduism are among the more well-known religions in Australia (Bouma, 2006). According to the Australian Bureau of Statistics' 2006 census, the main religious affiliations in Australia are: Christian (63.9 per cent), Buddhist (2.1 per cent), Muslim (1.7 per cent), Hinduism (0.7 per cent) and Judaism (0.4 per cent) (ABS, 2006), and hence we focus on such religions as opposed to those beliefs that fall outside the designation of 'organised religion', for example 'new age' religions. We also acknowledge that this chapter is predominantly written from our interviews and conversations with Christian women representing various denominations including Catholic, Protestant, Pentecostal, Reformist and Revivalist. In our time as researchers, we have interviewed thirty-five Christian women, three Muslim women, one Hindu woman and one Jewish woman about their experiences of domestic violence, reflecting the Australian context within which we are embedded.

Research studies have debated difference in prevalence rates of domestic violence in religious communities compared to the general population (Popescu & Drumm, 2009) and amongst different religions (Wang et al., 2009), with some arguing rates are higher in religious groupings and some arguing rates are similar to non-religious groups. It is not our intention to enter this debate; instead we want to focus on religion because it is widely accepted that beliefs about gender and the respective roles of men and women in society, and particularly the family, underpin explanations of domestic violence (Allen & Devitt, 2012), and religion is a major shaper of these gender positions. It has been argued that religion confers legitimacy on gender inequality and on gendered violence (Patel, 2000), and the question of whether or not religious beliefs and practices are at the root of domestic violence has been raised many times (Ellison, Bartkowski & Anderson, 1999; Ellison et al., 2007; Nason-Clark, 2009). In this chapter, we aim to illuminate gendered discourses and subject positions to show how gender shapes understandings and experiences of domestic violence in religious contexts. We do not engage in a theological discussion or debate on the complex teachings of various religions as we respect the diversity, divinity and spirituality within all religions. Rather, we argue that women from various religious backgrounds experiencing domestic violence face many complex and specific dynamics of abuse within their own religious contexts that impact on their spirituality. In short, religiosity is highly gendered and this context plays a pivotal role for women in understanding, experiencing and enduring domestic violence.

## Domestic violence and religion

Over the last decade, the emerging literature that has focused on religion and domestic violence has predominantly looked at either the views of the clergy on domestic violence and their responses to the phenomenon of abused women (Shannon-Lewy & Dull, 2005; Levitt & Ware, 2006), or the effects of religious teachings on abused women's understandings of domestic violence, and their use of religious beliefs and spirituality to cope with abusive relationships (Ellison et al., 2007). These studies provide insights into the complex role of religion in domestic violence, providing evidence that institutional religion can be a barrier when women seek help in addressing domestic violence (Bent-Goodley & Fowler, 2006; Wendt, 2008; Zimmer Schneider & Feltey, 2009), and that, paradoxically, religious practice and beliefs can be a significant source of strength for achieving resilience in the face of domestic violence and for contributing towards women's healing after leaving a relationship (Giesbrecht & Sevcik, 2000; Gillum, Sullivan & Bybee, 2006; Potter, 2007; Wendt, 2008). These studies have also shown that women can detach from organised religion due to loss of faith and distrust of religious beliefs and practices, or fearfulness of participating in services and other ceremonies at which the perpetrator may be present (Dehan & Levi, 2009). Research has also found that there are clear patterns in the use of religious beliefs and practices by men to justify and excuse their abusive and violent behaviour (Nash & Hesterberg, 2009).

Despite the growing research into religion and domestic violence, scholars have argued this area is under-theorised and under-researched for several reasons including: the personal nature of spirituality together with the apprehension from researchers and practitioners about invading privacy; the diversity of religious beliefs and practices; the tendency to subsume spiritual abuse within other forms of abuse such as emotional abuse; and the fear from researchers and practitioners of misunderstanding religious beliefs and practices and therefore offending adherents (Shannon-Lewy & Dull, 2005; Gillum, Sullivan & Bybee, 2006). We are aware of these factors as researchers ourselves, and have had much discussion about how to present a chapter on religion and domestic violence. We do not claim that all women experience religiosity similarly or that gender is fixed in religious settings; instead, we aim to use this chapter to show how discourses of gender and religiosity interweave in the lives of women experiencing domestic violence.

Furthermore, writing a chapter on the experiences of religious women provides the opportunity to identify and explore women's experiences of spiritual abuse as a form of domestic violence. There is no consensus on a definition of spiritual abuse (Ward, 2011), but it is a term of reference that is emerging within the field of domestic violence, meaning the denial or misuse of religious beliefs or practices to force victims into subordinate roles, or the misuse of religious or spiritual traditions to justify physical violence or other forms of abuse (Nason-Clark, 2004; Bent-Goodley & Fowler, 2006). Dehan and Levi (2009) reported from their study with ultraorthodox Jewish women that women stated their spirituality was damaged by spiritually guided violence from their intimate partner, which affected their identity, wellbeing and spiritual life. Other studies have reported several common behaviours used by perpetrators to spiritually abuse religious women, including women being stopped from attending religious services such as church or participating in religious activities, and using religious texts and teachings about submission, male leadership and the sanctity of marriage to control the woman and prevent her from leaving the relationship. Studies have also shown insight into how perpetrators use religious doctrines of forgiveness to absolve themselves of wrongdoing and insist that the woman forgive the abuse and continue the relationship (Bent-Goodley & Fowler, 2006; Wendt, 2008; Dehan & Levi, 2009). Ward (2011) concludes that spiritual abuse is evident when the abuser uses the realm of the woman's spiritual experiences and connectedness beyond the self to hurt her, and when the main damage does not occur at the interpersonal level, but rather at the transcendental one; that is, the focal dimension of the abuse is spiritual. Furthermore, Ward (2011) argues that spiritual abuse is a misuse of power in a spiritual context whereby spiritual authority is distorted to the detriment of those under its leadership.

The literature has to date shown many of the unique factors impacting on religious women when experiencing domestic violence, listed above. Furthermore, researchers have argued religious women often feel pulled and confused between what they perceive as the teachings of their religion and their personal safety and emotional and spiritual health (Nason-Clark, 2009). Consequently, domestic violence may not be considered a major concern because male dominance and female submission and subordination, together with forgiveness and hope, are advocated in family life and public life by their religions in various forms (Douki et al., 2003; Nason-Clark, 2009). Within the context of religion, it has been argued, domestic violence can be invisible or justified through religious commandments and teachings that preserve the honour and privacy of the family (Douki et al., 2003).

Knickmeyer, Levitt and Horne (2010) point out that, despite several theologians and domestic violence theorists implicating patriarchal religious ideologies, few studies have examined the actual experiences of women in domestic violence and their relationship to their religious beliefs and participation in faith communities. For example, Popescu et al.'s (2009) study found Adventist women held beliefs about marriage and divorce, stereotypes about Christians, and beliefs about Christian gender roles that were externally reinforced by other people in their lives such as clergy, church members, family members and partners. They argue domestic violence for women in faith communities is amplified by such belief systems and that religious teachings, as they are interpreted by others in the community, obscure the notion of partner abuse. Similarly, Knickmeyer, Levitt and Horne (2010) interviewed ten Christian women in the United States and found the enactment of Christian gender roles and the pressure to present as perfect, problem-free Christian couples concealed and prolonged domestic violence. They argued that religious beliefs and communities can function to promote secrecy around domestic violence. Specifically, they found women's experiences of feeling explicit and implicit pressure to perform the role of a good wife and to uphold Christian teachings about marriage was a dominant theme through which religion can operate to perpetuate abuse. Similarly, in Muslim communities, Baldry, Pagliaro and Porcaro (2013) argue that in order to better understand how domestic violence is justified, even in its most extreme forms such as killing, the commitment to the maintenance of masculine honour needs to be examined. In their exploration of attitudes about domestic violence amongst Afghani police, they found domestic violence was still seen as an acceptable means to restore masculine honour. They argue the role of masculine honour facilitates, justifies and even causes domestic violence, and religious contexts influence these gender role expectations.

Hajjar (2004) points out that, even though it has been argued across the world that gender inequality is the cause of domestic violence, within religious contexts gender equality is actually contested. She argues that many religions uphold beliefs that domestic relationships are legitimately hierarchical; that is, men and women's roles are naturally and divinely hierarchical. For example, Hajjar states that in Muslim societies this belief is both derived from and reinforced by *shari'a*, which tends to be interpreted to give men power over women family members.

Interpretations of *shari'a* accord men the status of heads of their families with guardianship over and responsibility for women. The complement to this is the expectation that women have a duty to obey their guardians. 'Men are superior to women on account of the qualities with which God hath gifted the one above the other, and on account of the outlay they make from their substance for them' (Quran, Sura 1V, verse 38) (Allen & Devitt, 2012). Similarly, Gallagher (2004) and Nason-Clark (2009) talk about the sanctity of marriage for Christian communities, whereby the promise to God to stay married until death places the intact family on a pedestal, and Christian women are positioned to be responsible for the marriage. Men are awarded access to power that women are unable to achieve (Gallagher, 2004), and this gender hierarchy is modelled in intimate relationships where men are the heads of the household and women the submissive partners (Gallagher, 2004). Allen and Devitt (2012) point out that St Paul was one of the most influential apostolic writers in shaping these Christian theological understandings of the roles of women and men with exhortations such as 'The head of the woman is the man … forasmuch as he is the image and the glory of God: but the woman is the glory of the man' (1 Corinthians 11:3, 7–9). Allen and Devitt (2012) argue these ideas are of central concern in relation to violence against women because they have a long history and are deep-seated in many societies. These religious teachings of male headship and wifely submission are high risk for women as they suggest that gender inequality is ordained by God, and therefore women are less likely to challenge such discourses (Nash & Hesterberg, 2009). Thus, in religious contexts, gender inequality is acknowledged and justified in religious terms on the grounds that God made men and women 'essentially' different; that these differences contribute to different familial roles, rights and duties, which are complementary; and that such complementarities are crucial to the cohesion and stability of the family and society (Hajjar, 2004).

Similar to writers such as Nason-Clark (2009) and Hajjar (2004), we too argue that for many religious women the experience of domestic violence is intricately intertwined with their spiritual life in such a way that it is difficult to understand one separate from the other. Hajjar (2004) points out that if we are to understand domestic violence for religious women, we need to examine the theological beliefs and ideologies that legitimise inequalities. It is within this context that we searched for gendered discourses and how they shape and justify domestic violence.

## Domestic violence, religion and gender

Avishai (2008) points out that many sociological studies of women's experiences with religions are typically framed by a paradox that ponders women's complicity. However, to see past this framing and to gain a greater understanding of how gender shapes domestic violence in religious contexts, Ward (2011) argues it is time to explore the subjective experience of women and men; that is, the deeply personal and spiritual. Avishai (2008) argues that women and men do not so much comply with gendered norms as they 'do' gender through modes of behaviour and comportment that are shaped by regulatory discourses. She points out that to understand religious women's experiences one needs to recognise that agency is not just about purposeful action such as resistance or the subordination–subversion dichotomy, but is grounded in the very constructions of gender. We aim to focus on these gender constructions in this chapter and we do this through the stories of religious women themselves.

As the literature has shown, the obvious place to start when examining gendered discourses in the context of religion is the subject positions of male headship and female submission. We found these constructions dominated women's stories of domestic violence. These positions were constructed predominantly through stories about Adam and Eve and quoting Ephesians 5:22–4 from the Bible:

> Wives, submit yourselves to your own husbands as you do to the Lord. For the husband is the head of the wife as Christ is the head of the church, his body, of which he is the Savior. Now as the church submits to Christ, so also wives should submit to their husbands in everything.

Women used the creation story and the concept of submission to try and grasp their own experiences of domestic violence and to explain why they personally endured such abuse for long periods of time.

The women spoke about Eve: her taking the forbidden fruit and giving it to Adam was constructed by partners and some religious leaders as a trait that all women potentially share; that is, women can be tempters, tricksters and ultimately the downfall of men. For example, Thea, a Christian woman, showed her Bible during her interview where her partner had underlined references to Eve as a way to exert his authority in their relationship:

> He defiled my bible. In Genesis, Chapter 2 and Verse 16 when after Adam and Eve had eaten the forbidden fruit, God said, 'Your desire will be for your husband and he will rule over you … I will greatly increase your pains in childbearing and with pain you will give birth to children.' He underlined and with exclamation marks 'he will rule over you'. My husband circled 'your desire will be for your husband and he will rule over you'.
>
> (Thea, 2013)

Magda, a Christian woman, also spoke about Eve and how domestic violence can be constructed as legitimate when women show the potentially dangerous traits of Eve. Magda left her partner after thirty-four years of marriage:

> There were sermons on marriage and they were for weeks long. On marriage and on women, the woman is the home maker and the home breaker and it's a woman's fault if the marriage fails. After all women nag and they want to rear their ugly head just like Eve did and a man has to put up with this all the time of course and he's going to be worn down, that is what you are taught. Eve is always blamed; she is the one who sinned.
>
> (Magda, 2013)

The creation story and the figure of Eve can be used within religious contexts to construct femininity as being potentially dangerous and something to watch out for; that is, Eve represents women as luring, tempting and tricking men in religious contexts. Through Eve, women are positioned with suspicion, as being sinful and not trustworthy, all positions that can be used to justify domestic violence if a man's headship is threatened in any way. Both Thea and Magda also spoke about their disappointment in their husbands for not fulfilling their role in headship. But they did not equate headship with ruling and dominance but as giving unconditionally to each other; that is, man and woman helping and complementing each other:

> Adam was standing right there behind her, did he go in and say Satan you get behind and leave my wife alone ... that should be what men are guilty of ... they're lacking in their care and their love, they're failing in their headship which actually is the sin of Adam but the churches just don't address men, it is always Eve, you know.
>
> (Magda, 2013)

> In the Bible when it says woman will submit to her husband, it means mutual submission but he would always say, 'You've got to do what I say, and you have to be in unison with me.' He didn't want unison, he wanted me under him and he wanted submission all the time from me, 'You've got to honour me, you've got to back me up, you've got to believe in the same things that I believe in.'
>
> (Thea, 2013)

Many women we interviewed spoke about their beliefs in mutual submission and therefore all reached a point in their lives where they could argue scripturally and spiritually that their partners had misinterpreted and misused readings from the Bible. However, during their lives with domestic violence they were seduced by the idea that masculinity and femininity frame and pervade their way of life. Discussions on submission were the most dominant theme in the interviews with religious women. First, women spoke about their perseverance and desire to understand submission as a way to please their partners and ultimately stop domestic violence in their lives, and second, they described moments in their lives when they realised spiritually that no matter how much submission was taught by their religious communities and practised by them as women, it was not going to stop the violence they were subjected to. Submission is highly gendered and women are offered particular subject positions of femininity that represent this submission. For example, Leona, a Christian woman who was married for twenty-one years, said:

> And in many ways it was a very nurturing church, incredibly nurturing, but very much about the submission of women and really quite extreme in that, for example, women wouldn't wear jeans or pants, would wear skirts. And some women wore them down to the ground because they thought that that was a feminine moral thing to do.
>
> (Leona, 2013)

Similarly, Haleigh, a Christian woman who married when she was eighteen years old and left her partner after seven years, said:

> There were three pastors who were very critical, just because of the way I dressed. It was so conservative, but they would say that this was tight, you know, just an average shirt was too tight. And like if I wore pants, I'd make sure like I was conservative, so you wouldn't see anything, because that's how I was brought up, you know? But everything was 'You can't wear this, you can't talk like this, we don't like your sense of humour, we just don't approve.'
>
> (Haleigh, 2013)

Discourses of submission offer women particular feminine subject positions such as conservative, hidebound, modest, quiet and restrained, all of which contrast with the image of Eve. These subject positions have influence and are taken up by both men and women in religious contexts because submission is embedded within theology, which reinforces religious entitlement to male power and control (Nason-Clark, 2009). Submission also offers subject positions that are highly valued within religious contexts because they contrast the potentially dangerous 'feminine' that Eve represents, for example, or femininity expressed within secular contexts (Avishai 2008). In addition, these subject positions construct domestic violence as a feminine problem and as feminine terrain because it is an extension of women's province of maternal authority and domesticity where women are recognised experts (Haaken, Fussell & Mankowski, 2007). Many women we interviewed spoke about times in their lives when they worked hard to perfect subject positions immersed in submission, believing it was their domain to master with the end result being a 'perfect' marriage and one without violence and abuse:

> Women in our church weren't allowed to speak much. Their role was to care for children and women could teach other women, but women were not allowed to teach men. It was very much from the women that I got the very clear picture that if I was experiencing domestic violence, I should look at myself and be more submissive and that would solve the problem. I remember doing a twelve-week program and it preached about women not wearing jeans or pants, being submissive, being there for their husband, never refusing sex, all that sort of teaching. And I was told that if I followed that, I wouldn't have any problems in my marriage. I would have a wonderful, happy marriage.
>
> (Leona, 2013)

While men are granted authority as head of the family, in many religious contexts the home is granted to women and positioned within the feminine or maternal authority (Haaken, Fussell & Mankowski, 2007). Consequently, religious communities look to the feminine domain to explain unhappiness, discontent or any forms of dysfunction within home life, and hence gendered subject positions can constitute an internal, spiritual barrier, contributing to women's tolerance of abuse in intimate relationships. Both Islam and Christianity place family and marriage as the bases of society and as essential for spiritual growth (Faizi, 2001; Nason-Clark, 2009). Saving the marriage and keeping the family intact are valued highly in religious contexts and we heard many stories about women's efforts, perceived responsibility and sacrifices to ensure the survival of their marriage. For example, Tammy, a Christian woman who married when she was nineteen years old and left after eight years, said:

> I definitely stayed in the marriage for the length of the time I did because of my faith, because I felt from the church that you do need to stay married and God honours marriage. Now I know right from my own personal experience with my prayer life and having a relationship with God – like, I feel that I am close with him. He does not want me staying in that abusive marriage, but trying to tell someone from the church that – I definitely stayed in the marriage as long as I did because of advice from others that you need to stay married.
>
> (Tammy, 2013)

Similarly, Leona and Haleigh spoke about marriage being highly valued within their religious communities and how much they wanted to be a part of that belonging:

> People would help me in very tangible ways like cook me dinner, help me move, but when it came to the issue of domestic violence, it was this very mixed message. Which I think is also why I stayed in a relationship that was unhealthy because nobody really – marriage is considered sacred as a Christian. And to be divorced is – you do become excluded. I've certainly experienced that since I became divorced and I've since left the church.
>
> (Leona, 2013)

> I was a bit ignorant at that time, because raised in that church from, you know, a very young age, you're kind of taught that any friends 'outside' of the church aren't your real friends, it's programmed in from a young age. But it was horrible to think that way only at eighteen years old, yeah, but at the same time to be so afraid that you weren't going to find a future husband, it was like, you were programmed that you've just got to find one. You've got to find one. Everyone else is finding one, so you have to as well.
>
> (Haleigh, 2013)

For some women, the advice of religious leaders from their own church communities impacted significantly on their decisions to get married and remain within their marriage. For others, we found they took it upon themselves to study and search for advice and teachings beyond their personal church communities about how to preserve their marriage. Their determination was backed up by the promise they had made to God, through marriage. They believed they were living the life God ordained for them and hence did not want to fail God:

I used to Google so much online that it took me a long time before I learned domestic violence. Before I got married I read thirty Christian books on marriage and listened to about forty tapes. I attended seminars – I have done a lot and during that time I have read a lot of books too.

(Nina, 2013)

I remember being told to leave your husband you would be the cause for him to commit adultery, man cannot go without sex. You must stay for the sake of your children. That caused a huge spiritual shift in me that I ended up totally dependent upon the Lord. I thought, right, from now on I'm going to find out who God is, I'm going to try and understand what is Christian marriage and I stuck my nose into the Bible, I stuck my nose into the book, every book I could read.

(Magda, 2013)

Discourses of marriage within religious contexts offer stark gendered roles of male headship and female submission. The centrality of religious belief systems such as submission supports men's sense of entitlement and expectations of women within the home, and ultimately justification for domestic violence if women are portrayed as failing to take up appropriate feminine subject positions associated with submission. Haleigh recalled how she reached a time in her spiritual life where she felt so confused about her relationships with her church and God that she could no longer attend church, and the consequent abuse she endured by her partner as a result.

So there was always that control. He doesn't want to be seen alone as it showed that I'm not supporting him, you know, I'm not showing I'm submissive to him as the head of the house, and that sort of trash. And it got to the point where I didn't want to go to church and so I was, I went under the blankets and said I'm sleeping in. The next thing the blankets were off, I felt myself, like he dragged me across. I fell onto the ground, he slapped me hard, I screamed because I was in shock, and then got strangled. So that was his way he knew he could force me to the car to go, because he knew how scared I was. And it was ridiculous, I was just thinking, so you strangled me and now you are like you should come to church.

(Haleigh, 2013)

Discourses of submission set up unrealistic notions of the ideal wife; that is, a wife that practices total submission and sacrifice for her husband and family will reach happiness, perfection and stability for all. Zakar, Zakar and Kraemer (2013) argue such constructions undermine any notions of equality in gender relations and position men in discourses of supremacy, which create spaces for the control and coercion of women, and justification for practices of discipline through abuse and violence. For example, partners can justify their abusive behaviour by quoting biblical texts that assert their perceived supremacy:

He always wanted me to dress a particular way, like wearing trousers and pants was just wrong, short hair was sinful. He would say you aren't priding yourself enough or if I then put fancy things in my hair he would say the scriptures tell you it's in excess. He would quote and pull parts of the scriptures to the point to shape you and to turn you into what he wanted. For example, Proverbs 31, there is a part about Pharaoh and the church and to prove that he and the church were perfect he would say that Pharaoh is of the outside world and that people find it easier to follow the Pharaoh rather than Christ. I was supposedly following Pharaoh.

(Haleigh, Christian, 2013)

But there is in religion, there are lots of things for men. For example, the women need to respect their husband, and lots of things about men. Not women. For example in Quran they are saying you need to have four wives, but they don't care about the reasons why, there is reason, yeah, their interpretation is very … unquestioning.

(Rabeea, Muslim, 2013)

This polarisation of male authority and female submission, seen as divinely prescribed, is used to justify men's abuse within the home, and contributes to women's ambivalence and indecisiveness when it comes to moving from abuse to safety in faith communities (Popescu & Drumm, 2009). This belief enables male supremacy, whereby male partners and religious leaders are positioned by doctrines and religious teachings to comment, assess, determine and judge women's performances in particular gendered subject positions. Consequently, as shown above, religious women are highly likely to critically examine themselves when they are struggling to understand domestic violence in their lives, and men from religious contexts are able to draw on and use religious doctrine to reinforce this lens and to justify their own abuse. Feminine subject positions are put under the spotlight in religious contexts, and there is the expectation that perfection in the home will be achieved when women become fully invested in these subject positions. Natasha, a Hindu woman, spoke of the importance of submission:

I've always been quiet, this girl who listens to everyone but after twenty years if you think that's right, and then suddenly speaking up for yourself you feel, 'Oh, am I doing something wrong, am I being rude, am I being mean?' I am Indian born, so, in our culture we respect everyone senior to us, everyone elder to us … so to be a good girl you have to shut up and listen and you are not very vocal about your opinions. There is a clear distinction between good and bad, so those who voice their opinions, they're known as the more rebel types in India, so, yeah I didn't want to fall in that bracket back then, so I kept to the submissive side.

(Natasha, 2013)

In religious stories, female characters can also be drawn upon to reinforce particular feminine subject positions of submission. We found in our interviews, particularly with Christian women, female characters in the Bible can be used to encourage submission and responsibility for domestic violence. For example, Madga spoke about Hannah who is mentioned in 1 Samuel of the Old Testament. Hannah was the wife of Elka'nah, and her distress is discussed in the Bible because 'the Lord had closed her womb'. She prayed and wept to God and poured out her soul to him in private, and in due time her prayers were answered and she conceived and bore a son, named Samuel. Madga said she aspired to be like Hannah and so prayed to God about her marriage for decades and believed remaining quiet and not telling others of her discontent, sadness and fear in her marriage, like Hannah, would lead one day to God answering her prayers for a loving, good, safe marriage: 'I kept quiet cause I thought I'm going to be like Hannah. I just pray and I'll shed my tears before the Lord' (Madga, 2013).

Haleigh spoke about Mary and Martha, two sisters in the book of Luke, Chapter 10. Jesus Christ visited their village and Martha received him into her house. Mary sat at Christ's feet and listened to his teachings, but Martha was distracted with serving and went to Jesus and said, 'Do you not care that my sister has left me to serve alone?' Jesus replied, 'Martha, you are anxious and troubled about many things, one thing is needful, Mary has chosen the good portion, which shall not be taken away from her.' Haleigh explained that her partner and religious leaders told her she was a Martha and not a Mary; hence she needed to be more like Mary; that is, more compliant:

> They use the scriptures in many ways, like do you know Mary and Martha, how Martha complained about everything, she had to do the serving, the cleaning, everything. And Mary just sat there to hear everything that was said, you know? So they used to compare me to that. Are you a Mary or a Martha? Like, is it wrong to want help, or isn't she holy and humble enough to be able to cope with it all on her own? I was so confused. But they were basically comparing me to them saying 'Are you a wife that whinges or are you a wife that complains? Are you a wife that's not happy with your husband's choices? Are you this, are you that?'
>
> (Haleigh, 2013)

Female characters can be used and drawn on by women, male partners and religious leaders to reinforce discourses of submission and appropriate feminine subject positions such as quiet, non-argumentative, meek and compliant. We found characters like Eve, mentioned earlier, Hannah, Mary and Martha were used by male partners and other religious leaders to shift focus to women's responsibility or sin in contexts of domestic violence, therefore reinforcing male subject positions of supremacy. Using such prominent female characters featured in the Bible provides another way to place a lens on women's behaviour in the home and their intimate relationships, simultaneously moving the focus and scrutiny away from the abuse and the abuser.

However, when male partners were willing to accept responsibility for a violent or abusive act, or expressed a willingness to work at their relationship, many women described the pressure they felt from their partners, religious communities and leaders to forgive the abuse, particularly if the partner displayed remorse and sadness. For many religions, like Christianity, to forgive is a valued attribute (Haaken, Fussell & Mankowski, 2007), which is viewed as a call from Christ, or taught as following in Christ's example and being willing to share in Christ's suffering (Crisp, 2007). Forgiveness also has important ecclesiastical undertones, whereby clergy are ordained to forgive sins in the name of God, Christ and the Holy Spirit and so it represents divinity (Ward, 2011):

> I think the belief of forgiveness certainly impacted on me and I felt that pressure on me to forgive rather than pursuing a legal line. It was also about to reconcile and to stay in the marriage. And I guess also the pressure, the consequences that I actually believed, certainly when I was in the fundamentalist church, that if I left my husband, that would be it. Forgiveness is not seen in its correct context. I think I've certainly been judged and asked to forgive things that are so hard to forgive.
>
> (Leona, 2013)

Our interviews with religious women also showed that male partners shift focus away from their abusive behaviour by drawing on concepts of female fidelity and sexual morality. In addition to submission, discourses of femininity within religious contexts also offer subject positions of purity, virtue, chastity and modesty. Religious doctrines teach that sexual relationships outside marriage are sinful, and sex before marriage is included in the definitions of sexual immorality. We found, in particular, that for women who have experienced sexual abuse as children or who found God and practised a religion later in life, their sexual morality was highlighted by their partners as a way to belittle and judge them, positioning them as sinful, and making women feel that the sin of sexual immorality was the cause of unhappiness in their relationships. We also found women subscribed to this idea at particular times in their lives because sexual immorality was seen as damaging to their spiritual essence or being. The shame of sexual abuse or sexual relationships outside of marriage was deeply felt by religious women. For example, Thea's story was common:

> I thought, well this Christian man, a good Christian man who knows the Bible, he wants to marry me, a sinful, you know, dirty rotten rag. So, when I had met my husband I was only a baby Christian. I still didn't understand, I didn't know that I was loved, that I was worthy, that I was washed clean of my sins. I was still stuck in the fourteen-year-old, you're a naughty girl, you're bad, sinful and shameful, you should be ashamed of yourself and all those things that I grew up with as a child and a teenager. And so, all the time that he was abusing me, I was like, 'Oh, I just have to put up with it because, you know, I'm rotten …' And so, because I wasn't a virgin when I married him, he underlined that

verse in the bible about women and virginity … but then it's like, 'Hello, you weren't a virgin either and you've got a son', but anyway, but when Jesus saved me, he cleansed me, he threw all my sin and shame and guilt in the sea of forgetfulness. He not only forgave me, he forgot. No-one should dredge it up but he did. He even brought up that I was sexually abused as a child.

(Thea, 2013)

Similarly, Ameena spoke about how she could never return to Iran because it is known amongst her family circle in Iran that she came to Australia to have a relationship with a man and they were not married:

My family are Muslim and for Muslim people they cannot marry to like Christian or other religion. My parents don't know I am now living by myself. I don't want them to think that there's nothing now. So when they ring and say 'Where is your son?' I say 'They have gone to the shops or playground.' Then I think I must be happy, if I was in Iran I was stoned to death now. I mean sex with no marriage. I am not involved in Muslim community here because I am not religious now and they don't want to understand and we don't need them.

(Ameena, 2013)

Within religious contexts, because discourses of femininity provide subject positions that promote submission, compliance and quietness as well as the potentially dangerous temptress, sinner and sexual provocateur, there is very little space for religious women to talk about sexual abuse by their partners in contexts of domestic violence. In most religions, historically, sex has been constructed as potentially an unruly force in human affairs, and hence its rightful place is within the constraints of marriage (Browning, Green & Witte, 2006). In our interviews with women, sex was often constructed as a duty women had to perform as part of their role as wife, which equated with the perception that men are entitled to and in need of sexual gratification. It is a woman's duty to keep the potentially unruly under control:

I was told if you're going to be raped you're better off submitting to it than fighting and resisting. So I thought 'I have to be that submissive wife, I must give in even if I don't want it and even if my period's not quite finished yet, even if you're not comfortable with it.' I was told if you want to keep your man you give him as much sex as you can and he won't want to leave. Anyway so I just put up with it. I've gotten to the point that my skin crawls if my husband touches me. I tried to be a loving, understanding wife. I was married for over thirty-four years. I gave it my uttermost, I gave it my best, I was dying … sex is supposed to be a loving, wondering thing and gift from God and I believed it could be. But I got to a point where I was dead. I made a vow before the Lord and I took that vow serious. And it was extremely difficult my leaving.

(Madga, 2013)

Marriage and sexuality constructed within religious contexts exert a particular pressure on women to be sexually receptive to their partners. Sexuality being tied up in duties of wifehood and submission constructs a belief that a woman should always be sexually available to her partner, irrespective of domestic violence (Hoel & Shaikh, 2013). Many women we interviewed grappled with feelings of guilt, ambiguity and confusion at performing this role. For them, sex was supposed to represent a mutually satisfying action that brings wife and husband together, transformed through marriage into a new person, completeness (Browning, Green & Witte, 2006); however this was often not their experience, particularly when domestic violence featured and grew within their relationships. Penny, a Jewish woman, spoke about her younger years when she felt lost spiritually and how she believes, upon reflection as an older woman, that her vulnerability was targeted by her first partner:

> I found him very spiritually draining. He would tell me he was a Buddhist. But he knows nothing about Buddhism because I have done my own reading on that. He actually knows zip. He would say Buddhists don't kill other things – they just love each other through sex, they're all harmony, harmony but then he had extreme temper tantrums. I thought I had no value as a person other than to have sex really, and it took me years and years – I was very stressed – I found it very hard to concentrate and focus on working or feeling comfortable in group situations or I overact if someone makes a pass at me because I think that they're just playing their game.
>
> (Penny, 2013)

Similarly, Jimin, a Christian woman, spoke about her spiritual confusion between religious teachings of sexual relationships and her first experiences of an intimate relationship and sex:

> I mean he was brilliant, he was an Oxford graduate, and he knew the Bible very well. I thought he was very charming but all he actually wanted was to … sleep with me, take advantage … Men looking for women who they can take advantage of, which I didn't know before, I had no knowledge, but last year, this man approach me with Bible verses, he would actually lead the Bible group, and I thought, 'Wow, he's really charming, he knows Bible, and maybe he's the one who god send me', that's what I thought, but really no. He was sleeping around, you know, I was one of his targets.
>
> (Jimin, 2013)

During our many years of interviewing women about domestic violence, we have found it is common for all women to struggle with talking about sexual abuse as a form of domestic violence. This difficulty comes about because the context of marriage can often erase the ability to name rape and sexual abuse, and because sexual abuse has broader personal and spiritual implications for all women, irrespective of where the abuse occurred and their religious beliefs and practices or lack thereof (Crisp, 2012). However, sex, sexuality and sexual abuse are often positioned as taboo subjects within religious contexts, evoking particular shame within gendered discourses, whereby shame is positioned with the feminine. Women's sexual lives often become the focus in religious contexts and are often read through subject positions of temptress, unclean and one who beguiles men with their sexuality (Messina-Dysert, 2012). Men are able to use these gendered ideas to justify their own sexual behaviour and abuses, and simultaneously shame women by invoking their sexual histories, encounters and experiences. This context creates a space where women are unable to express pain, confusion or grief, which potentially grows spiritual trauma, shame and self-blame in domestic violence (Messina-Dysert, 2012).

In summary, we argue, for religious women in particular the pressure to forgive, coupled with the promotion of submission within marriage, and the concept of feminine sin portrayed through tempting and beguiling, come together to create another layer of fear, a spiritual trauma for women experiencing domestic violence. This trauma can also be targeted by perpetrators of abuse by creating fear of the afterlife. Male partners or leaders are able to use this fear to their advantage in stopping a woman from leaving a marriage. The threat of evil and damnation adds another layer of complexity to understanding women's endurance in violent relationships:

> I think because abusers are so skilled at abusing, using whatever means they have – for a person in the church they've just got this extra weapon which is spiritual and in any form. For example when I was trying to break up with him – he quotes Matthew 18 that states where two or three are gathered and I am like, that doesn't even make sense, but he insisted that it meant that you had to be in unity, but even as stupid as it sounded after a while he convinced me. And the other one was the Bible says that you can't withhold sex and that's it – no excuses. Yes and so it's not just abuse from him, he gets his allies from his friends and they aim teaching at me. When I talk back and ask why are you assuming this and why do you say that, then they, oh say, we get so discouraged with you – the devil has got me!
>
> (Nina 2013)

> He put the fear of God into me. He would tell me, 'I'm going to come back to haunt anyone that does bad by me' and he used to terrify me and I know that sounds stupid if you don't believe in that sort of thing. My mum had drummed it into me, that if you do the wrong thing you will go down there [hell] and if there is evil spirits and all this sort of thing … he would say constantly 'I am going to come back and haunt you if you do the wrong thing and when I die this house will be …' He was always saying, 'I am going to be dead and put on an evil face.' I still had imbedded beliefs from being a child, that mum would, being a Roman Catholic would, there's the chalkboard and that's the good marks, that's the bad marks. You'd get more of those then you'll go down there.
>
> (Hannah, 2013)

In understanding domestic violence in the lives of religious women, we argue that the relationships women have with God and their religious communities, in whatever representation, cannot be ignored. Throughout domestic violence women are forever negotiating and renegotiating their image of self and God, and their relationship with God (Crisp, 2007). In the majority of religious contexts, women are immersed in theology and religiosity that teaches selfless submission, subservience and forgiveness, and that marriage is a divine, special promise, oath or contract. Hence understanding, responding to and grappling with domestic violence is shaped by this context. The coercion, manipulation and control featured in domestic violence are given another layer of power and influence when claims are highly gendered through the authority or divinity of God and the afterlife:

> There's a spiritual element to it, they confirm it with a scripture. That's why I was never able to report it to the police because he's not going to be able to get to heaven is he? You know, I didn't want to put anything in his way, do you know what I mean? It's just ridiculous now when I sit here and go, 'is there a heaven?'
>
> (Haleigh, 2013)

Despite the horrendous stories of physical, sexual and emotional abuse, and despite the high value placed on marriage, and the effort and endurance women described to change their circumstances and relationships, all the women we interviewed eventually left their partners. However, we found this event came about as either a result of their partner's adultery, giving them legitimate permission to leave their marriage (Browning, Green & Witte, 2006); or women describing a spiritual enlightenment or message from God that allowed them spiritual peace to leave their marriage (Ward, 2011). Again, women's decisions are immersed in their spirituality and relationship with God:

> Because the Bible says that's the only – so I thought back then – the Bible says that's the only reason for divorce is infidelity, and only if you can't forgive the person. So, I thought, yes! So, I, actually I waited until a perfect opportunistic time and I went, 'Right. I found this, and you need to get out. We're finished.'
>
> (Thea, 2013)

> I found who I am. I had to know the truth, that's why I read and studied the Bible because if God is real I need to know what he is saying, and from there I understood what spiritual abuse is. The Bible is everything that I've got, because I know when you have nothing, God is everything you've got.
>
> (Jimin, 2013)

> One day I remember thinking 'Holy God I've got to have an answer from you or I'm dead' and this day I read a devotion, a reading from Exodus and the Red Sea and there is a verse where Moses cries out to God because the sea is in front of him – and God says 'What are you doing that for? Just move

on' – and then the Pastor write 'if you've got a toxic relationship – just move on' and I am like … I grabbed that, thinking that's it, this was a little opening for me, the start of my journey.

(Nina, 2013)

Gendered discourses are particularly powerful and influential in religious women's lives because they have an established base or social institution, which is religion. This discursive field shapes women and men's lives by offering 'appropriate' subject positions and ways of thinking in everyday life, including experiences and understandings of domestic violence (Weedon, 1997).

## Conclusion

Domestic violence has been explained through gender inequality for decades; however, in religious contexts, how gender is represented and taken up means that domestic violence is understood and positioned as virtually non-existent. Masculine authority and feminine submission is constructed as divinely ordained and this reinforcement of gender relations diminishes women's beliefs in their right to, or their sense of, equality (Allen & Devitt, 2012). The theological and spiritual context, together with a sense of community and family that religious contexts provide, gives women and men a sense of identity, connection and order. In most religions, the feminine is positioned as the subordinate yet given status, and the spotlight is on the realm of home life (Zakar, Zakar and Kraemer, 2013). Gender and family life are intertwined with spiritual life in complex ways for religious women, whereby ideas of compliance and submission are powerful in shaping women's gendered subjectivity. Women can gain respect, status and forms of satisfaction, affirmation and affection by fulfilling particular subject positions embedded in religiosity. However, if they are perceived as acting in other subject positions that are not so desirable or positioned as dangerous, femininity can be loathed and constructed as usurping male power (Baldry, Pagliaro and Porcaro, 2013).

If male partners and religious leaders, and even women themselves, perceive they are not conforming to or fulfilling their purpose or role as part of their marriage – a promise, oath or contract they made with God – domestic violence is positioned as a legitimate way to regulate femininity and reposition masculine supremacy; its acceptability makes it invisible. However, for women living with domestic violence, we argue that this not only threatens their physical lives and emotional wellbeing but also threatens their spiritual self and security in religious contexts; hence the enormity of questioning, challenging and leaving their relationships and communities cannot be overstated. Religious teachings, beliefs and rules are inscribed, felt and lived; they are about essence, faith and life in relation to the divine. Gender is disciplined and done through behaviours and comportments that are shaped by these regulatory religious and spiritual contexts (Avishai, 2008). This context produces highly valued feminine and masculine subjectivities where we can understand women's experiences of domestic violence, including spiritual abuse, how men and religious leaders use gender to abuse women and to justify it, and also why women often take ownership of changing their circumstances (Nason-Clark, 2004).

# References

Allen, M. & Devitt, C. (2012) Intimate partner violence and belief systems in Liberia. *Journal of Interpersonal Violence*, 27(17), pp. 3514–31.

Australian Bureau of Statistics (ABS) (2006) Census data. Available at: www.censusdata. abs.gov.au

Avishai, O. (2008) 'Doing religion' in a secular world: women in conservative religions and the question of agency. *Gender & Society*, 22(4), pp. 409–33.

Baldry, A., Pagliaro, S. & Porcaro, C. (2013) The rule of law at time of masculine honor: Afghan police attitudes and intimate partner violence. *Group Processes & Intergroup Relations*, 16(3), pp. 363–74.

Bent-Goodley, T. & Fowler, D. (2006) Spiritual and religious abuse: expanding what is known about domestic violence. *AFFILIA: Journal of Women and Social Work*, 21(3), pp. 282–95.

Bouma, G. (2006) *Australian Soul: Religion and Spirituality in the Twenty-First Century*, Cambridge University Press, Melbourne.

Browning, S., Green, C. & Witte, J. (2006) *Sex, Marriage, and Family in World Religions*, Columbia University Press, New York.

Crisp, B. (2007) Spirituality and sexual abuse: issues and dilemmas for survivors. *Theology & Sexuality*, 13(3), pp. 301–14.

Crisp, B. (2012) The spiritual implications of sexual abuse: not just an issue for religious. *Feminist Theology*, 20(2), pp. 133–45.

Dehan, N. & Levi, Z. (2009) Spiritual abuse: an additional dimension of abuse experienced by abused haredi (ultraorthodox) Jewish wives. *Violence Against Women*, 15(11), pp. 1294–1310.

Douki, S., Nacef, F., Belhadj, A., Bouasker, A. & Ghachem, R. (2003) Violence against women in Arab and Islamic countries. *Archives of Women's Mental Health*, 6, pp. 165–71.

Ellison, C., Bartkowski, J. & Anderson, K. (1999) Are there religious variations in domestic violence? *Journal of Family Issues*, 20(1), pp. 87–113.

Ellison, C., Trinitapoli, J., Anderson, K. & Johnson, B. (2007) Race/ethnicity, religious involvement, and domestic violence. *Violence Against Women*, 13(11), pp. 1094–1112.

Faizi, N. (2001) Domestic violence in the Muslim community. *Texas Journal of Women and the Law*, 10(2), pp. 209–30.

Gallagher, S. (2004). The marginalization of evangelical feminism. *Sociology of Religion*, 65, pp. 215–237.

Giesbrecht, N. & Sevcik, I. (2000) The process of recovery and rebuilding among abused women in the conservative evangelical subculture. *Journal of Family Violence*, 15(3), pp. 229–48.

Gillum, T., Sullivan, C. & Bybee, D. (2006) The importance of spirituality in the lives of domestic violence survivors. *Violence Against Women*, 12(3), pp. 240–50.

Haaken, J., Fussell, H. & Mankowski, E. (2007) Bringing the church to its knees: evangelical Christianity, feminism, and domestic violence discourse. *Psychotherapy and Politics International*, 5(2), pp. 103–15.

Hajjar, L. (2004) Religion, state power, and domestic violence in Muslim societies: a framework for comparative analysis. *Law and Social Inquiry*, 29(1), pp. 1–38.

Hoel, N. & Shaikh, S. (2013) Sex as ibadah: religion, gender, and subjectivity among South African Muslim women. *Journal of Feminist Studies in Religion*, 29(1), pp. 69–97, 188, 190.

Knickmeyer, N., Levitt, H. & Horne, S. (2010) Putting on Sunday best: the silencing of battered women within Christian faith communities. *Feminism & Psychology*, 20(1), pp. 94–113.

Levitt, H.M. & Ware, K. (2006) 'Anything with two heads is a monster': religious leaders' perspectives on marital equality and domestic violence. *Violence Against Women*, 12(12), pp. 1169–90.

Messina-Dysert, G. (2012) Rape and spiritual death. *Feminist Theology*, 20(2), pp. 120–32.

Nash, S. & Hesterberg, L. (2009) Biblical framings of and responses to spousal violence in the narratives of abused Christian women. *Violence Against Women*, 15(3), pp. 340–61.

Nason-Clark, N. (2004) When terror strikes at home: the interface between religion and domestic violence. *Journal for the Scientific Study of Religion*, 43, pp. 303–10.

Nason-Clark, N. (2009) Christianity and the experience of domestic violence: what does faith have to do with it? *Social Work & Christianity*, 36(4), pp. 379–93.

Patel, P. (2000) Southhall black sisters: domestic violence campaigns and alliances across the divisions of race, gender, and class. In J. Hanmer & C. Itzin (Eds) *Home Truths About Domestic Violence: Feminist Influences on Policy and Practice, a Reader*, Routledge, London, pp. 167–84.

Popescu, M. & Drumm, R. (2009) Religion, faith communities, and intimate partner violence. *Social Work & Christianity*, 36(4), pp. 375–8.

Popescu, M., Drumm, R., Mayer, S., Cooper, L., Foster, T., Seifert, M., Gadd, H. & Dewan, S. (2009) 'Because of my beliefs that I had acquired from the Church …': religious belief-based barriers for Adventist women in domestic violence relationships. *Social Work and Christianity*, 36(4), pp. 394–414.

Potter, H. (2007) Battered black women's use of religious services and spirituality for assistance in leaving abusive relationships. *Violence Against Women*, 13(3), pp. 262–84.

Shannon-Lewy, C. & Dull, V. (2005) The response of Christian clergy to domestic violence: help or hindrance? *Aggression and Violent Behavior*, 10, pp. 647–59.

Wang, M., Horne, S., Levitt, H. & Klesges, L. (2009) Christian women in IPV relationships: an exploratory study of religious factors. *Journal of Psychology and Christianity*, 28(3), pp. 224–35.

Ward, D. (2011) The lived experience of spiritual abuse. *Mental Health, Religion & Culture*, 14(9), pp. 899–915.

Weedon, C. (1997) *Feminist Practice and Poststructuralist Theory*, 2nd edition, Blackwell, Malden, MA.

Wendt, S. (2008), Christianity and domestic violence: feminist poststructuralist perspectives. *AFFILIA: Journal of Women and Social Work*, 23(2), pp. 144–55.

Zakar, R., Zakar, M. & Kraemer, A. (2013) Men's beliefs and attitudes toward intimate partner violence against women in Pakistan. *Violence Against Women*, 19(2), pp. 246–68.

Zimmer Schneider, R. & Feltey, K.M. (2009) 'No matter what has been done wrong can always be redone right': spirituality in the lives of imprisoned battered women. *Violence Against Women*, 15(4), pp. 443–59.

# 6 Refugee women

I think that men, yeah, they are thinking 'This is our culture and we have to
have power on the women otherwise they, maybe they will divorce, they will
go.' They [the men] are afraid of that … that's why they are showing their
power over women.

(Rabeea from Afghanistan, 2013)

## Introduction

In this chapter we explore the unique factors that impact on refugee women's
experiences of domestic violence. While the experiences of refugee women are
situated in and have significant continuities with the broader experiences of
women from culturally and linguistically diverse (CaLD) backgrounds, we have
chosen to focus on refugee women in this chapter for two main reasons. First, the
wars of the last decade have produced inordinate numbers of people who are
displaced across the globe. Most recently, the war in Syria in 2013 has produced
close to two million refugees, with these numbers coming on the back of those
people already displaced by the wars in Iraq, Afghanistan and Africa. During
2012, a worldwide average of 23,000 people per day were forced to abandon their
homes due to conflict and persecution (Australian Human Rights Commission,
2013). The sheer numbers of displaced persons across the globe and the increasing
numbers seeking asylum in countries such as Australia underscores the exigencies
of understanding domestic violence in refugee communities in countries of
resettlement.

Second, there are significant differences in circumstances between those who
migrate voluntarily and those who are forced to leave their countries of origin.
For refugees, migration is the inexorable consequence of the horror of war and
persecution; that is, survival is often dependent upon fleeing their homes and
attempting to find safety elsewhere. Broader discussions about the experiences of
CaLD women tend to gloss over the different circumstances between voluntary
and forced migration but it is precisely these circumstances that both underpin
and create particular complexities in situations of domestic violence for refugee
women. This is not to argue that gender constructions are not similar in contexts
of domestic violence for refugee communities and CaLD communities in general.

For example, racism and a sense of 'not belonging' are likely to affect both refugees and voluntary migrants in similar ways, particularly those from non-Western societies. In this sense, the intersections of gender and culture are likely to produce and expose discourses that similarly position refugees and voluntary migrants. What is significant for refugees, however, is how dominant gendered discourses and the subject positions they offer are re-interpreted and reconfigured by the unique circumstances of refugee life. In this chapter we examine the specific circumstances that increase the complexity of domestic violence for refugee women, such as their previous experiences of sexual and gender-based violence in contexts of war and flight, the impact of trauma and resettlement on husbands and partners and the significance of culture and connection to communities brought about by the events of displacement and loss. These circumstances are further compounded by language barriers, unemployment and poverty, and Western and Anglo-centric understandings of domestic violence.

This chapter is informed by two small qualitative studies involving refugee women and human service workers. The first of these was carried out as part of a larger project involving a South Australian domestic violence service in partnership with the Liberian community in South Australia. The larger project was developed in response to challenges faced by workers in the domestic violence service sector to provide culturally relevant and supportive services to women and children from new and emerging communities. Consultation with the Australian Refugee Association revealed that, although Liberian women had identified domestic violence as a significant issue affecting their lives and their community, women from this community were not accessing or receiving domestic violence support or information. Qualitative data were collected through focus group discussions with Liberian women. Focus groups have been found to be a useful way of gaining insight into cultural norms and collective beliefs about sensitive topics (Shiu-Thornton, Senturia & Sullivan, 2005). The focus groups were facilitated by two senior workers from the domestic violence service and a Liberian worker from the Australian Refugee Association. The second study was focused on the impact of encampment on domestic violence in refugee communities. This study involved individual interviews with refugee women who had spent time in camps overseas and in Australian detention centres. Human service workers in refugee and domestic violence services in South Australia were also interviewed about their experiences of supporting refugee women affected by domestic violence.

While we had some moderate success in recruiting refugee women for these studies, recruitment, overall, was a challenging process due to the extreme vulnerability of this group of women. Many refugee women continue to endure the shame and humiliation of being a victim of rape and torture during war and flight and in refugee camps, and these events are so often shrouded in secrecy and shame that they can prevent women from speaking about any kind of violence in their lives. As well, we understood that past experiences of abuses of power and betrayals of trust carried out by systems of rule or authority in their home countries may make refugee women fearful to speak to people outside of their cultural communities or trusted relationships, especially about an issue as sensitive as domestic violence. We were also aware of the need to overcome language and other barriers so that women would be able to provide authentically informed consent to participate in our research. In order to address these issues to the best of our ability, we attempted to recruit refugee women through the services from which they were already seeking support. This ensured that only those women who were already well supported by services and assessed by workers as being comfortable with such a process were invited to participate in the research.

However, we encountered workers in services who acted as gatekeepers in response to our requests for assistance in the recruitment of refugee women. One of the main concerns put forward by human service workers was women's safety. As one worker noted: 'There are significant safety risks involved in divulging domestic violence, both personally and from community. Given that most women would still be in the relationship, their safety would be the primary consideration.' Another primary concern was that many refugee women would not be ready or prepared to discuss domestic violence, particularly if they are within twelve months of becoming settled into the community following detention. As another worker noted: 'This is still a period where resettlement worries and issues, particularly housing, are a major feature.' Human service workers were also concerned about refugees 'becoming over-researched', given their relatively small numbers and the ever-expanding quantum of research projects focusing on refugee health and welfare. However, during our many face-to-face meetings with workers and managers in a number of services providing support to refugee women, we came to understand more fully that workers tread a fine line between a desire to protect refugee women and the need to provide these women with reasonable opportunities to be involved in research that may be of benefit to them. Many refugee women have experienced such high levels of sexual violence and humiliation prior to their arrival in Australia that speaking about current experiences of domestic violence can trigger painful memories and post-traumatic stress. In turn, workers appeared to gain some reassurance by our focus on the ethical conduct of research with vulnerable communities as well as our desire to make research a mutually beneficial process in which there would be some practical benefit for participants. For example, the focus group interviews with Liberian women were structured to provide women with opportunities to engage in therapeutic counselling both during and immediately following the interviews, and on most occasions these opportunities were taken up by the women. Our meetings with workers also encouraged our decision to involve them in our research and to conduct interviews with them about their perspectives and experiences of providing services to refugee women affected by domestic violence. These interviews enriched our research findings by providing context and depth to the narratives and stories provided by refugee women.

## Domestic violence and refugee women

As foreshadowed, there are similarities in women's experiences of domestic violence across CaLD communities due to factors relating to being a member of a minority culture and learning about and adapting to a dominant culture that can be hostile and impenetrable. However, there are particular factors that increase the complexity of domestic violence for refugee women and which differentiate their experiences from other CaLD women. Due to the circumstances of forced migration, many refugee women are dealing with the challenges of the present while dealing with the horrors of the past (Pittaway & Eckert, 2013). That is, they are faced with the complex challenges of settlement in a new and often very different culture, while also having to deal with the often horrific effects of war, loss, displacement and encampment. Many refugee women are resettled in countries of asylum, such as Australia, with an already accumulated set of traumatic experiences resulting from the violence and atrocities they have witnessed, their long endurance of human rights violations, and the impact of persecution and flight (Pittaway & Eckert, 2013):

> The killing … that was the big reason why we left … that's the big issue for, especially for Hazara people; that's why they escaping but even now in Pakistan they don't have safety. There is lots of killing of Hazara people, but I don't know who are the bad people; Taliban or non-Taliban, I don't know.
>
> (Saleema from Afghanistan, 2013)

> Yeah, where I come, the people have no life. They don't know about next, in a second what happened with you. There is only death in your school, in your language centre, in your … everywhere is similar. It's a very scary place now … when we want to come here in Australia, we thought 'Here is death if we go on the journey we, our boat is splash, anything bad with us; everywhere is death, but we have a hope.'
>
> (Hamasa from Afghanistan, 2013)

> From everywhere you have a scare when you move from your country to another country, and you have no documents and illegal; it's very dangerous … you live in a jungle with animals with dangerous snakes, like these things, and especially if police catch you, it's very trouble for you.
>
> (Zahra from Pakistan, 2013)

Almost all refugees have either witnessed or been subject to violence, including rape, torture, public humiliation, murder and the loss or disappearance of family members (Pittaway & Eckert, 2013). Women who have endured such experiences have an increased vulnerability to further abuse or sexual exploitation in their countries of origin (Rees, 2004; Allen & Devitt, 2012), and are more vulnerable to domestic violence and sexual abuse upon resettlement in a new country (Pittaway, 2004; Schmidt, 2005, Pease & Rees, 2008). Moreover, domestic violence taps into women's prior experiences of trauma and can be internalised as a continuation of their ordeal (Zannettino, 2012b):

> We are away from the war now but when the men get violent it is just like we are back there because we are scared and we are worried and we don't

know what mood he will be in and we are in fear all the time ... we feel just like we feel when we were in Liberia but there is no war here, it is only the relationship that makes us scared.

(Christiana from Liberia, 2009)

There are significant continuities between the refugee experience and domestic violence because gender is central in both. Systematised sexual abuse and gender-based violence is the most pervasive form of violence against women in the context of war (Heineman, 2011; Leatherman, 2011). Sexual violence against women and girls is commonly used as a strategy to terrorise, control, displace and even eliminate targeted groups (Leatherman, 2007, 2011; Khanna, 2008; Longombe, Claude & Ruminjo, 2008; Leiby, 2009; Bartels et al., 2010; Burnet, 2012), and perpetrators are often motivated by a desire for power and domination (Longombe, Claude & Ruminjo, 2008). The United Nations High Commissioner for Refugees (UNHCR, 2003) estimates that 80 per cent of all refugee women experience rape and sexual abuse. The raping of women in combat and occupation zones is a nearly universal condition of military campaigns (Mullins, 2009). While men generally comprise the majority of victims of human rights abuses during armed conflict, patterns of victimisation indicate that women are targeted more often in ways that are directly linked to their gender and sexual identity, and to their identity as the bearers and protectors of a community's culture and future generations (Leiby, 2009). When women are targeted for rape in conflict situations, it is often the enemy's way of humiliating and showing their power over the men in the community. Refugee women and girls are targeted for rape and sexual exploitation and abuse in flight and in refugee camps and urban refugee sites (Pittaway & Eckert, 2013).

The effects of violence, torture and the trauma of flight from home are amplified by conditions in countries of asylum. Existence is often a daily struggle, with poor access to food, water, housing and health. People live in a state of insecurity and uncertainty. Many live in protracted refugee situations, or what has been called 'warehoused', where they have been in camps and urban areas from eight to thirty years (Pittaway & Eckert, 2013). Women and children are exposed to rape, forced marriage and forced sex through economic abuse, which has been termed 'survival sex'. Many women experience anxiety about family and friends left behind, guilt and shame, feelings of helplessness in an unfamiliar environment, fear and insecurity and cultural dislocation (Pittaway & Eckert, 2013).

Refugee women experience a heightened risk of domestic violence due to the traumatic experiences that they and their families have endured prior to their arrival in a new country (Pittaway & Rees, 2006; Pittaway, Muli & Shteir, 2009; Zannettino, 2012b). Pittaway and Rees (2006) apply a framework of cumulative risk to draw attention to some of the specific and compounding issues that can make refugee women more vulnerable to domestic violence. They identify several cumulative effects that impact on domestic violence in the refugee context, including more extreme cultural practices concerning women and girls than in the traditional society arising from efforts to protect traditional family and community norms broken down by war and displacement, and an increase in men's violent behaviour resulting from threats to their traditional identities and roles brought about by their experiences of trauma, persecution and time spent in refugee camps. In addition, women who have experienced rape and sexual abuse in situations of armed conflict are more vulnerable to rejection, abandonment and further abuse by the male members of their family. Pittaway and Rees (2006) conclude that there are universal causative factors in cases of domestic violence, such as male power and patriarchal cultures, that are exacerbated by the abuses and disadvantages faced by both refugee men and women in their countries of origin and when living in refugee camps.

Refugee women are at particular risk of domestic violence in countries of asylum and resettlement (Pittaway & Rees, 2006; UNHCR, 2008; Hajdukowski-Ahmed, Khanlou & Moussa, 2009) which is largely due to the impact of trauma, torture, displacement and loss of family dynamics and relationships (Doney, Eckert & Pittaway, 2009; Zannettino, 2012b). For example, an Australian study conducted by Pittaway, Muli and Shteir (2009) found that, despite the great potential of refugees and migrants from the Horn of Africa to successfully integrate into Australian society, women in the study reported that their histories of rape, engaging in sex in order to survive, and having children born of rape made them vulnerable to further sexual exploitation and abuse, and prevented them from connecting with their own community, which exacerbated their loneliness and social isolation in the wider community. In addition to the traumas and after-effects of their pre-arrival experiences, the challenges and stresses of resettlement in a new country can also increase women's vulnerability to domestic violence. Issues such as separation from family members, disruption to traditional gender roles, racism and discrimination, low socioeconomic status, a lack of knowledge about or access to support services, difficulties with English language acquisition, lack of access to appropriate and affordable housing and a lack of education have all been identified as markers of risk in domestic violence (Rees, 2004; Rees & Pease, 2006; Pittaway, Muli & Shteir, 2009; Zannettino, 2012b). In addition, issues such as the potential for family shame if abuse is disclosed, the need to maintain community connections and marital commitments taking precedence over concerns for the welfare of individual women have also been shown to contribute to refugee women's vulnerability to domestic violence (Bhuyan et al., 2005; Tse, 2007).

Refugee women's experiences of domestic violence are invariably interwoven with their experiences of sexual and gender-based violence in contexts of war, flight and encampment. This interweaving underscores the need to understand the ways that gender manifests in refugee women's experiences of domestic violence. Their own and their family's experiences of violence and trauma prior to resettlement in countries of asylum both contribute to and exacerbate the occurrence of domestic violence in their lives. In some cases, war is a contributing factor in the perpetuation and normalisation of domestic violence because the oppression of women is reinforced through a heightened exposure to sexual and gender-based violence (Meffert & Marmar, 2009; Allen & Devitt, 2012). What is clear from the literature is that the boundaries between 'political violence' in contexts of war and 'domestic violence' in contexts of intimate relationships are almost indistinguishable because both forms of violence are inherently gender-based. That is, both forms of violence involve the abuse of women simply because they are women. These boundaries are further blurred by the fact that 'political violence' almost always involves rape and sexual abuse (Leatherman, 2011), which means that women are abused at the most private and intimate level. Paradoxically, it is the 'intimacy' of political violence against women that is so often the catalyst for domestic violence, as women are viewed by their husbands as deserving of punishment for the sexual 'transgressions' that have brought shame upon them and their families. Hence, both in war zones and in the home, the bodies and sexual identities of refugee women become the battlefield for gender control and subjugation. As two workers noted, the first in relation to Afghani women refugees and the second in relation to African women refugees:

> In many cases, the women are the private property of male relatives where they are subjected to sexual objectification and forced or arranged marriage.
>
> (Dana, 2013)

> Refugee women are sexually victimised in almost every area of their lives, in war, in camps, and in their own relationships because of the shame of what has happened to them.
>
> (Elaine, 2012)

## Domestic violence, refugees and gender

The literature concerning domestic violence in refugee communities has focused on two broad areas. The first challenges aspects of culture that promote women's victimisation (e.g. James, 2010). The second focuses on the psychosocial effects of war and persecution and post-migration experiences and how these contribute to domestic violence (e.g. Rees, 2004; Parris, 2013). Feminist arguments in relation to gender have centred on the human rights of refugee women, particularly in relation to their experiences of sexual and gender-based violence (e.g. Pittaway & Bartolomei, 2001). In relation to domestic violence in particular, feminist arguments have sought to examine the intersections of gender and culture (e.g. Rees & Pease, 2007; Pease & Rees, 2008) and to critically examine culture as a contributing factor (e.g. Pittaway & Eckert, 2013). A dominant discourse in both domestic violence and settlement service sectors is that domestic violence in refugee communities is 'culturally acceptable' and therefore inevitable. In many cases, 'culture' is used to explain domestic violence in refugee and CaLD communities (Pittaway & Eckert, 2013). However, feminist authors in this area have argued that many of the fundamental causes of domestic violence in refugee and CaLD communities are shared with the dominant culture (Pease & Rees, 2008; Pittaway & Eckert, 2013). Hence, the subjugation of women by men is a universal phenomenon that is embedded in systems of patriarchal power relations that transcend culture, nationality and religion (Pease & Rees, 2008; Pittaway & Eckert, 2013).

However, when understanding particular contexts of domestic violence for different groups of women, examining how refugee women engage with gender discourses is critical. For many refugees who have endured protracted refugee situations, the significance of culture and tradition is reinforced by a 'refugee culture', which is built up over years in refugee sites in countries of asylum (Pittaway & Eckert, 2013). This 'refugee culture' is often intensely protective of family and community norms in order to maintain some remnant of traditional life in conditions that threaten and often destroy these structures (Carlson, 2005; Pittaway & Eckert, 2013). For example, refugees have reported that adherence to traditional gender norms is far stricter in camps and urban areas than before flight (Pittaway & Eckert, 2013). Rigid gender roles are often valued and constructed as integral to the functioning of particular cultural communities, and to dismantle them is to destroy the very foundation of that culture and its community. In contexts that defend tradition and conventional norms, gender differences are often magnified through discourses of masculinity that are hegemonic and discourses of femininity that are extremely submissive. These discourses support the superiority and power of men and the inferiority and powerlessness of women and, in so doing, they offer women very restricted subject positions such as weak, passive, obedient and subservient to husbands and men. These subject positions are given further verisimilitude and power through their entanglement with discourses of culture and religion. For example, an Afghani woman who was herself a refugee and currently works with refugee women affected by domestic violence stated that:

> I think it's from the religion as well and from the culture but many times it's they have lots of power that's why they are just using the religion or culture, yeah, but not, not really about the religion or culture, but just if anyone have power they want to do something and no one is there to stop them, especially for men, they want to have that power on women and children.
>
> (Rabeea, 2013)

The refugee position itself reinforces the subject positions of weak, passive and obedient because, as Szorenyi (2013) points out, refugee discourse relies on the construction of asylum seekers as victims, and victimhood is often presented in specifically gendered ways – as a state of passivity, helplessness and neediness. In this way, refugee and gendered discourses are mutually reinforcing because discourses of femininity also offer subject positions of passive, helpless, needy, weak and obedient. Moreover, through the use of systematised sexual and gender-based violence, these subject positions are exploited and galvanised by an enemy that uses women's sexual subjugation to humiliate men and destroy communities. As pointed out earlier, rape as a weapon of war is supported by global gender inequality and discourses of hegemonic masculinity (Leatherman, 2011). It has its greatest power in patriarchal cultures and communities because it strikes at the heart of men's strength, power and honour while reinforcing women's weakness and subservience to men, as well as women's infidelity and sexual impurity.

These sexual violations and the discourses of shame that overlay them (Pittaway & Eckert, 2013) offer restricted subject positions for women such as 'damaged goods', 'lacking in moral virtue' and bringing dishonour to her husband and family (Ostapiej-Piatkowski & Allimant, 2013). Hence, for refugee women, we argue these subject positions are reinforced by both gender and refugee discourses and, as such, alternative ways of being gendered are even less visible or accessible. In this chapter we aim to show how these discourses and associated subject positions impact on refugee women's experiences of domestic violence.

Using culture to explain men's violent behaviour towards women in the context of domestic violence sanctions and normalises behaviour that in other contexts would be considered abnormal and unacceptable. Such positioning is given legitimacy through discourses of cultural relativism, which posit that beliefs and values are relative to a particular culture, and that the values of one culture should not be used to judge the worth of another (Abercrombie, Hill & Turner, 2006). While discourses of cultural relativism have rightfully challenged ethnocentric discourses and practices, they have also been used to justify the acceptability of particular traditions and customs that violate women and girls in some cultures. Pease and Rees (2008) argue that there is a conflict in Australian/Western societies, which, on the one hand, legally prohibit rape and violence against women and, on the other, demonstrate standards that resonate with the patriarchal values of male defendants on the grounds of cultural beliefs and traditions. Refugee women have had claims for justice following a rape or sexual assault undermined when the perpetrator invokes the cultural defence of his traditional right to have sex with his wife at his discretion (Dimopoulos & Assafiri, 2004). To sanction and normalise men's violent behaviour on cultural grounds is to not only ignore how gender features in this context but also to disregard the existence of domestic violence altogether. In other words, it is to say that domestic violence does not exist in this context because this is just how men and women relate to each other in this culture. As one worker pointed out:

> When people talk about culture in domestic violence often what they're saying is that it's expected that these women will be treated badly because it's cultural – that's just how men treat women in that culture. So what they're saying is that it's OK for one group of women to be treated badly but it's not OK if it happens to Anglo-Australian women, and this is all justified by arguing culture for one group and not the other.
>
> (Michelle, 2013)

Moreover, domestic violence can often be viewed as less extreme or secondary to the abuses that women have already encountered in situations of war, flight and encampment. Within such a discourse, refugee women are positioned as needing to be grateful for the safety they experience in countries of resettlement. Speaking out about domestic violence could make them appear ungrateful or even unworthy of asylum in the first place. As one Cambodian woman who was hospitalised after an incident of domestic violence recalled:

At that time I got only $37 in my bag, I still not permanent resident yet. And I feel like 'what's going to happen, what if they will send me back to Cambodia?' because like in Cambodia you know, the lady with three kids, I can't survive, and even looking for job, no-one going to, you know? It's ... with three kids it's hard in Cambodia.

(Mia, 2013)

Szorenyi (2013) makes the point that refugee women may be caught in a double bind where speaking out about domestic violence can undermine the status of victimhood upon which refugee discourse is so heavily reliant. One of the outcomes of this double bind is that refugee women may feel that they have no choice but to stay silent about domestic violence, which has the unintended consequence of making domestic violence appear to be non-existent in their lives. Feminine and refugee discourses produce similar subject positions of submissive, helpless and unquestioning, and therefore needing to be forever grateful. This double bind can be inadvertently reinforced in service provider contexts where the focus of interventions is on the traumatic pre-arrival experiences of refugees. As one worker noted:

Refugee and domestic violence services really need to work together more or talk to each other more because refugee services don't always know about or pick up on domestic violence because their focus is on dealing with past traumas and other issues of resettlement.

(Elaine, 2012)

Being positioned as a refugee not only focuses attention on pre-arrival experiences but simultaneously positions refugees as 'unlawful non-citizens' or stateless peoples with 'no rights to rights' (Arendt, 1979; Zannettino, 2012a). For example, in Australia in the last decade government policies have included mandatory detention and offshore processing of asylum seekers, and politicians of all persuasions have focused on strict border control and 'stopping the boats', emphasising the illegality of asylum seekers. This discursive field has served to propagate the public perception that Australia is being swamped by refugees and that these people are to be feared, loathed and ultimately controlled (Zannettino, 2012a). As two Afghani refugee woman noted:

We spent eight months in detention ... it was very long time, because when we were in here September eleven happened, that's why Government of Australia they say you need to go back to your country. That's why all the process work it was very slow for us and after we had the hunger strike in here for nearly two weeks, and after that they allowed us to come outside.

(Saleema, 2013)

They were children when they came in here [Australia] so they didn't understand ... But sometimes there was some discrimination about refugees;

yeah sometimes I am feeling in here discrimination, but it's happening everywhere.

(Anita, 2013)

Being constructed as 'stateless people' provides fertile ground for fear and hostility around discourses of refugee status, and positions refugees as 'other' and as 'strangers' and 'outsiders' in the wider community. Gendered and refugee discourses not only position women refugees as submissive, helpless, quiet and thankful but also as suspect and untrustworthy. Women refugees are caught up in contradictory subject positions, which they are required to navigate in order to prove their worthiness in a new country. The feminisation of these subject positions is galvanised by the proliferation of images of female refugees that are intended to evoke compassion and charity from the wider community (Szorenyi, 2013). However, these feminised images also show cultural and religious traditions, such as the wearing of the burqa, that evoke suspicion and fear in the wider community. Hence, feminised images of refugees reinforce gendered discourses that position refugee women as passive, weak and in need of assistance, but they also give power to discourses that position refugee women as 'other' by presenting them as objects of suspicion. These subject positions can make it extremely difficult for women to reach out to the wider community for help and support for domestic violence. The status of victim and its associated subject positions of weak, passive and needy are undermined by speaking out about domestic violence, while discourses that position women as 'other' further silence women by making them feel that disclosing their suffering may be met with disdain or suspicion. As one worker noted, 'They fear being judged – they feel judged by their community and then they are judged by the wider society about their colour, their way of living, so adding domestic violence to this is just too much' (Elaine, 2012).

Women were also fearful that speaking out about or accessing support for domestic violence would hurt their husbands and fracture their families:

The men know that the women will not call the police ... she will just go into her room and hope that he stops what he is doing. The man knows that she is worried about him having to leave the home or that he might lose his job ... we don't want the men to be taken from us even when they hurt us because we need the man to be with his family.

(Esther from Liberia, 2009)

We are worried about getting help from domestic violence services because we are scared that we will have to leave our families and our children. We want to get help for our problems but we don't want to leave our husbands and families.

(Sofia from Liberia, 2009)

These fears were exacerbated for those women whose pre-arrival experiences have instilled in them a well-founded distrust of systems of authority and power. For example, in Liberia it was not uncommon for men to be exploited and brutalised by a legal system that was often violent and corrupt, and women expressed a great fear that men would be similarly victimised in Australia (Zannettino, 2012b). Moreover, women were concerned that interventions from outsiders would publicise their problems, thereby bringing notoriety and shame onto their family and community:

> We try to work out our problems within our own community because if we go outside our community, people might take things the wrong way and think that the problem is much bigger than what it really is and then it makes us look bad.
>
> (Sarifina from Liberia, 2009)

> In Liberia, a woman would only call the police about domestic violence if her situation had become very bad … this was because going outside for help would show that the family was not able to help themselves and this would be a very shameful thing for the family.
>
> (Theresa from Liberia, 2009)

> Many people they just judging, yeah … she wasn't good wife, she does not care about her children, about reputation, that's why many women just, they don't, they just stay. Even some men they have one wife in here, one wife in Afghanistan, but the wife in here they can't say anything because of reputation.
>
> (Saleema from Afghanistan, 2013)

As the above quotations illustrate, refugee women also position themselves as protectors of their family and culture, which involves protecting their husbands and partners from public scrutiny and suspicion. This subject position stems from the loss of family members, cultural identity, community structures and social networks (Carlson, 2005) and is galvanised by the discourses of the refugee culture, which emphasise the importance of defending culture and tradition. In this context, what remains of family and culture is precious and great value is placed on protecting and nurturing it. Hence, the subject position of protector can become very important to refugee women because it allows them to exert agency and strength in contexts where they are likely to have very little power and control. Consequently, the woman's positioning as protector of family and culture may be more powerful than her need for safety and support, and this may prevent her from seeking help for domestic violence. The woman and her partner share the positioning of other, suspect and untrustworthy that is set up by refugee discourses. In this way, the subject position of protector can be both empowering and subjugating for women. Moreover, because it often involves putting the needs of husbands and family ahead of their own, it is inexorably interwoven with the gendered discourses of subservience and obedience of wives and mothers. As one Afghani worker noted:

The women are not in that position to speak up, they are afraid of their husbands. Men think that if a woman goes to work and supports herself, they will be compromised with their wife. In our culture women are quiet. It is very shameful to argue. Even if they argue, their husbands don't care ... Many women have the same issues here as they had in Afghanistan – depression, many have lots of children and can't leave the house, they can't speak English, and they don't have any power. Sometimes the husband doesn't give money for the wife and children for food, clothes, education.

(Rabeea, 2013)

Women and men can and do share particular subject positions offered by refugee discourses as shown above; however, there are others that are highly gendered for refugee women that cannot be ignored when understanding domestic violence. As experiences of systematised sexual and gender-based violence against women in contexts of war, flight, displacement and encampment are extremely common, it is probable that many refugee women are living with the trauma of sexual violation. Refugee women are likely to feel a profound sense of shame and humiliation from these experiences because they occur within societies and cultures that place a high value on women's sexual purity: 'In our culture sex is not talked about openly even among women and especially before marriage ... the woman is meant to be pure and only be with her husband' (Paree from Iran, 2012).

As Ostapiej-Piatkowski and Allimant (2013) point out, a woman who experiences sexual violence within a society where women are required to keep their bodies 'pure' may draw different conclusions about herself as a victim than a woman in a society where clear laws place responsibility for such violence on the perpetrator. They state further that:

> On countless occasions, we have been reminded that one woman may retain a strong sense of identity and resilience in spite of her severe conflict-related experiences, while another woman's perceptions of self-worth after similar experiences is that she is 'nothing' and 'deserving of such violence'.
>
> (Ostapiej-Piatkowski & Allimant, 2013, p. 17)

The gendered discourses surrounding rape and sexual violation in some refugee communities offer victims only very negative subject positions such as damaged, shamed and dishonoured. Refugee women who are positioned in these ways are more likely to view themselves as deserving of domestic violence because such violence is often viewed as punishment or chastisement for humiliating and shaming her family. As one worker noted, 'Many women view themselves as being worthless and they see their husband's violence as just a reminder or confirmation of this' (Michelle, 2013).

Often, these subject positions are lived out by women in extreme secrecy and with a heightened sense of fear that members of their community will find out about their victimisation, bringing further shame or even reprisal and expulsion from the community. The disclosure of domestic violence is likely to bring unwanted attention as well as the risk that their history of sexual violation will be revealed so these women are less likely to seek help for domestic violence either from within or outside of their community. As one worker stated:

> They don't want to tell members of their own community that their husbands are beating them because they are ashamed that this is happening and they don't want people to talk and to think that she has done something wrong for him to do this – it just opens everything up about her past … But they don't want to talk to people outside their community because they are worried about what might happen there too.
>
> (Elaine, 2012)

Perpetrators of domestic violence can also use women's shame and humiliation to justify their violence against their wives or threaten to reveal women's previous sexual violations in order to prevent them from disclosing or seeking help for domestic violence. As one worker noted:

> We know of quite a few situations where the husband has threatened to shame the woman in her community if she tells anyone about what he is doing to her … in this situation she will continue to be a victim and he will never be held to account because she will do anything to prevent the humiliation.
>
> (Michelle, 2013)

Domestic violence in the lives of refugee women becomes hidden by atrocities that occur in war. Rape and sexual violation produce gendered discourses that position them as damaged, shamed and dishonoured. These subject positions, therefore, prevent women from disclosing abuse through fear of further shaming and humiliation and potential expulsion from their cultural communities. The threat of physical or social exclusion from one's cultural community is a powerful deterrent to women speaking out about domestic violence because their connection to culture and community may be the only source of social support available to them (Ostapiej-Piatkowski & Allimant, 2013). As one worker noted, 'Those women who are single refugees have family to feed. Take them away from that culture because they decided to leave the husband it becomes unsafe, culturally unsafe for them' (Elaine, 2012). Moreover, maintaining a connection with their community is one of the few ways that refugees can retain their cultural identity and come to terms with the loss of both home and loved ones:

> We had to leave so many people behind … I think about them all the time … I want to go back to Liberia to be with them but I don't know where some of them are and we can't go back now to be with them.
>
> (Ariana, 2009)

> I was so worried about my family back in Afghanistan, my mother and sisters … this made me very sick … even now after all these years many time

I am not very good here … sometimes I have depression, I have anxiety, I want to cry, I want to shout, I don't like anyone, I don't want to talk, and this is the effect of worrying about my family.

(Saleema, 2013)

While rape in the context of war is acknowledged through discourses and subject positions of shame and dishonour, we found in our interviews that rape in marriage is viewed as non-existent in some refugee communities. As one worker noted:

I've learnt the hard way when I introduced the idea of rape within marriage it was like if I could be eaten alive – 'What do you mean, we don't have that, that's part of woman's role. If the man wants it …' – and that's hearing it from the mouth of a community leader saying if there is marriage there is no rape.

(Elaine, 2012)

As there is no discourse for rape in marriage, women are positioned to view unwanted or forced sex from their partners and husbands as an aspect of their lives that they must learn to accept as it is part of their wifely duties. As one Liberian woman noted:

We want our men to leave us alone when we don't want to have relations with them but this makes them very angry sometimes … They think it's their right and they think we are not doing what we should be doing if we turn them away. In Liberia the woman does what the man wants but here it is different.

(Anna, 2012)

Hence, the missing discourse of rape in marriage positions women as dutiful wives rather than as rape victims and this positioning is given power through its association with gendered discourses that position women as subservient and obedient to husbands and partners. In addition, the positioning of the dutiful, subservient and obedient wife is reinforced by the shame and humiliation associated with being raped by a stranger in the context of war and flight. Being raped by one's husband or partner does not bring the same kind of shame and humiliation as being raped by a stranger because the former is wrapped up in subject positions of the dutiful and obedient wife. These subject positions give women legitimacy and respect, because they are valued by some cultures and are reinforced by the religious and institutional discourses extant in those cultures. In other words, if particular cultures place high value on these positions, and they are reinforced by religion, they become valuable for women to engage with, particularly in contexts where connections to one's culture have been suddenly and brutally torn away. Hence, refugee women can find a sense of agency within and gain legitimacy from the subject positions of devoted wife and mother because they are culturally valued. As one worker noted in relation to her work with young refugee women:

So they're so desperate to have a boyfriend because if you don't then you're not worth it, then there is something … so their self-esteem gets really affected … The link, the common ground amongst all of those women I've dealt with, it's cool to have a boyfriend … Because those young girls are not allowed to have boyfriends because of the culture so they look at forced marriage as a good thing because then I can go to my girls and say 'I too have a man'.

(Elaine, 2012)

Refugee women's engagement with discourses of wife and mother is also reinforced by their being positioned as 'outsiders' and 'suspect' in countries of resettlement. While the subject positions of wife and mother give refugee women cultural value within their own communities, they also give them legitimacy and credibility in their new country because the almost universal playing-out of such discourses means that they are also subscribed to and given value by the dominant culture. The subject positions of wife and mother therefore give refugee women common ground with other women in post-settlement contexts, thereby reducing their positioning within discourses of the 'other'. At the same time, however, these subject positions and their entanglement with discourses of duty and obedience can make refugee women more vulnerable in contexts of domestic violence because they reaffirm the acceptability and normality of men's violence against women in intimate relationships.

In refugee contexts, we argue, women embrace the subject positions of protector of family and culture and of dutiful wife and mother because they offer legitimacy, agency and hope within discourses and contexts of 'othering', rape and shame. In understanding domestic violence in refugee contexts, the ways that men engage in these discourses and subject positions cannot be ignored as men share with women the subject positions of other, suspect and untrustworthy. Even though we did not interview men, women pointed to how men engaged with the subject positions offered by refugee discourses. We argue that understanding men's violence against their wives in refugee communities needs to go beyond those arguments that explain men's violence as a defence of their superiority to and power over women. For many refugee men, domestic violence becomes a way of denying or burying the 'un-masculine' feelings evoked by the traumas of war, loss and displacement (Parris, 2013). For example, Liberian women indicated that their traumatic experiences were often overwhelming and that the inability of family members to cope with the impact of these experiences was a contributing factor in violent and abusive behaviour among family members (Zannettino, 2012b). This was especially the case for men, whose masculine identities rely heavily upon their capacity to deal with and overcome adversity but whose lived experience, including the complexities of resettlement, prevents the fulfilment of this identity. The disjuncture between what is expected of men in Liberian culture and what they were able to deal with given their past and current circumstances was extremely frustrating for men, often leading to their lashing out at other family members. Many of the women spoke about how important it was to minimise conflict or to avoid situations and behaviours in their relationships that may provoke men, whom they perceived were frequently on the verge of becoming violent. As one Liberian woman stated:

> The men in our community want to be strong and the leader of their families but so much has been taken from them and they can't always hide their anger at what they have been through ... The women are careful around the men because she knows that he will put his anger on her because she is always there and the one closest to him.
>
> (Hawah, 2009)

Refugee men, like all men, are exposed to discourses of masculinity that position them as inherently stronger and more powerful than their wives and children, and therefore rightfully and justifiably placed as the rulers and protectors of their families. These constructions of masculinity, however, are threatened by the refugee experience at a number of levels. As previously discussed, the experiences of war, cultural dislocation and hostility in many settlement contexts have positioned women as protectors of family and culture, a positioning usually reserved for men. Second, men's experiences of war and conflict may have involved traumatic events such as torture and the loss of loved ones that are likely to make them feel scared, sad and in need of protection – feelings and experiences that are in direct conflict with the subject positions of the strong and capable leader and protector. As one Afghani woman noted:

> For men it would be very hard as well to settle in here. I am seeing them, I am talking with them. Many of them they are very, very worried about their families when they are coming here: 'what will happen with our family when we can't find job, how we can support them?'
>
> (Rabeea, 2013)

The literature has clearly shown that war is often conducted along gendered lines where there is a clear intent by the enemy to humiliate the strength and honour of men by sexually violating their wives and other female members of their family and community. This gendering of war is particularly evident where the subjugation and often sexual exploitation of women and children is the primary weapon used against men. That is, men are often the targets of the abuse carried out against women and children, with women and children being the collateral damage in attempts to destroy cultural communities of which men are the leaders and protectors. In this situation, men are unable to defend and protect the virtue of 'their women' and have thus failed as protectors of their families and communities. This failure is felt and lived out as a personal failure in their manhood. Even though a man may feel traumatised, sad and scared by his experiences, such feelings are prohibited by dominant constructions of masculinity in his culture – he must push them aside or bury them in order to live out the discursively prescribed masculine subject positions of leader and protector of his family. In this context, domestic violence becomes one way for him to reassert his male power and control. Rabeea explains again:

Yeah, for lots of them it's very hard, yeah, how they can accept? Yeah, it's very, very hard for them. That's why when sometimes they talk they are saying 'we want to live in here like in Afghanistan. We don't want to change anything here', but I think the women they need to bring the changes, yeah, men doesn't want to change anytime.

(Rabeea, 2013)

The refugee context depicts loss, suffering and trauma. The events of war, persecution and flight set up and construct refugee discourses but such discourses are also created within and mobilised by actual and lived experiences; families have lost so much and gendered subject positions offer security, loyalty, identity and purpose in a context that is hostile and frightening. Thus, gender provides a way to maintain culture and identity. Moreover, the refugee culture offers women an important role to play as protectors and preservers of culture and family, which gives them much needed legitimacy, agency and personal power. However, unlike their male partners who share in the subject positions offered by refugee discourse, their femininity positions them as dutiful, subservient and obedient, creating a context of gendered exploitation and abuse. In contexts of domestic violence, these subject positions silence women and hide the existence of rape and domestic violence in refugee communities. This silence becomes double as women also share the subject positions of 'other' and outsiders with their partners. Hence, the feminine subject positions offered by the melding of refugee and gendered discourses produce a see-sawing effect in which refugee women are simultaneously empowered but more vulnerable in contexts of domestic violence:

Yeah it is, and this make me – even for now, now at the moment in Australia new generation they have this issue like forcing marriage and they don't have – because often they don't have, want to wear a scarf but the family force them to wear it because of the culture, because of the people. Yeah, but they don't have that freedom, and some of them they are forcing them into marriage, the family, and after a while they just get divorced many of them. Same thing, this happen, it was happening in Afghanistan and now happening in here as well. There are not too many changes for women or for girls, it's the same.

(Rabeea, 2013)

## Conclusion

Domestic violence in refugee communities is situated in contexts of inherent vulnerability brought about by the traumatic experiences of war, violence, persecution, flight, encampment and resettlement. The refugee culture that is developed in response to such horrors offers women very restricted subject positions such as weak, passive, obedient and subservient to husbands and men. These gendered subject positions, which are reinforced by refugee discourses that construct asylum seekers as both victims – passive and grateful – and outsiders – 'other' and suspect – silence women in contexts of domestic violence. Within this discursive field, refugee women position themselves as protectors of their family and culture, a subject position that is highly valued because it gives women agency and strength in contexts of powerlessness. However, this subject position can prevent women from seeking help for domestic violence as they also share with their partners the positioning of 'other', suspect and untrustworthy.

Women's experiences of rape and sexual violation produce gendered discourses that position them as damaged, shamed and dishonoured because they occur in cultural contexts that place high value on women's sexual purity. These subject positions create fear, shame, and humiliation, which impact on women's decisions to disclose domestic violence. While rape in the context of war is acknowledged through discourses and subject positions of shame and dishonour, rape in marriage is viewed as non-existent in some refugee communities. The missing discourse of rape in marriage positions women as dutiful and obedient wives rather than as rape victims, and these subject positions are valuable to women because they are afforded legitimacy and respect by religious and institutional discourses in some cultures. However, these subject positions can make refugee women more vulnerable in contexts of domestic violence because they hide rape and reaffirm the acceptability and normality of men's violence against women in intimate relationships. For some refugee men, domestic violence can be a way of re-establishing manhood and burying the 'un-masculine' emotions stemming from their experiences of destruction and loss, rather than a demonstration of their superiority to and power over women. It is clear that gender and refugee discourses make gender a highly contested and paradoxical space for refugees, which for women can be simultaneously empowering and subjugating in contexts of domestic violence.

# References

Abercrombie, N., Hill, S. & Turner, B.S. (2006) *The Penguin Dictionary of Sociology*, 5th edition, Penguin Books, London.

Allen, M. & Devitt, C. (2012) Intimate partner violence and belief systems in Liberia. *Journal of Interpersonal Violence*, 27(17), pp. 3514–31.

Arendt, H. (1979) *On Revolution*, Penguin Books, Harmondsworth, Middlesex.

Australian Human Rights Commission (2013) *Asylum Seekers, Refugees and Human Rights: Snapshot Report 2013*, Australian Human Rights Commission, Sydney.

Bartels, S., Scott, J., Leaning, J., Mukwege, D., Lipton, R. & VanRooyen, M. (2010) Surviving sexual violence in eastern Democratic Republic of Congo. *Journal of International Women's Studies*, 11(4), pp. 37–49.

Bhuyan, R., Mell, M., Senturia, K., Sullivan, M. & Shiu-Thornton, S. (2005) Women must endure according to their karma: Cambodian immigrant women talk about domestic violence. *Journal of Interpersonal Violence*, 20(8), pp. 902–21.

Burnet, J.E. (2012) Situating sexual violence in Rwanda (1990–2001): sexual agency, sexual consent, and the political economy of war. *African Studies Review*, 55(2), pp. 97–118.

Carlson, S. (2005) *Contesting and Reinforcing Patriarchy: An Analysis of Domestic Violence in the Dzaleka Refugee Camp* (Working Paper 23), Refugee Studies Centre, University of Oxford, Oxford.

Dimopoulos, M. & Assafiri, H. (2004) Pathologising NESB women and the construction of the 'cultural defence'. In C. Ralfs, J. Cunningham, K. Jennings, J. Breckenridge & P. Carden (Eds) *Point of Contact: Responding to Children and Domestic Violence*, Partnerships against Domestic Violence (PADV), Commonwealth of Australia, Canberra, pp. 1–45.

Doney, G., Eckert, R. & Pittaway, E. (2009) *African Women Talking: We Want the Best Thing for our Family*. Centre for Refugee Research, University of New South Wales, Sydney.

Hajdukowski-Ahmed, M., Khanlou, N. & Moussa, H. (2009) Setting the context: reflection on two decades of an evolving discourse on refugee women. In M. Hajdukowski-Ahmed, N. Khanlou & H. Moussa (Eds) *Not Born a Refugee Woman: Contesting Identities, Rethinking Practices*, Berghahn Books, New York, pp. 1–24.

Heineman, E.D. (Ed) (2011) *Sexual Violence in Conflict Zones: From the Ancient World to the Era of Human Rights*, University of Pennsylvania Press, Philadelphia, PA.

James, K. (2010) Domestic violence within refugee families: intersecting patriarchal culture and the refugee experience. *Australian and New Zealand Journal of Family Therapy*, 31(3), pp. 275–84.

Khanna, R. (2008) Communal violence in Gujarat, India: impact of sexual violence and responsibilities of the health care system. *Reproductive Health Matters*, 16(3), pp. 142–52.

Leatherman, J.L. (2007) Sexual violence and armed conflict: complex dynamics of re-victimization. *International Journal of Peace Studies*, 12(1), pp. 53–60.

Leatherman, J.L. (2011) *Sexual Violence and Armed Conflict*, Polity Press, Malden, MA.

Leiby, M.L. (2009) Wartime sexual violence in Guatemala and Peru. *International Studies Quarterly*, 53, pp. 445–68.

Longombe, A.O., Claude, K.M. & Ruminjo, J. (2008) Fistula and traumatic genital injury from sexual violence in a conflict setting in eastern Congo: case studies. *Reproductive Health Matters*, 16(31), pp. 132–41.

Meffert, S.M. & Marmar, C.R. (2009) Darfur refugees in Cairo: mental health and interpersonal conflict in the aftermath of genocide. *Journal of Interpersonal Violence*, 24(11), pp. 1835–48.

Mullins, C. (2009) 'We are going to rape you and taste Tutsi women': rape during the 1994 Rwandan genocide. *British Journal of Criminology*, 49, pp. 719–35.

Ostapiej-Piatkowski, B. & Allimant, A. (2013) Best practice considerations when responding to people from CaLD backgrounds, including refugees, with mental health issues and experiences of domestic and sexual violence. In L. Zannettino, E. Pittaway, R. Eckert, L. Bartolomei, B. Ostapiej-Piatkowski, A. Allimant & J. Parris, *Improving Responses to Refugees with Backgrounds of Multiple Trauma: Pointers for Practitioners in Domestic and Family Violence, Sexual Assault and Settlement Services*, Practice Monograph 1, Domestic and Family Violence Clearinghouse, University of NSW, Sydney, pp. 14–18.

Parris, J. (2013) Responding to refugees affected by domestic and sexual violence: working with men. In L. Zannettino, E. Pittaway, R. Eckert, L. Bartolomei, B. Ostapiej-Piatkowski, A. Allimant & J. Parris, *Improving Responses to Refugees with Backgrounds of Multiple Trauma: Pointers for Practitioners in Domestic and Family Violence, Sexual Assault and Settlement Services*, Practice Monograph 1, Domestic and Family Violence Clearinghouse, University of NSW, Sydney, pp. 19–26.

Pease, B. & Rees, S. (2008) Theorising men's violence towards women in refugee families: towards an intersectional feminist framework. *Just Policy*, 47, pp. 39–45.

Pittaway, E. (2004) *From Horror to Hope: Addressing Domestic Violence in Refugee Families Resettled in Australia*, Centre for Refugee Research, UNSW and Office for Women, NSW Premiers Department, Sydney.

Pittaway, E. & Bartolomei, L. (2001) Refugees, race and gender. *Refuge*, 19(6), pp. 21–32.

Pittaway, E. & Eckert, R. (2013) Domestic violence, refugees and prior experiences of sexual violence: factors affecting therapeutic and support service provision. In L. Zannettino, E. Pittaway, R. Eckert, L. Bartolomei, B. Ostapiej-Piatkowski, A. Allimant & J. Parris, *Improving Responses to Refugees with Backgrounds of Multiple Trauma: Pointers for Practitioners in Domestic and Family Violence, Sexual Assault and Settlement Services*, Practice Monograph 1, Domestic and Family Violence Clearinghouse, University of NSW, Sydney, pp. 10–13.

Pittaway, E., Muli, C. & Shteir, S. (2009) 'I have a voice – hear me!' Findings of an Australian study examining the resettlement and integration experience of refugees and migrants from the Horn of Africa in Australia. *Refuge*, 26(2), pp. 133–46.

Pittaway, E. & Rees, S. (2006) Multiple jeopardy: domestic violence and the notion of cumulative risk for women in refugee camps. *Women Against Violence: An Australian Feminist Journal*, 18, pp. 18–25.

Rees, S. (2004) Human rights and the significance of psychosocial and cultural issues in domestic violence policy and intervention for refugee women. *Australian Journal of Human Rights*, 10(2), pp. 1–19.

Rees, S. & Pease, B. (2006) *Refugee Settlement, Safety and Wellbeing: Exploring Domestic and Family Violence in Refugee Communities*, Violence Against Women Community Attitudes Project, Paper 4, Victorian Health Promotion Foundation, Melbourne.

Rees, S. & Pease, B. (2007) Domestic violence in refugee families in Australia: rethinking settlement policy and practice. *Journal of Immigrant and Refugee Studies*, 5(2), pp. 1–19.

Shiu-Thornton, S., Senturia, K. & Sullivan, M. (2005) 'Like a bird in a cage': Vietnamese women survivors talk about domestic violence. *Journal of Interpersonal Violence*, 20, pp. 959–76.

Schmidt, S. (2005) *Liberian Refugees: Cultural Considerations for Social Service Providers*, Bridging Refugee Youth and Children's Services (BRYCS), Baltimore, MD.

Szorenyi, A. (2013) Asylum as a gendering process: exchanges and intersections. Paper presented at Standing Together to End Gendered Violence against CALD Women Conference, Adelaide, 1 November.

Tse, S. (2007) Family violence in Asian communities: combining research and community development. *Social Policy Journal of New Zealand*, 31, pp. 170–94.

UNHCR (2003) *Sexual and Gender-Based Violence against Refugees, Returnees and Internally Displaced Persons: Guidelines for Prevention and Response*, UNHCR, Geneva, http://www.unhcr.org/3f696bcc4.html

UNHCR (2008) *Handbook for the Protection of Women and Girls*, UNHCR, Geneva, http://www.unhcr.org/protect/PROTECTION/47cfae612.html

Zannettino, L. (2012a) From Auschwitz to mandatory detention: biopolitics, race, and human rights in the Australian refugee camp. *International Journal of Human Rights*, 16(7), pp. 1094–119.

Zannettino, L. (2012b) '… There is no war here; it is only the relationship that makes us scared': factors having an impact on domestic violence in Liberian refugee communities in South Australia. *Violence Against Women*, 18(7), pp. 807–28.

# 7 Rural women

The family is all about male and female roles ... If you don't follow the ways of doing things you are not being a good wife to your husband. Family has to stay together regardless ... to pass on property in this area and if you separate then properties get lost. This is probably a reason why keeping family together is so strong.

(Candice, 1999)

## Introduction

In this chapter we explore the unique factors that shape rural women's experiences of domestic violence, and how gendered discourses feature in contexts of rurality. The term 'rural' is complicated and has been debated within the literature (Wendt, 2009b; DeKeseredy & Schwartz, 2009; Bryant & Pini, 2011). The purpose of this chapter is not to enter these debates because they can be read elsewhere; instead we acknowledge that rurality is considered unstable and diverse, and that there are many cultures of particular rural communities, rather than unitary notions of a rural culture. Rural can be classified according to population and occupation; hence, for this chapter, rural can be considered the generalised understandings of places with small population sizes and/or densities that exhibit variable levels of collective efficacy (DeKeseredy & Schwartz, 2009, p. 20; Sandberg, 2013).

This chapter is written from the work of Wendt (2009a, 2009b). During 1999–2004, Wendt interviewed twenty-one women living in a rural region in South Australia aged between 18 and 60 years. Fourteen of the women lived on farming properties and seven lived in towns with populations ranging from 1,000 to 4,000. The majority of women had been living in the region for ten years or more, and eight had lived in their communities for their entire lives. This chapter draws on Wendt's work but also brings new understandings of gender by examining the interview transcripts to theorise gendered discourses and particular subject positions offered to rural women and how these impact on their experience of domestic violence.

We wanted to include a chapter on rural women's experiences because research has shown there are unique factors stemming from rural environments that shape experiences and perceptions of domestic violence. Furthermore, gender divisions in rural families, such as farming families, have tended to be more rigid and enforced than in urban communities. This context has fostered constructions of rural people as conservative and traditional or as backward, dumb and unable to cope with the modern world (Alston, 1995, 1997; Hogg & Carrington, 1998; DeKeseredy & Schwartz, 2009; Sandberg, 2013). In addition, within many constructions of rural life, rurality is often associated with men's experiences more than those of women (DeKeseredy & Schwartz, 2009).

## Domestic violence and rurality

In researching domestic violence in rural communities, studies often attempt to determine whether domestic violence is more prevalent in such contexts compared to their urban counterparts. Sandberg (2013) points out that findings often suggest that it is either higher in rural locations than in metropolitan cities, or that rates are similar. Other research has also assessed the prevalence of different types and experiences of domestic violence in selected rural and urban communities; for example, Balogun, Owoaje and Fawole (2012) reported in a sample of 600 women in south-western Nigeria that more urban women experienced controlling behaviours, while more rural women experienced physical violence. Peek-Asa et al. (2011) also found that rural women in the United States reported significantly higher severity of physical abuse than their urban counterparts, and concluded that rural women experience higher rates of domestic violence and greater frequency and severity of physical abuse yet they live much further away from available resources.

Although available research indicates that the rates of domestic violence are at least similar across rural and urban areas (with some reporting higher rates in rural areas), professionals in the field have long recognised that factors contributing to the incidence and response to domestic violence are different for the two areas. It is this difference that domestic violence research has focused on. Research has established that the rural context, particularly geographical isolation, can amplify the control exerted by the perpetrators, and the subordination and loneliness of many rural women (Gagne, 1992; Hornosty, 1995; Websdale, 1998). Isolation can become another aspect of abuse, which can be used by perpetrators to increase their control and create fear. For example, control tactics such as removing the telephone, hiding heating and cooling devices in winter or summer, disabling transport, firing guns as threats and threatening to harm or kill animals have been reported in research (Hornosty, 1995; Websdale, 1998; Bagshaw et al., 2000). In fact, Lanier and Maume (2009) argue that isolation is an important concept to consider in understanding the unique factors for rural women, which is, how geographic isolation not only compounds limited formal services but also amplifies the lack of social contact with others. This double-edged sword of isolation impacts on the victimisation of rural women in domestic violence contexts.

Earlier studies have examined structural barriers that keep rural women trapped in domestic violence relationships such as geographic isolation, limited access to services, the absence of employment opportunities, financial issues, insufficient housing and the absence of public transportation. Websdale and

Johnson (1997) argue that domestic violence in rural areas is structurally an economic, public health, labour, housing and educational issue, and therefore structural solutions to domestic violence are needed to alleviate the pressure on women to return to their partners. These structural factors and solutions have therefore been the focus of research. For example, financial insecurity, stress and financial dependency are common factors affecting rural families and women. Incomes on rural properties are often spasmodic, women often have little access to cash and property, and assets and money are often controlled by men, or by men's extended families, for example through family trusts. Rural women's and children's labour is often essential on rural properties and economic and emotional attachment make it extremely difficult for them leave (Alston, 1997; Wendt, 2009b). In rural communities women also face limited employment opportunities because occupational choice is limited should they leave. Moreover, seeking out other employment or educational opportunities becomes difficult when balancing the demands and intensity of working long hours in the family business (Alston, 1997). Physical distance and isolation also compound rural women's lives. Distance and isolation often prevent women from leaving violent relationships, accessing services, information and resources, and establishing and maintaining supportive networks (Hogg & Carrington, 2006). Research has also recognised that little or no assistance from police and legal justice systems can contribute to women's vulnerability in domestic violence. Rural police work is performed under different constraints than metropolitan police work, as police officers in rural areas are often isolated and under-resourced. Furthermore, police officers in rural communities are likely to know many people in the community personally and may find it difficult to maintain a balance between their police work and their personal relationships (Knowles, 1996; Eastman et al., 2007).

Research concerning domestic violence in rural contexts continues to focus on structural factors through comparisons with urban contexts. For example, in a qualitative study comparing rural and urban domestic violence victims, Logan et al. (2003) found that rural victims had less social support, lower education and income, and more experiences of child abuse and mental and physical illness compared to urban victims. Other studies have extended research in rural contexts by examining how different opportunities and barriers to escape domestic violence impact on specific groups of women in rural areas. For example, Grossman et al.'s (2005) study highlights how African American families in rural environments are the poorest, and hence how race and location operate together in ways to create different opportunities and barriers in contexts of domestic violence. Shuman et al. (2008) found that older, rural women were more likely to report severe domestic violence. Such research suggests that solutions sit within the structural realm of empowering women through access to services, education, employment, finance and housing (Sarkar, 2010).

Other researchers have turned their attention to exploring how rural women cope and make decisions within contexts of domestic violence. For example rural women use more placating and safety planning strategies rather than separating from or leaving their abusive partners (Riddell, Ford-Gilboe & Leipert, 2009;

Davis, Taylor & Furniss, 2001). More recently, Bhandari et al. (2011) studied rural women who were pregnant and experiencing domestic violence, and found that seventeen women permanently left the abusive relationship, six dated a new partner or went back to their former partner and three women remained in the abusive relationship. Wanting a father figure for their children was particularly important to those women who returned to partners. Studies have also established that many rural women in domestic violence relationships attempt to reach out to informal and formal support networks for assistance but often receive responses that negate, discount or minimise their experiences, and hence they are treated in a non-supportive manner. Research has established that rural women's use of information support networks, and their effectiveness, is pivotal in their attempts to leave domestic violence (Bosch & Bergen, 2006; Davis et al., 2001). Studies have also found that rural women often prefer to rely on family and friends for domestic violence help, and when informal support is unavailable or not helpful they hesitate to contact formal services, particularly legal support. In addition, rural women fear lack of anonymity and confidentiality when accessing formal support networks (Ragusa, 2012). Schuler, Bates and Islam (2008) argued from the findings of 110 in-depth interviews with women and sixteen small discussion groups in rural Bangladesh that poverty and gender inequality, inequities in legal frameworks, and patriarchal attitudes and corruption in both formal and informal institutions at the local level discouraged abused women from seeking recourse and decreased the likelihood of a favourable outcome when they do. Finally, studies have found, similar to other groups of women, that when rural women leave the abuser the violence and abuse do not necessarily stop. For example, Shepard and Hagemeister (2013) reported the perceptions of rural women on custody and visitation arrangements with abusive ex-partners in the United States and found that most reported experiencing ongoing abusive and controlling behaviour by their ex-partners related to custody and visitation arrangements.

How rural women cope and access informal or formal support networks has also been researched from the perspectives of service providers in rural areas. For example, Eastman et al. (2007) used a non-probability purposive sample to investigate the perceptions of domestic violence service providers in rural regions of North Carolina and Virginia. Findings identified deficits in public knowledge, agency and community resources, and professional development as being the most problematic issues. Victims were perceived in this study as having to face multiple issues and barriers when seeking services. Other studies have explored how rural communities understand and try to respond to the issue of domestic violence. For example, Wendt (2010) found in a rural community in South Australia that, once barriers to coordination were identified in rural communities and talked about amongst relevant stakeholders, workers were able to visualise a local response to move past these barriers. She argued that keeping coordination at the forefront of service provision can help build strength at the community level. Similarly, Sukhera et al.'s (2012) study conducted in rural Honduras demonstrated the importance of examining how a rural community defines and responds to domestic violence in order to lay the foundation for future interventions.

More recently, research that has focused on rural women's coping has aimed to establish psychological impacts of domestic violence on their lives. For example, Hayati et al. (2013) aimed to deepen understandings of how rural Javanese women cope with domestic violence and they found experiencing chronic violence ruined the women's personal lives because of the associated physical, mental, psychosocial and financial impairments. Hayati et al. (2013) found that it was common for rural women to cope using what they labelled the 'elastic band strategy'. This strategy implied a constant stretching, by making efforts to oppose the violence, for example, through spiritual framing, seeking outside support, being assertive and trying to make a positive diversion. However, the stretching was often followed by withdrawal and surrender through submissiveness, keeping silent or ignoring their husband's behaviour. Even though this 'elastic band strategy' was a mechanism to survive, Hayati et al. (2013) argue that it also prompted conflicting impulses to seek support versus remaining in the relationship, contributing to chronic stress experienced by the women. Similarly, Stephenson, Winter and Hindin (2013) found in their study with 6,303 rural married women (aged 15–49) in four Indian states – Bihar, Jharkhand, Maharashtra and Tamil Nadu – that experiencing physical, verbal or sexual intimate partner violence is associated with an increased risk of adverse mental health outcomes.

Studies exploring domestic violence have also identified and explored cultural factors that exist in rural contexts that prevent women from seeking assistance or leaving violent relationships. For example, researchers have identified that factors such as tolerant attitudes towards or minimising of domestic violence, positioning domestic violence as a private family issue, gossip networks, and family and community values and beliefs about gender roles impact on rural women's experiences and decisions about domestic violence (Eastman et al., 2007; Wendt 2009b). Furthermore, studies have found that expectations about marriage being forever are particularly strong in rural contexts because of practices surrounding inheritance and the influences of religion and church, which often play vital roles in rural communities (Eastman et al., 2007; Wendt, 2009b). Such research shows that, in addition to addressing structural factors such as education, employment, law and poverty, solutions sit within understandings of the prevailing cultures of particular places (Wendt, 2009b; Kaur & Gaug, 2010). For example, Kaur and Gaug (2010) found that in rural India most women in their sample agreed that wife beating was a deeply ingrained behaviour and most of the husbands believed that it was their right to beat their wives. They also found that in 60 per cent of the cases the mother-in-law was involved in domestic violence. Wilson-Williams et al. (2008) also found in rural India that violence was normalised, or considered acceptable, if women did not adhere to expected gender roles. Bhandari et al. (2011) argue that rigid gender norms in many rural areas of the United States contribute to the attitude that there is nothing wrong with women facing violence from their intimate partners, as it is part and parcel of maintaining the subordinate status of women. In summary, most research agrees that both structural and cultural factors intersect in complex ways in shaping domestic violence experiences in rural contexts. For example, Schuler, Bates and Islam (2008) argue that in rural

Bangladesh domestic violence is intertwined with poverty and gender inequality. They reported that women in their study often made symbolic statements about the importance of marriage and maintaining fidelity to the husband, but they argued that the significance of such statements is situated in the dignity that the cultural ideology provides for women whose decision to remain in abusive marriages is mainly driven by economic imperatives. They argue that women are vulnerable to domestic violence in rural settings because few alternatives are open to them in terms of economic and social resources and hence they have virtually no viable life options outside marriage (Schuler, Bates & Islam, 2008; Schuler & Islam, 2008). Sabarwal, Santhya and Jejeebhoy (2014) report similar findings, indicating the significance of financial autonomy and freedom of movement in reducing the risk of domestic violence.

Over the years, research about domestic violence in rural communities has found that rural women are particularly vulnerable to intimate partner violence because of the difficulty in seeking assistance or recourse due to the potent combination of structural and cultural factors within rural contexts. Recently, Sandberg (2013) wrote a piece on the importance of understanding rural contexts and domestic violence to challenge the assumption that urban research can be generalised to cases outside urban areas. Studies on rural domestic violence have been vital in making visible the experiences of women living in diverse rural locations and hence have increased knowledge about urban and rural differences. However, at the same time, Sandberg (2013, p. 351) eloquently and sensitively reminds us that in such research there is the possibility of contributing to the 'othering' of rurality; that is, reinforcing images and perceptions of rural locations and rural inhabitants as deviant, which may further marginalise rural women experiencing domestic violence. In terms of domestic violence and assumptions about gender relations, rural communities have been constructed or categorised as particularly patriarchal; that is, rural people are constructed as being more traditional and conservative than urban people or as being backward compared to urban people (Wendt, 2009b; Sandberg 2013). Sandberg (2013) points out that discourses that position rurality as particularly patriarchal, traditional or backward in terms of gender relations contribute to the 'othering' of rural communities and locations. Such discourses can position domestic violence as part and parcel of backward rural culture (Sandberg, 2013, p. 359), which can overshadow the nuances and complexities of gender relations and identities in rural contexts.

## Domestic violence, rurality and gender

Rawsthorne (2008) reminds us that research that has explored gender relations in rural communities often concludes that patriarchal structures and attitudes remain embedded in rural cultures. Furthermore, researchers often argue there is a greater emphasis on traditional gender roles of male breadwinner and female homemaker in rural communities, which reinforces male power and control over women's lives, and that rural life and values increase men's ability to abuse women (Sudderth, 2006; Eastman et al., 2007). We do not argue against these insights and Wendt's

(2009b) work has also supported such conclusions. However, we also argue that rural communities are exposed to many of the same cultural discourses as the wider community (Little, Panelli & Kraack, 2005). Hence, when rural women are given the label of 'traditional and conservative', and therefore 'other', we run the risk of missing the dominance of particular gendered discourses that influence many groups of women, and therefore the similarities in how women engage with and take up particular feminine subject positions in contexts of domestic violence. Furthermore, positioning rural women as more traditional and conservative than their urban counterparts assumes that rural identity is stable and fixed, a binary entity associated with urban, which is positioned as progressive and modern. Bryant and Pini (2011) argue that viewing gender as a process intricately connected to discourses is more helpful because there is a range of discourses by which we constitute ourselves as 'feminine' or 'masculine' but these do not all have equivalent status. Some discourses are more powerful than others in particular contexts and hence once a discourse becomes 'normal' or 'natural' it is difficult to think and act outside it. There are powerful discourses that constitute feminine and masculine in rural contexts and perhaps they are easier to find because they have specific historical, social and institutional bases reinforcing them, making them more visible. In other words, the rural environment constitutes a site from which gender relations can be examined and highlighted. In this chapter we aim to highlight gender relations in rural contexts of domestic violence but not to position rural women as more traditional and conservative. Instead, we attempt to show how rurality shapes the ways that women construct themselves and what this means for domestic violence.

By re-examining the interviews with rural women living in South Australia that Wendt conducted between 1999 and 2004, we found that rural women predominantly constructed themselves within the context of loyalty to family life, and farming or property life. Within the context of family life, women positioned themselves as being responsible for keeping the family intact, happy and functioning, drawing on feminine discourses of devoted wife and mother. Despite recalling severe episodes of domestic violence and living with fear, the majority of women identified the family unit as being extremely important to them and consequently they were committed to maintaining the functionality of the family for the sake of their children and the farm or business. However, when they could no longer endure domestic violence and made the decision to leave their partner, their stories about the blame and criticism they endured from extended family and community members demonstrated the dominance of the devoted wife and mother discourse, which often positioned them as weak or as a failure for leaving their family. Feminine discourses were constructed around family, whereby women were positioned as primarily responsible for the wellbeing of their families:

> I think I would have gotten out quicker if family wasn't so important to me. I believe very much in the family and really wanted it to work … and I do value what people think of me and I didn't want to get out and people say 'it is my fault you left' … I am afraid of people saying 'don't be so weak'.
>
> (Belinda, 1999)

Anything to keep your family together, you have to try and keep your family unit operating no matter how bad it gets, that fitting in and appearing normal and average is very important. If you are not this it is like you are threatening to the in-laws and the community.

(Nelly, 1999)

Cultural messages of women being responsible for the wellbeing of family were reinforced by the women's own extended family and community networks. Despite domestic violence being perpetrated by intimate partners, the dominance of such feminine discourses shifted the focus from the perpetrators' behaviour to an examination of what women were or were not doing to stop or fix domestic violence. Domestic violence was implicitly constructed as a consequence of women's poor choices or behaviour:

I went to a lawyer who was appalled by the behaviour, I couldn't sleep, been bashed, dragged around by my hair … but he was sometimes belittling, for example he said 'do you know what's wrong with you women, you are intelligent women, why do you let this happen' … there is underlying beliefs that women are women and men are men and they don't cross.

(Vivian, 1999)

His family told her, my mum, that she was weak putting up with it for all those years … but as far as the community went, her friends knew but sort of blamed her, expected her to stick at it and change him.

(Brigitte, 2002)

Furthermore, as the above two quotations show, rural women are often positioned to navigate contradictory cultural messages. On the one hand, feminine discourses position them as responsible for the wellbeing, functionality and happiness of the family, which reinforces messages of staying and persevering in a relationship despite abuse; yet on the other hand, feminine discourses can be used to position them as weak and stupid for living with domestic violence. These contradictory constructions of femininity shift the gaze to women and their actions in domestic violence, ultimately making the perpetrators' actions and behaviour invisible, harmless or in some cases necessary.

With feminine discourses being constructed around family, where women were positioned as responsible for the wellbeing of their families, women also gave examples of trying to protect the image of their husbands or partners. Feminine discourses of responsibility for family also positioned women as protectors of men's reputations. In this way, femininity was constructed as loyal to and protective of masculinity, and attests to the power of gendered discourses that position women as the dutiful and loyal wife. Women gave many examples of keeping domestic violence hidden from others in their social and family networks for long periods of time to ensure that the reputation of their family, particularly their husbands, remained intact:

I tried very hard to keep the house clean and tidy, he continually threatened suicide so I was always careful that I wouldn't say or do anything that would make him threaten it again. I tried to concentrate on community things and friends ... when we had people around for meals, he wasn't cooperative and sometimes would not turn up. I had to organise and entertain on my own like nothing was wrong ... I kept it hidden for years because I felt ashamed and I kept trying my responsibilities at home, ensuring they were on track.

(Fay, 1999)

Part of it is you don't want anyone to think there is something wrong, you want to blend in and be accepted, don't want to be blamed, and so you play ostrich well. I also wanted my family to be happy and didn't want my husband to be treated differently or have his friends find out things. I hung in there longer than I ever imagined, I felt my husband has worked all those years to get his property and so didn't want to jeopardise that and so hung in there. I felt I needed to help him fulfil his dream. I was his wife and I needed to support my husband.

(Nelly, 1999)

The construction of femininity as loyal, dutiful and protective of masculinity extended to loyalty to marriage and children. Nearly all rural women interviewed described their devotion and dedication to marriage and providing a family unit for their children. First, we found rural women tended to cope with and endure domestic violence for long periods of time because marriage represented to them their commitment to their husbands and the survival of farming life. Second, for many women, it also demonstrated their commitment to their religion:

The expectations of being a woman, I had the belief that the marriage will last forever and I had to be there no matter what. Family is important to me and I was worried about how the situation would affect my son, and my son is the only grandson his family will ever have and I was worried about how that would affect them. Extended family are important but people don't think much of you when you are the one that walks out of the marriage. But now I don't care, stuff them. God knows the truth about what happened and he will judge us both accordingly.

(Gene, 1999)

It all comes back to family values, I wanted to make my marriage work, I wanted to keep my parents happy, the values you are brought up with, the morals are part of you. I felt if I walked out of that marriage I wouldn't be living up to the expectations, I would be sinning ... I used to be a strong believer in marriage, but after what I have experienced I don't see myself getting married ever again. I am too scared.

(Eden, 1999)

From my point of view the first person you sleep with is the person you are supposed to spend the rest of your life with. I was dedicated to that and had given my trust to this one person ... I didn't front up to church after I had my baby because I was so embarrassed about not having a partner, I was so worried what people would say about me ... I didn't want to be seen as a slut, the fact that I slept with someone ... I felt like I let my family down, mum, dad, grandparents, getting pregnant while not being in marriage.

(Belinda, 1999)

We found there was a strong discourse of marriage as a marker of women's morality, despite it often being an arrangement of enduring abuse. Marriage was one of the few ways that rural women could show their moral worthiness and not being married made them appear as 'less than' or 'sinful', particularly if they had children out of wedlock. As with other groups of women, particularly religious women and older women, marriage discourses create feminine subject positions that are tied to morality, dignity and respect.

We also found that women endured domestic violence for long periods of time because loyalty to partners, children and family extended to loyalty and responsibility to rural life. That is, they were positioned to view femininity as being tied to the domestic sphere because duty to home and family allowed their husbands to run the property unencumbered, thereby setting up a secure and stable future for their children.

Everyone has the attitude if you have a child you should be at home with the child. You should be the primary carer. If anything goes wrong in your family it's the mother ... women are supposed to be there and dishing out what everyone needs, it is the love, caring, they are supposed to be everything to everyone. I think fathers have no option but to be the one that brings in the money.

(Belinda, 1999)

There are expectations of being a good mother, loving towards my partner and it is hard to talk about not wanting to accept those roles because I have to accept a domestic role because I am a mother and regardless and so what I try and do is give everything a lot of value in my life so I feel I am doing it for a reason ... women need to be domesticated in rural areas, you have that responsibility on the farm.

(Candice, 1999)

The importance of the domestic sphere in sustaining farming life and their children's futures reinforced feminine discourses of loyalty to family and children because it legitimised women's roles and feelings of self-worth in rural contexts. However, such discourses of femininity position women as solely responsible for the wellbeing of their children and for enabling and maintaining a relationship between children and fathers. This responsibility also remained with women in their plans to leave domestic violence, creating a paradoxical set of circumstances in their lives. As femininity for rural women is most often played out in the domestic sphere, with farming work and the like hidden within the many layers of domestic labour, women often have no way of providing economically for themselves and their children. However, because femininity is, in actuality, so closely tied to family livelihood in rural contexts, women's responsibility for the wellbeing of their children extends well beyond the domestic sphere. In other words, leaving the marriage is also likely to mean that the family's livelihood will be at risk or lost, making the children even more vulnerable. Hence, for rural women, loyalty to and responsibility for children often means that they are forced to take up a position of having to sacrifice their own safety for the sake of their children's economic survival. For example, Fiona spoke about the importance of ensuring a future for her children, as well as her employees, and this was a major reason she remained in her marriage:

> If I walked away I would want my share and that means the place would have to be sold and [my son and daughter] would miss out … I feel that is not fair on them. I just feel that I have an obligation to try and repay the loan … we also have an obligation because we employ people and they rely on us for work … I just think that when I am getting on I would like to know that I am passing something onto my children … they are our children and we do owe them something for their future … and my grandchildren.
>
> (Fiona, 2002)

We found that for rural women, femininity was constructed as subservient to masculinity, and hence women's positions of mother and wife, and their responsibility for keeping families together, was considered vital in the success and survival of farming properties. Consequently, rural women often endure domestic violence for long periods of time, and look to themselves and their own abilities to cope with domestic violence (Hayati et al., 2013). Rural women support and promote masculinity even in contexts of domestic violence because the success and survival of the farm or business is important to them too as it reaffirms their femininity and the importance of their role and ensures their children's future. As such gendered discourses are tied up in rurality and impact on domestic violence experiences. For example, the woman leaving her husband and family can be viewed as failing to hold up her end of the bargain in the context of rural life. We found that rural women were aware of such perceptions of responsibility and some women held these views themselves for periods of time because the feminine subject positions of wife and mother were of particular importance to them and their perceived purpose in life. Consequently, the women told many stories about their efforts over time to try and please their partners and extended families as a way to stop domestic violence. However, after years of living in fear, and experiencing deteriorating health and despair, many women left their partners but the majority of women interviewed left with nothing or, at the very most, with some possessions or a small amount of money. Many of the women interviewed accepted this outcome because it ensured the survival of farming properties and businesses for the sake of their partner's success and a future inheritance for their children. In addition, the majority of rural women interviewed made a point of saying they would never get married again. Some women felt disappointment and sadness that they personally 'failed' in their marriages because they could not resolve the domestic violence, while others questioned their identification with discourses of femininity and the responsibilities associated with being a wife and mother. These women expressed anger about their experiences of domestic violence, explaining it as exploitation and oppression resulting from such discourses. They also expressed anger about not experiencing the fulfilment and happiness that these feminine discourses and associated subject positions promised:

> It was always my fault, I wasn't trying hard enough to fit in. He has a background in the church and he is respected. I thought no one would believe me. I had all these expectations on me. I was trying to adjust, trying to fit in but he had all these expectations like he still went to the pub and expected to come home to a meal and the bed warm. It wasn't what I expected. I felt like a servant.
>
> (Liz, 1999)

As the stories in this chapter have shown, rural women predominantly constructed themselves not only within the context of family life but also farming or property life. Gendered discourses of femininity not only position women as carers and supporters of partners within the home but also as helpers and supporters of their partners' farming work. Many of the women used descriptions like 'superwoman' or 'workhorse' to describe their work on the farm and expressed being overwhelmed by the expectations these descriptions imposed. For some women, not being able to meet these high expectations gave their partners a reason for perpetrating violence and abuse; that is, domestic violence was positioned as stemming from partners' understandable frustration or pressure associated with farming life.

> Women are meant to be home looking after the children, doing the housework and keeping the house going. But you are expected to go out and do the vineyard as well. I had to be superwoman, weren't to question anything, no control over finances, just live and do what is expected ... If you didn't work at home or in the vineyard, gee, did that cause frictions but I don't understand, they didn't look at the time you used up helping with the banking and accounts. I couldn't win, expected to be in the vineyard but I can't leave the babies home alone sleeping, so much friction ... I agree that family unit produces strength, routine and structure, I understand that system, but it was unrealistic and not practical, which caused friction.
>
> (Nelly, 1999)

> I never felt free to do anything for myself. He would get me to do lots of work with him, very heavy work. I didn't mind helping but as soon as we stopped he

would expect tea to be ready within ten minutes and a nice good meal. I would have to unpack everything from that day and get everything ready for the next day. I was expected to be the perfect wife, business person, and everything.

(Isis, 1999)

Constructions of femininity as carer, helper and supporter flowed between home and property life, with femininity being positioned as assistant or collaborator to masculinity. However, some women recognised that this perceived partnership was often one-sided; that is, they were expected to be available to help and work on the farm but the expectation for partners to help and work in the home was not reciprocated. The different expectations assigned to femininity and masculinity can be used to create hierarchy and gendered power relations within family and farming life, which diminishes the visibility and identification of domestic violence. DeKeseredy and Schwartz (2009) use the term 'proprietariness' to explain the discrepancy in expectations of women and men across home and farm life. They suggest that the emotional force of the male partner's sense of entitlement over property flows into domestic life, bringing with it a pervasive attitude of ownership and control towards social relationships with intimate female partners.

Women are there to help, help the property and rural interest expand … we are like workhorses. I suppose it is important to keep a property running but we don't benefit from it in the same way as men might benefit. Men will inherit as much as possible, set up family trust, women second best … and we are expected to help them a lot but men rarely help women in domestic duties and raising children, which is a full-time job, but that is not important for the man in the child-rearing. He said I should always be available for the children and helping out on the farm … it was always about the farm so the son could take it over and I accept those values, but at the cost of everything?

(Fay, 1999)

Inheritance of property, by sons in particular, was a theme that featured in many of the rural women's interviews. Women endured domestic violence for years so either their husbands or their sons could inherit property. Many women felt pressure to stay in a marriage to enable inheritance of property and some sacrificed their own safety, wellbeing and financial compensation so that properties and businesses could remain and flourish for future generations:

Because I was on a farm I have been shunned by certain members of the farming community. I think they are frightened but I took a low settlement so my husband could keep the property but certain people think after eleven years of marriage I shouldn't get anything.

(Fay, 1999)

I do want things with my life that would be considered useless in the rural community, like being an artist. I think it is slowly accepted by my partner's parents but there is still 'you should learn to prune because that would give 3–4 months of work a year …' I loved him and didn't want him to lose his life. He wouldn't have got the farm if we broke up. They would have written him off and they would say he is a fuck up and I wanted to think that we could work it out.

(Candice, 1999)

Hard working towards life and make your living, work your block and run your farm, get everyone to put their bit in to make it work. You all pitch in but also at the same time a woman's place is in the home because she makes the family and these are handed down generation to generation. It comes from the family.

(Eden, 1999)

However, it is also important to point out that, for some women, being part of establishing and working on a family farm, property or business was personally fulfilling and part of their identity. Identification with farming life made it difficult for women to leave relationships because they gained a lot from living and working in rural contexts. Rural women's and children's labour is often essential on rural properties, and economic and emotional attachment make it extremely difficult for them to leave (Alston, 1997; Wendt, 2009b).

There was a really strong connection there. My partner and I had similar interests, the business kept me there for a long time … I helped create it … I set up all the administrative side of it … by the time I left we had a major business … we built a magnificent house and I knew when I left that I would leave with nothing. I think I left seven times to go back.

(Cathy, 2002)

I put so much into that business, the hard manual yakka, so I just feel I have put far too much in to walk away.

(Fiona, 2002)

The women's stories have shown that, despite domestic violence in their lives, they gained much from being a mother, homemaker, partner and helper to the family business, and hence they did not construct themselves as 'traditional' or 'conservative'. In fact, like other Australian research has found, rural women often find great satisfaction and identification with feminine discourses that allow them to move between family and farming life (Alston, 1995). For some women, femininity was therefore constructed as strong and as the necessary foundation to enable and keep rural properties alive; domestic violence is threatening because it erodes such foundations. DeKeseredy and Schwartz (2009) argue that patriarchal discourses provide women and men with a social rationale; that is, constructions of femininity and masculinity endure because people come to believe that it is natural and right that women are in inferior positions and therefore men feel justified and supported in excluding women and, up to a point, women feel that this exclusion is correct. From the stories of rural women, it can be further argued that, due to rural women's strong identification with and understanding of rural life, they make extraordinary sacrifices when they leave domestic violence relationships, often leaving with nothing to ensure survival of their partners' and families' businesses. Sacrifice became a feminine subject position offered by rural and gendered discourses. Rural women often sacrifice their own safety when they persevere in domestic violence relationships for their children and for inheritance of property and then they often sacrifice all they have worked for when they leave. While sacrifice was a dominant discourse in women's lives, such a discourse positioned them as strong and stoic rather than as victims or martyrs:

> The only good thing that came out of all this is that it has made me stronger. It has made my skin thicker and made me wiser and stronger. I am very independent and very capable and I have got that determination which is also positive.
>
> (Elizabeth, 2002)

> The old value of persistence or putting up with everything. People consider it a good attribute to have to be steadfast, not let anything get to you.
>
> (Candice, 1999)

> My upbringing has helped me cope enormously. It gave me strength that I would never have had ... I was never 'poor me' and so that gave me strength, to cope with things.
>
> (Nelly, 1999)

## Conclusion

Research has shown that there are unique factors rural women experience and endure when living with and seeking help for domestic violence compared to urban women. However, our examination of the gendered discourses that feature in contexts of rurality shows that rural women do not position themselves as conservative, traditional or backward. Instead, rural women view femininity as being strong and essential to the survival of rural and family life. The high value placed on femininity can make it difficult for rural women to identify and name domestic violence, and to leave domestic violence relationships because women, men, family and extended family look to them for explanations and answers about domestic violence, leaving the perpetrator's actions invisible. Domestic violence is positioned in family life, the domain of the feminine, and hence the gaze becomes directed towards the woman's roles, expectations and actions. In addition, it contributes to rural women focusing on themselves, rather than their abusive partners, to address and stop domestic violence. The subject positions of helper, homemaker, partner and mother provide legitimacy and purpose to rural women, because they are constructed as demonstrating feminine strength and power. As these gendered subject positions are widely shared in rural communities, discourses of loyalty to male partners and property become ubiquitous, making it extremely difficult, if not impossible, to talk about domestic violence and abuse of gender power relations. As Pruitt (2008) argues, the point is not that rural women are worse off than their urban counterparts or, as we argue, not more conservative or backward in how they engage with gendered discourses and subject positions; it is that their spatial circumstances and the consequences of those circumstances are pivotal to the phenomenon of domestic violence. Rurality shapes gendered discourses and offers particular subject positions that align with rural life. How women and men engage with such discourses shapes how domestic violence is lived, experienced, identified and responded to in rural communities.

## References

Alston, M. (1995) *Women on the Land: The Hidden Heart of Rural Australia*, UNSW Press, Sydney.

Alston, M. (1997) Violence against women in a rural context. *Australian Social Work*, 50(1), pp. 15–22.

Bagshaw, D., Chung, D., Couch, M., Liburn, S. & Wadham, B. (2000) *Reshaping Responses to Domestic Violence: Final Report*, Partnerships Against Domestic Violence, Canberra.

Balogun, M., Owoaje, E. & Fawole, O. (2012) Intimate partner violence in southwestern Nigeria: are there rural–urban differences? *Women & Health*, 52, pp. 627–45.

Bhandari, S., Bullock, L., Anderson, K., Danis, F. & Sharps, W. (2011) Pregnancy and intimate partner violence: how do rural, low-income women cope? *Health Care for Women International*, 32(9), pp. 833–54.

Bosch, K. & Bergen, M. (2006) The influence of supportive and non-supportive persons in helping rural women in abusive partner relationships become free from abuse. *Journal of Family Violence*, 21, pp. 311–20.

Bryant, L. & Pini, B. (2011) *Gender and Rurality*, Routledge, London.

Davis, K., Taylor, B. & Furniss, D. (2001) Narrative accounts of tracking the rural domestic violence survivors journey: a feminist approach. *Health Care for Women International*, 22, pp. 333–47.

DeKeseredy, W. & Schwartz, M. (2009) *Dangerous Exits: Escaping Abusive Relationships in Rural America*. Rutgers University Press, New Brunswick, NJ.

Eastman, B., Bunch, S., Williams, A. & Carawan, L. (2007) Exploring the perceptions of domestic violence service providers in rural localities. *Violence Against Women*, 13(7), pp. 700–16.

Gagne, P. (1992) Appalachian women: violence and social control. *Journal of Contemporary Ethnography*, 20(4), pp. 387–404.

Grossman, S., Hinkley, S., Kawalski, A. & Margrave, C. (2005) Rural versus urban victims of violence: the interplay of race and region. *Journal of Family Violence*, 20(2), pp. 71–81.

Hayati, E., Eriksson, M., Hakimi, M., Högberg, U. & Emmelin, M. (2013) Elastic band strategy: women's lived experiences of coping with domestic violence in rural Indonesia. *Glob Health Action*, 6: 18894. http://dx.doi.org/10.3402/gha.v6i0.18894

Hogg, R. & Carrington, K. (1998) Crime, rurality and community. *Australian and New Zealand Journal of Criminology*, 31(2), pp. 160–81.

Hogg, R. & Carrington, K. (2006) *Policing the Rural Crisis*, Federation Press, Sydney.

Hornosty, J. (1995) Wife abuse in rural regions: structural problems in leaving abusive relationships – a case study in Canada. In F. Vanclay (Ed) *With a Rural Focus – Conference*

*Papers of the Australian Sociological Association*, Centre for Rural Social Research, Charles Sturt University, Wagga Wagga, NSW, pp. 21–34.

Kaur, R. & Gaug, S. (2010) Domestic violence against women: a qualitative study in a rural community. *Asia-Pacific Journal of Public Health*, 22(2), pp. 242–51.

Knowles, J. (1996) *Police culture and the handling of domestic violence: an urban/rural comparison*, Criminology Research Council, Canberra.

Lanier, C. & Maume, M. (2009) Intimate partner violence and social isolation across the rural/urban divide. *Violence Against Women*, 15(11), pp. 1311–30.

Little, J., Panelli, R. & Kraack, A. (2005) Women's fear of crime: a rural perspective. *Journal of Rural Studies*, 21, pp. 151–63.

Logan, T.K., Walker, R., Cole, J., Ratliff, S. & Leukefeld, C. (2003) Qualitative differences among rural and urban intimate violence victimization experiences and consequences: a pilot study. *Journal of Family Violence*, 18, pp. 83–92.

Peek-Asa, C., Wallis, A., Harland, K., Beyer, K., Dickey, P. & Salflas, A. (2011) Rural disparity in domestic violence in prevalence and access to resources. *Journal of Women's Health*, 20(11), pp. 1743–9.

Pruitt, L.R. (2008). Place matters: domestic violence and rural difference. *Wisconsin Journal of Law, Gender & Society*, 23, pp. 347–414.

Ragusa, A. (2012) Rural Australian women's legal help seeking for intimate partner violence: women intimate partner violence victim survivors' perceptions of criminal justice support services. *Journal of Interpersonal Violence*, 28(4), pp. 685–717.

Rawsthorne, M. (2008) Violence against women in rural settings. In B. Fawcett & F. Waugh (Eds) *Addressing Violence, Abuse and Oppression: Debates and Challenges*, Routledge, London, pp. 93–105.

Riddell, T., Ford-Gilboe, M. & Leipert, B. (2009) Strategies used by rural women to stop, avoid, or escape from intimate partner violence. *Health Care for Women International*, 30, pp. 154–9.

Sabarwal, S., Santhya, K. & Jeejeebhoy, S. (2014) Women's autonomy and experience of physical violence within marriage in rural India: evidence from a prospective study. *Journal of Interpersonal Violence*, 29(2), pp. 332–47.

Sandberg, L. (2013) Backward, dumb, and violent hillbillies? Rural geographies and intersectional studies on intimate partner violence. *Affilia: Journal of Women and Social Work*, 28(4), pp. 350–65.

Sarkar, M. (2010) A study on domestic violence against adult and adolescent females in a rural area of West Bengal. *Indian Journal of Community Medicine*, 35(2), pp. 311–15.

Schuler, S., Bates, L. & Islam, F. (2008) Women's rights, domestic violence, and recourse seeking in rural Bangladesh. *Violence Against Women*, 14(3), pp. 326–45.

Schuler, S. & Islam, F. (2008) Women's acceptance of intimate partner violence within marriage in rural Bangladesh. *Studies in Family Planning*, 39(1), pp. 49–58.

Shepard, M. & Hagemeister, A. (2013) Perspectives of rural women: custody and visitation with abusive ex-partners. *Affilia: Journal of Women and Social Work*, 28(2), pp. 165–76.

Shuman, R., McCauley, J., Waltermaurer, E., Roche, W.P., Hollis, H., Kilgannon Gibbons, A., Dever, A., Jones, S. & McNutt, L. (2008) Understanding intimate partner violence against women in the rural south. *Violence and Victims*, 23(3), pp. 390–405.

Stephenson, R., Winter, A. & Hindin, M. (2013) Frequency of intimate partner violence and rural women's mental health in four Indian states. *Violence Against Women*, 19(9), pp. 1133–50.

Sudderth, L. (2006) An uneasy alliance: law enforcement and domestic violence victim advocates in a rural area. *Feminist Criminology*, 1(4), pp. 329–53.

Sukhera, J., Cerulli, C., Gawinski, B. & Morse, D. (2012) Bridging prevention and health: exploring community perceptions of intimate partner violence in rural Honduras. *Journal of Family Violence*, 27, pp. 707–14.

Websdale, N. (1998) *Rural Women Battering and the Justice System: An Ethnography*, Sage, Thousand Oaks, CA.

Websdale, N. & Johnson, B. (1997) Reducing women battering: the role of structural approaches. *Social Justice*, 24(1), pp. 54–81.

Wendt, S. (2009a) Constructions of local culture and impacts on domestic violence in an Australian rural community. *Journal of Rural Studies*, 25(2), pp. 175–84.

Wendt, S. (2009b) *Domestic Violence in Rural Australia*, Federation Press, Sydney.

Wendt, S. (2010) Building and sustaining local co-ordination: an Australian rural community responds to domestic and family violence. *British Journal of Social Work*, 40, pp. 44–62.

Wilson-Williams, L., Stephenson, R., Juvekar, S. & Andes, K. (2008) Domestic violence and contraceptive use in a rural Indian village. *Violence Against Women*, 14(10), pp. 1181–98.

# 8   Aboriginal women

I am with my people. I haven't moved outside of where my people are from, I am never comfortable anywhere else … the people from the land are here and we all have a basic understanding of our culture, which has been lost through the past events of the government. I am part of a group rebuilding our language, to help identify us. The reason I live or do anything is for my people, for my family, and if I am not comfortable with it, then I don't do it. This is my home.

(Mayree, 2007)

## Introduction

In this chapter we will explore the unique factors that impact on Aboriginal women experiencing family violence in Australia, and examine how Aboriginal women think about and construct gender. We write this chapter with the acknowledgement of Australia's history of colonisation, oppressive legislation, racism and stolen generations, and hence we made the decision to focus solely on the Australian context. We listened to Larissa Behrendt (1993), who writes that for Aboriginal women the difference in Australian history cannot be ignored and assumptions cannot be made that Aboriginal women in Australia share the same experiences as black American women or other First Nations people. This assumption, she argues, is dangerous and stems from white privilege.

Historically, non-Aboriginal women have been involved in the marginalisation, removal and dispossession of Aboriginal women from their traditional lands, and thus we have benefited and profited from this oppression of Aboriginal people (Frederick, 2010). Despite the struggle for women's rights and the growth of the women's movement in Australia, the societal and economic positioning of Aboriginal women has remained stagnant for many years (Greer, 1994; Wilson, 1996; Frederick, 2010). Aboriginal women experience the potent combination of racism and sexism in their lives as a result of colonisation and dispossession, and non-Aboriginal women are very much part of this history and present-day context.

We are non-Aboriginal women writing a chapter on Aboriginal women's experiences of family violence and gender. We hesitated before deciding to write such a chapter because of our Australian history. Howe (2009), a non-Aboriginal feminist, lists the many reasons for such a hesitation in Australia, including fear of exacerbating a problem we want to try to help remedy, fear of being criticised, through to knowing that Aboriginal women are quite capable of speaking on their own behalf. However, after reading Irene Watson's discussion with Mary Heath (Watson & Heath 2004), we recognised that this fear is about ourselves and retreating can only occur from a position of privilege (Alcoff, 1991; Howe, 2009). We need to experience doubt, fear and discomfort as part of 'growing up the space for conversation' (Watson & Heath, 2004), for silence is the language of complicity (Aboriginal and Torres Strait Islander Women's Taskforce on Violence, 1999). At the same time, we cannot forget that we write this chapter in the context and history of colonisation, and that it is only our own perspectives that can be produced, not Aboriginal women's; hence, what we write will impact on Aboriginal and non-Aboriginal readers in different ways. We accept we are not immune to criticism, responsibility and accountability. We take responsibility for the power we wield as researchers.

Behrendt (1993) also states that in Australia the differences in experiences for Aboriginal people including traditional, rural and urban Aboriginal women cannot be ignored. Similarly, an Aboriginal woman we interviewed, working as a health worker in her community, said: 'It's recognising you know within Australia we have many different Aboriginal groups with different beliefs and you can't lump everyone into one group' (Dale, 2007). It is therefore important to note that this chapter is informed by interviews with seventeen Aboriginal women living in Adelaide, South Australia, land of the Kaurna people. However, some of the women we interviewed experienced life as a child growing up on the Yorke Peninsula Aboriginal Mission, later called Point Pearce, land of the Narungga people, and some women grew up in regional towns and centres in South Australia such as Ceduna (land of the Wirangu people), Port Augusta (Nukuna people) and Murray Bridge (Ngarrindjeri and Bangerang people). The interviews were conducted in 2007 and 2010 as part of research projects that focused on family violence service provision and community understandings and responses to family violence (Wendt, 2010; Wendt & Baker, 2013). However, we are also aware that many of the nation names we have used are contested, as are boundaries, and thus we recognise these are contested spaces.

In writing this chapter we do not start with the premise that it is acceptable to write about Aboriginal women, men, families and community as the problem. Instead, our intention is to explore how gender is constructed by the Aboriginal women we have interviewed, and simultaneously be guided by the work of Aboriginal women writers, scholars and activists to somehow lessen the dangers of speaking for and about, if that is even possible (Alcoff, 1991). As Irene Watson states, we have to begin the process of talking to each other more deeply than ever before, and we need to engage with the discomfort and with the difficulty and put thoughts and ideas out there to deconstruct old colonial paradigms (Watson & Heath, 2004). As non-Aboriginal women in Australia writing about sensitive experiences of violence against women, we need to feel our way through fear and discomfort, and be challenged, but at the same time admit to the limits of our knowing and writings as non-Aboriginal women (Moreton-Robinson, 2000).

Aboriginal and Torres Strait Islander people make up approximately 2.5 per cent of the total Australian population, with approximately 32 per cent living in major cities, 21 per cent in inner regional areas, 22 per cent in outer regional areas, 9 per cent in remote areas, and 15 per cent in very remote areas (Dudgeon et al., 2010). In this chapter we will be using the term family violence instead of domestic violence, except where directly reproducing quotations from the women we have interviewed or direct quotations from other sources. Mainstream concepts of domestic violence underpinned by Western models of female oppression may not fit the experiences of Aboriginal women whereby the interconnections of family and social systems are important. But at the same time we note it is difficult to identify terminology that is appropriate and acceptable to the many First Nations languages and cultures in Australia. In this chapter, we will use the term Aboriginal to refer to people of Aboriginal and Torres Strait Islander descent because it is frequently used, except where directly reproducing quotations or information from other sources or referring collectively to First Nations peoples from more than one country (Purdie, Dudgeon & Walker, 2010; Arney & Westby, 2012).

## Family violence and Aboriginal women

Even though domestic violence transcends all cultures and boundaries and similar experiences can be extracted across groups, family violence in Aboriginal society has its own unique factors created from colonisation (Brownridge, 2003). In Australia, Aboriginal people are and have been asserting their own world view and understanding of domestic violence. Such understandings focus on how the historical context of colonisation, oppression, dispossession, disempowerment, poverty and cultural, social and geographical dislocation impact on individuals, families and entire communities (Cheers et al., 2006, p.52; Day et al., 2012, p.106). The term family violence has been used instead of domestic violence by Aboriginal communities to highlight how Aboriginal society has been impacted on, and experienced powerlessness, collectively as a result of ongoing colonisation (Zellerer, 2003). In 1999, the Aboriginal and Torres Strait Islander Women's Taskforce on Violence (referred to as the Taskforce from hereon) reported that the history of Australia cannot be isolated in any discussions of violence in the lives of Aboriginal people in the contemporary context. Dispossession, cultural fragmentation and marginalisation have contributed to the current crisis in violence that many Aboriginal people find themselves in today, as well as high unemployment, poor health, low educational attainment, poverty, and alcohol and drug abuse (Allan & Kemp, 2011). Colonisation has eroded Aboriginal cultural and spiritual identity and, as Cripps and Davis (2012) state, the term family violence is used to describe the range of violence that takes place in Aboriginal communities including the physical, emotional, sexual, social, spiritual, cultural, psychological and economic abuses that may be perpetrated within a family. The term recognises the broader impacts of violence on extended families, kinship networks and community relationships. It has also been used in the past decade to encompass acts of self-harm and suicide, and has become widely adopted as part of the shift towards addressing intra-familial violence in all its forms. In summary, Memmott (2010, p. 335) argued that the causal factors of family violence can be considered under three categories including: the 'catalysing' or 'precipitating' causes that 'trigger' a violent behavioural episode by a perpetrator; the 'situational factors' in the social environment of the antagonist, which can include such aspects as substance abuse, other people encouraging one or both of the antagonists to act, and social differences between the antagonists' geographical or economic situations; and third, the 'underlying factors' are the deep historical circumstances of precolonial, colonial and postcolonial Aboriginal existence that place many contemporary Aboriginal people in a circumstance of vulnerability, leading to their perpetrating, or being the victim of, violent behaviour.

Aboriginal writers and researchers have established that due to colonisation, domestic violence in non-Aboriginal contexts and family violence in Aboriginal contexts cannot be assumed to be the same, and hence managing and preventing it requires different strategies. For example, as well as poverty, poor housing, high unemployment, mental health problems and intergenerational anger, resentment, shame, frustration and discrimination, many Aboriginal families carry memories of government policies that violated their most basic human rights. Aboriginal people in Australia have experienced or witnessed massacres, the forcible removal of children from families, brutal treatment by police and incarceration at higher rates than non-Aboriginal people (Davis & Taylor, 2002). Cripps (2008) highlights that Aboriginal communities are small, tight-knit places, where inevitably everybody knows everybody else; hence, this context creates follow-on effects from an incident of violence, which can directly and indirectly affect everyone within that community. Cripps (2008) argues that this context adds layers of complexity for victims of family violence when negotiating choices and decisions available, compared to those experienced by non-Aboriginal women. For example, most non-Aboriginal women do not experience marginalisation as a minority and direct or indirect racism, which often compounds high levels of distress for Aboriginal women in seeking assistance.

The Taskforce (1999) points out that we cannot assume the same experience for all Aboriginal people; that is, some families were able to escape past atrocities and find ways to heal and recover, and many families and communities are fighting to address the consequences of colonisation. However, at the same time, physical acts of brutality and sexual violence are being perpetrated within families and across communities to degrees previously unknown. For example, Davis and Taylor (2002, pp. 69) state while Aboriginal women 'comprise only 2% of the total female population, Aboriginal femicide accounts for approximately 15% of all femicide in Australia', and the 'greatest proportion (98.5 per cent) of deaths are caused by someone close to the victim'. Similarly, Berry, Harrison and Ryan (2009) conducted a descriptive analysis of the National Hospital Morbidity Database using data from the Northern Territory, Western Australia, South Australia and

Queensland for the period 1 July 1999–30 June 2004. They found that Aboriginal people were twice as likely as non-Aboriginal people to be hospitalised for injury, and had 17-fold greater hospitalisation rates for interpersonal violence. Aboriginal males and females were most commonly injured by a family member or intimate partner and females constituted 54 per cent of cases. Most non-Aboriginal cases involved males, 82 per cent of whom were injured by strangers. The study also found the largest differential between Aboriginal and non-Aboriginal injury-related hospitalisation was for interpersonal violence, particularly for women. Aboriginal and non-Aboriginal writers have both highlighted that using the term family violence should not hide the fact that Aboriginal women and children are predominantly the victims of family violence (Arney & Westby, 2012; Kennedy, 1999; Taskforce, 1999; Atkinson, 1990b).

Judy Atkinson points out that Aboriginal people are experiencing ongoing stress in their everyday lives that is repeated and of great severity, and that many of these stressors are inflicted by people well known to the victims. She argues that continued and severe family violence is the cost of unresolved trauma. For example, her studies have consistently found that Aboriginal men incarcerated for violent offending reported traumatic and violent events in childhood and youth, and that child sexual abuse trauma triggers later in life, the results of which are played out on members of the extended family and others. Finally, her work has also successfully linked the historical events associated with the colonisation of Aboriginal lands (accidental epidemics, massacres, starvation and removal of people to reserves) to increases in the rates of family violence, child sexual abuse and family breakdown in Aboriginal society (Atkinson et al., 2010).

## Family violence, Aboriginal women and feminism in Australia

In Australia, historically, the paradigms used to understand family violence and Aboriginal women's experiences have been informed by Western feminist perspectives, resulting in well-intentioned but often unworkable solutions. The feminist paradigms have traditionally focused on abuse of power in intimate relationships as a consequence of patriarchal power, and how social and economic structures make women dependent upon and vulnerable to abuse by men, as outlined in Chapter 2. Aboriginal scholars have criticised this focus for being too narrow and ignoring the social context of colonisation, loss of culture and disruption of spiritual and environmental dimensions for Aboriginal people (Taylor et al., 2004; Nancarrow, 2006). Aboriginal women have been trying to say for quite some time in Australia that they do not have a purely gendered experience of violence.

In 1989, Bell and Nelson co-authored a paper raising their concerns about violence against Aboriginal women, arguing feminist social scientists have a responsibility to identify and analyse those factors that render women vulnerable to violence, and the fact that violence is happening to women from other ethnic or racial groups cannot be a reason for ignoring the abuse. They raised the question of non-Aboriginal women speaking for and interfering in Aboriginal matters as well as the question of universality in experiences of rape, violence and abuse by men (Bell & Nelson, 1989). Bell (1991) presents an argument for feminism by drawing on female friendship, 'owning to be a woman', and using feminism to provide a critique of the wider society. Aboriginal women responded to these arguments, pointing out that Aboriginal women have a unique consciousness and understanding of Australia's history that non-Aboriginal women do not. For example, Lucashenko (1994) argued that oppressions of racism, violence and economic struggle are not interchangeable with gender, and non-Aboriginal Australian women cannot deny they are part of colonisation, oppression and history. Huggins (1994) argued that tension persists within Australian feminism because Aboriginal women are concerned that non-Aboriginal women do not appreciate how racism shapes sexism. Behrendt (1993) stated that women will feel their Aboriginality more than their gender in the Australian context, and Bennet (1997) pointed out that non-Aboriginal women cannot assume a shared gendered experience of violence and abuse because of differences in class, culture and status. Huggins (1994) makes the point that women's social, political and spiritual position in Aboriginal culture, both traditional and contemporary, puts them in a far better position than white women could ever imagine in understanding the intricacies of violence in their lives, but that this is not understood or appreciated by non-Aboriginal women. In understanding violence against women, such as rape and sexual assault or intimate partner violence, Aboriginal women have been arguing that interpersonal violence in Aboriginal communities is ultimately a manifestation of sexism and racism brought about by colonisation (Lucashenko, 1994; Huggins, 1994; Bennet, 1997).

Atkinson (1990b) pointed out some time ago that Aboriginal women have been speaking out strongly about the violence they can no longer accept but a patriarchal mentality within Western systems and structures creates a context that is unable to hear what Aboriginal women have to say. Aileen Moreton-Robinson (2005) names this patriarchal mentality the operations of patriarchal whiteness. She argues that patriarchal whiteness is Anglicised, institutionalised and culturally based and it is an invisible, unnamed organising principle that shapes Australian social structure and culture. Irene Watson (2009) points out that violence amongst Aboriginal peoples, and in particular against women and children, has been misrepresented throughout Australia's colonial history, and that patriarchal whiteness contributes to this misrepresentation because it presents such violence as inherent to Aboriginal culture and law. She argues that colonisation and patriarchal whiteness demonise Aboriginal culture, providing an opening for the state to appear as a crusader and rescuer of Aboriginal women and children. This crucible of white race privilege and advantage has allowed white people and feminism historically in Australia to position Aboriginal communities as more violent than non-Aboriginal communities, and hence in need of intervention and saving. Patriarchal whiteness is ubiquitous but invisible and identifying it can help us to understand why we have not heard other narratives and images that show a more comprehensive range of Aboriginal experiences. For example, Aboriginal writers have argued, and still do, that Aboriginal women do not consider men to be their cultural superiors (Huggins,

1994; Watson, 2007; McGlade, 2012). However, Aboriginal women occupy a subordinate position because this is what has been and still is imposed on them by colonisation and the patriarchal nature of Anglo-Australian culture. Atkinson (1990a) writes that over time, myths about Aboriginal women have emerged and have been kept alive by paternalistic thinking, such as Aboriginal women are inferior and exist as servants for their male partners, and that their sexuality is something that can be exploited and abused. Colonisation brought an entrenched patriarchal system that legitimised the acculturation and dispossession of Aboriginal people and positioned Aboriginal women as inferior; hence socialising young Aboriginal men and women over time to restructure gender relationships (Taskforce, 1999). Or, as McGlade (2012, p. 65) explains, traditional Aboriginal society was not utopian and free of violence, but the categorisation of gender-based violence as traditional culture is very problematic. That is, colonisation has not only impacted on Aboriginal law ways; it has also resulted in a form of internalised abuse within Indigenous communities that is inherently gendered.

Aboriginal women have been saying for a long time that they want family violence to stop but they also want men to be helped and to be part of the solution. This message was strong throughout the consultations of the Taskforce in 1999, with Aboriginal women reporting if there is to be a break in the cycle of violence, working collectively to reunite families is essential. Similarly, Nancarrow (2006) reported on a study that looked at using restorative justice for family violence and found that Aboriginal and non-Aboriginal women prioritised justice objectives differently. While they all agreed that 'stopping violence' was the most important priority and that 'supporting women by validating their stories' was in the top three priorities, only non-Aboriginal women placed 'holding men accountable' in the top three. Aboriginal women placed 'sending a message to the community that violence is wrong' and 'restoring relationships' in their top three (equal third). Cripps and McGlade (2008) point out that typical 'Western' responses to family violence like women's refuges, criminal justice responses and programs of a therapeutic nature have mostly been culturally inappropriate and ineffective for Aboriginal families because they have focused on separating victims and perpetrators, with a particular focus on the criminal justice response. This approach to addressing violence relies on the institutionalisation of the offender to protect the victim which, as Cripps and McGlade (2008) point out, does not resonate with Aboriginal families, who often find these approaches disempowering. Separation from partners, families and communities risks access to cultural resources and creates a sense of conflicting loyalty for Aboriginal women (Coker, 2006).

The presence of gendered power relations and imbalances in family violence has been and continues to be debated in Australia. Lucashenko (1997, p. 148) writes that if Aboriginal Australians have been invisible generally, this has been doubly true for Aboriginal women, and this has been demonstrated by the dominance of Aboriginal men in the mainstream images of the sportsman, the political figure and the romanticised stockman as well as decades of increased Aboriginal agitation for land rights, and community initiatives in health, education and legal reform. She points out that, although Aboriginal women have struggled in the past to highlight issues of family violence, rape, child abuse and parental neglect, it has taken years to have these problems even acknowledged by some Aboriginal men; because talking about the bashings, rapes, murders and incest for which Aboriginal men themselves are responsible is seen as threatening in the extreme. Lucashenko (1997, p. 149) talks about the difficulties Aboriginal women experience in trying to support their communities to critique and challenge the state, and at the same time try to understand and respond to levels of 'black-on-black violence' in Aboriginal communities. She raises the concern that interpersonal violence is often overlooked as a secondary issue or portrayed solely as the dysfunction arising from colonisation by Europeans. Lucashenko's (1997, p. 156) discussion reminds us of the difficulties involved in speaking about gender in contexts of colonisation for Aboriginal women, particularly when she wrote that black women have been struggling for years to find appropriate ways to conceptualise violence and abuse in their lives; that is, to speak about Aboriginal men's violence leaves Aboriginal women open to accusations of 'coconut or feminist'. Racism within feminism has not helped this forced dichotomy, which silences issues of crucial concern. Langton (2007) also picked up this theme regarding the difficulties of talking about race and gender, when she wrote about the Australian Northern Territory Emergency Response, which followed the Northern Territory Government Inquiry into the Protection of Aboriginal Children from Sexual Abuse and the release of the 2007 report *Little Children Are Sacred*. She argued that, even though she can understand the feelings of an oppressed 'racial' collective, solidarity for its own sake does not permit a clear-cut rejection of wrongdoing. Langton (2007) argued that her own research showed several additional contributing factors driving some Aboriginal communities into the 'inner circles of hell': illicit drugs, alcohol, addictive substances, pornography and permanent unemployment. She argued that it was not just the historical and continuing exclusion from the economy, lack of intergenerational capital or vicious governments, but the practices of Aboriginal people themselves that transform mere poverty into a living hell. She concludes by asking: how much longer will this abuse of Aboriginal women and children be tolerated and when will the focus turn to the wheel of suffering?

The tension of discussing gendered power relations and imbalances in family violence is also seen in contexts of justice forums and responding to and addressing violence and abuse of Aboriginal women and children. For example, Marchetti (2010) explored the extent to which gendered power imbalances are present in the hearings of Indigenous sentencing courts concerning intimate partner violence, and how such power imbalances are managed by a process that aims to be more culturally appropriate than mainstream sentencing hearings. She points out that Aboriginal people are very aware of how colonisation has affected the life of the offender on a day-to-day basis, and this awareness can lead to excusing violent behaviour, thus it needs to be balanced by a clear opposition towards using violence against partners. She argues that minimising the harm done to Aboriginal women and children cannot be the primary response. Similarly, Cripps and McGlade (2008) and Price (2009) warn of the unintentional consequences of focusing on support for the offender at the cost of appropriate ongoing recognition and support of the victim and further warn of the potential harm of focusing on Aboriginal justice measures that presuppose a healed community. Watson (2009) also discusses how courts have shown sensitivity towards Aboriginal men in matters of rape where 'culture' is taken as a mitigating factor. She uses this point again to remind us that the process of translating Aboriginal law in Australian courts contributes to the harm that is done to Aboriginal women, while at the same time constructing Aboriginal men as inherently violent and inferior to white men. The mistake, she argues, is that the court's reading of Aboriginal law and culture is translated by a non-Aboriginal process that excludes from consideration the impact of more than two hundred years of colonial violence. Cripps and McGlade (2008) argue that a transformation of existing structures of gendered domination within Aboriginal communities needs to take place because women fear that restorative justice reforms may fail to address the underlying power inequity that is present in communities from years of oppression. However, Watson (2009) warns that turning to traditional law and culture and having these translated by non-Aboriginal people who presume to 'know' tradition is dangerous and fails to understand the effects of colonisation on Aboriginal relationships to kin and country, and assumes those relationships have remained intact and unaffected by colonisation and modernity (Watson, 2009). In summary, McGlade (2012, p. 69) argues that, while the family violence paradigm emphasises the collective Indigenous experience of powerlessness and leans towards practices of family healing, she is concerned that this paradigm ignores 'the very real power imbalances that exist between predominantly adult male perpetrators and the children they victimise' and the gravity of men's use of violence against women, resulting in very high rates of homicide of Aboriginal women.

In trying to move beyond this tension, Irene Watson (2007) points out that, if Aboriginal male violence is understood as an acting-out of being denied male power in other spheres, it seems counterproductive to embrace constructs that implicitly link the solution to domestic violence to the acquisition of greater male power. Instead, she argues that it is Aboriginal women who should be returned to and empowered by the place of their grandmothers' law, which has been silenced as a result of colonisation. Similarly, Nicole Watson (2011) has argued that historically state interventions such as the Northern Territory Emergency Response, income management and compulsory acquisition of land in the name of Aboriginal women's protection have invariably resulted in a binary that simultaneously renders their rights invisible while subjecting them to further regulation. For writers like Irene Watson, Nicole Watson and Aileen Moreton-Robinson, solutions to family violence will not come from patriarchal Western societies, but from Aboriginal women – who have a connection to land that is not based on a white, Anglicised, male conceptualisation of property and ownership but on the strengthening of women's law, self-determination, cultural sustenance and political and economic empowerment (Watson, 2007; Watson, 2011; Moreton-Robinson, 2005). In short, the solutions are embedded in cultural practices derived from knowledge that is outside the experience and knowledge of patriarchal whiteness (Moreton-Robinson, 2005).

In summary, gender, gender power relations and gender-related crimes of violence are difficult to discuss and debate because colonisation and patriarchal whiteness are interlocked and interwoven systems of oppression that impact on Aboriginal men, women and children in differing ways (Moreton-Robinson, 2005; McGlade, 2012). Such politics embedded within these systems of oppression largely allow us, by our inherent privilege, to not hear and therefore inadvertently, if not deliberately, enforce the silencing of Aboriginal women in relation to family violence, despite their attempts over decades to speak about such problems (Moreton-Robinson, 2005).

## Aboriginal women, family violence and gender

In Australia, Howe (2009) points out that a gendered analysis of violence against women and children within Aboriginal communities has been silenced by non-Aboriginal women, perhaps for the reason introduced at the start of this chapter. Throughout our years of interviewing women about domestic violence, we want to acknowledge that Aboriginal women took a great risk in speaking to us about family violence experiences in their lives (Wendt, 2010; Wendt & Baker, 2013). As Mayree said at the beginning of this chapter, 'the reason I live or do anything is for my people, for my family, and if I am not comfortable with it, then I don't do it' (Mayree, 2007). While nowhere near as courageous, we too have taken the risk to explore gender in this chapter, and we have done so with the knowledge that we could choose to retreat from such a discussion because of our place of privilege (Howe, 2009). But we know that this also works the other way: that our choice to take this risk is also a marker of our privilege. The difference is that choosing not to retreat from such a discussion challenges this privilege because it lays it bare to examination and critique. Moreover, we recognise that all women are characterised by different and dynamic types of femininity or social practices according to the specific cultural values placed on factors such as class, race, ethnicity, age, religion, sexuality and disability such that different femininities also represent different social positions of power, with none being fixed (Cossins, 2003). We, as authors of this chapter, therefore do not presume to know everything about the lives, histories, families, cultures and experiences of family violence of the Aboriginal women we interviewed. We respect in the act of storytelling, particularly in the context of research interviews, that the Aboriginal women decided what they wanted to tell us (Haaken, 2008). We also acknowledge the limits to our knowing due to our acting from a subject position of dominance; that is, white academic feminist researchers, compounded by our involvement in histories of domination through which our thinking and behaviours have been shaped (Moreton-Robinson, 2000; Haaken, 2008).

By using feminist post-structuralist ideas to re-examine gender in the contexts of family violence, we aim to show the gendered reality of social relations, and at the same time produce new generalisations about the lives of Aboriginal women that are inclusive and which recognise the diversity of women (Eudine Barriteau Foster, 1992). Furthermore, we do not want to replicate the existing discourses portraying Aboriginal communities as 'damaged', 'conflict ridden' and 'culturally violent'. We are guided by Irene Watson's (2007) ideas of focusing on other narratives, hence the quotations we provide come directly from the Aboriginal women we interviewed and our interpretations of their subject positions come from their constructions during the interviews. However, at the same time, the body of their voices and this text is contained by us as authors and the framework and approach we have taken.

Feminist post-structuralist ideas challenge the construct of woman in relation to man by suggesting that the gendered woman interacts with and is acted upon by her environment. This frame, we argue, is potentially useful in understanding how Aboriginal women construct gender in their lives because it disrupts the hierarchical binary opposition between woman and man, which has been unhelpful to Aboriginal people in understanding family violence. Furthermore, this shift from defining women as 'not men' to women as a construct of gender does not assume the shared experience of all women, which has been criticised and exposed in the Australian colonisation context.

In our interviews with Aboriginal women, in trying to understand family violence, many of the women remembered and acknowledged the past and reflected on the history of colonisation for their families and communities. Discourses of colonisation gave them space to try to remember family structures, cultures and men and women's roles before invasion. Gender was therefore positioned in history as something that was lost and different to Western understandings of masculinity and femininity. Similar to Atkinson (1990a), Huggins (1994), Watson (2007) and McGlade (2012), the women reflected on positions of subordination imposed by colonisation and hence expressed grief about the loss of men and women's positions in Aboriginal society:

> The family structure is different since colonisation. The culture has been destroyed, men haven't got the part in the family that they used to have, the women haven't got the role they had, children aren't getting taught what men and the women used to teach the children because we are living by white man's ways and white man's rules and we can't go back to our own culture.
>
> (Dale, 2007)

> I believe it is grief and loss of culture, identity, possession of land and you have got to know all this stuff inside you. I am just trying to explain it … but you have got all these things that you don't know, you aren't aware of but you want to know … don't fit in anybody's world and so where do you go?
>
> (Kara, 2007)

> Family violence, it is that being from the men, the men lose a lot of power and control over what's happening in their own lives as well as the family and with the loss of power it backfires on the women and the women tend to suffer more for it.
>
> (Mayree, 2007)

The grieving process is never complete. You are holding all that hurt and anger inside and it is sometimes easier to let that out on someone that you love because you know they will always love you.

(Gemma, 2007)

In reflecting on the past, the women also spoke about family obligation and the importance of family systems and extended family. They spoke about such themes in the context of finding it difficult to leave violent and abusive relationships and finding and maintaining accommodation. They constructed women as being vital to and embedded within family systems and the consequent dilemmas they often felt in trying to fulfil expectations and obligations to family but at the same time keep themselves and their children safe from violence and abuse. Cheers et al. (2006, p. 57) reported in their study on family violence that Aboriginal people emphasised family and its deep cultural roots as the community's structural foundation. Each person knows, and is located in, his or her family genealogy. The relationship between family strength and culture goes both ways: strong families maintain strong culture while strong culture keeps families strong. Similarly, for the women we interviewed, their family was a source of identity, providing a place for them in the social universe, linked together by extensive family networks that interweave throughout the community. Women positioned themselves as being part of this interweaving, bonding and mutual support but feared their ability to fulfil this obligation due to the stress of family violence. For example:

It is pretty hard for me because with my family, they are always hassling me about things with money or moving in … If I say no it would start a big conflict with the whole family and so it is hard to say no.

(Ali, 2010)

He would come back and stay a while and I was pretty much seeing myself as helping him out because he didn't have a home or anything like that and I just wanted him to have that time with the kids as well but it wasn't working out … I have felt pressure from family. Aboriginal people have always been around a lot of family and that support is important to maintain. But then I want to move or have a change from living so close to family and just concentrate on my own family and try and get a bit further ahead with myself.

(Jan, 2010)

The family system is much broader than for non-Aboriginal people. Like, if you had a domestic dispute with your partner it won't be just with the partner, the whole family or extended family get involved, and that is so hard to pull yourself out and being in a small community.

(Sally, 2007)

Specifically, some of the women constructed themselves as being responsible for ensuring their children had a relationship with their father and extended family.

Ensuring their children had a sense of their family history and networks was vital to building their Aboriginal identity, something the women did not want them to lose. Moreton-Robinson (2005) makes the point that Aboriginal women are culturally aligned with Aboriginal men because, irrespective of gender, they are tied through obligations and reciprocity to kin and country, and share a common history of colonisation. As Cripps (2008) reminds us, it can be difficult for victims of family violence to makes decisions within this context. As some women noted:

> I was living with my ex-partner's family and I felt like I was sort of under their wing and did what they wanted and didn't want to upset them because he was in jail. I just felt a pressure ... I couldn't be me and do what I wanted ... my daughter still sees his family, they love her, she's got to have contact with her other family as well, not just mine.
>
> (Rebecca, 2010)

> I was in domestic violence for a long while and didn't realise it until I started talking to others, counselling and my study years because you are like with the man and you live with the man, you're with him and you've got his kids and you do whatever he wanted to do. He was a good man and we would do family stuff but the drinking ... and then abuse.
>
> (Sara, 2010)

> My son still sees his father which was a hard thing but I thought, well you know, that's the only way that you know that's going to benefit my son is keeping that friendship, connection, even though we might not say much to each other.
>
> (Frieda, 2010)

Similar to other women represented in this book, Aboriginal women engaged with discourses of motherhood; that is, positioning themselves as protectors, providers and carers for their children, all roles they constructed as important within Aboriginal communities but especially important in contexts of family violence:

> I wanted to get off the mission and then I noticed the difference in my kids, big change. Like they stopped their swearing and everything ... being kids now, when they were there they were just ratbags and teasing all the time ... my goal was to get them away from there so they could grow up different to the other way. Everyone growing up now because kids having kids, I was looking at my daughter and thinking we are not staying here, my first cousin's fifteen-year-old daughter has a baby there and my daughter will be fourteen next month.
>
> (Marg, 2010)

Some women reflected on the strength they drew from their positions of being a mother to survive violence and abuse; that is, they often left families and communities to seek reprieve and protect children. We also found that some women cared for siblings and nieces or nephews when their own mothers or aunties were suffering from violence and abuse, depression or addiction:

> I don't know how to describe it but I wasn't very confident in being ... because of being around family violence and stuff, being, I could be like a better mum, I am a better mum. I got control of my life and I was in control of my daughter.
>
> (Rebecca, 2010)

> I am happier, got my own space and it feels good and settled because you know your family, your kids, will be alright and have a home to live in.
>
> (Felicity, 2010)

> I just felt with my partner and the starting over and over again ... I just thought to myself 'it isn't good, it is not happy, it is not healthy for me and the kids, to start over and over and have everything destroyed' so now I'm doing it on my own and hope everything will turn out.
>
> (Jan, 2010)

> I was eighteen and my baby sister was one and mum was going through a lot and I had to step in and take care of my baby sister because my mum kind of didn't really care what happened to herself, she doesn't care if she has a place to live or not, she is really sad after my dad died ... so I am legal guardian of my sister, just trying to break this cycle ... I just want to be a good mother to my children and just concentrate on them.
>
> (Ali, 2010)

Valuing motherhood, and embracing subject positions of protector, provider and carer, we also found the women positioned themselves as using their experiences of family violence to build and grow other subject positions, and these were mainly teacher and guide or someone with strength, power and confidence. During family violence some women constructed themselves as powerless, suffering and desperate, yet did not spend large amounts of time focusing on these positions; instead they used these positions to construct their potential role as one of healer and guide in their communities and families. As the Taskforce (1999) points out, women construct themselves in a space in which men, women, families and extended families provide support for one another and socialise children, and they see this as central to reviving family and overcoming adversity. For example, women constructed teacher and guide in the following ways:

> I want to do a community service course. I want to work with youth, so like a youth care worker. I just thought because I was a young girl that wasn't like trouble but someone they can relate. I could help other kids.
>
> (Rebecca, 2010)

I have grown so much as a person. I am strong for it and I would never have been able to sit here and talk about it and work in my role … a lot of women think they are stupid or dumb because they haven't been out working for a while but they are running a whole household and they are trying to manipulate everything at home so that their kids don't get to see as much of the stuff … and they are out doing things for their kids even though they may be hurt, they organise, they try and budget, they try and organise their kids and homes and they don't realise they have all that skill.

(Mayree, 2007)

For other women, they constructed themselves as confident, more powerful and fearless:

Like now, I stand up and say … 'You walk in my door? It's either you or me.' And I have actually pushed him out the door. I wouldn't have been able to do that in the past. I am not scared anymore … It is my home now. I have been in rough relationships and I have always just done what I am told but now I speak up for myself and say 'Get stuffed, don't come into my house.' My kids feel happy and settled and content and stable and everything, like it is our house.

(Jo, 2010)

He has a lot to do with the kids now and I just feel like I can stand up to him now, you know where I don't let him put it over me anymore which is good. So it's sort of like built my confidence up as well. I feel so much better, I'm in control now which is good.

(Kay, 2010)

Throughout the stories of women's experiences of family violence and associated navigations of trying to understand it, manage, respond and survive it, the women constructed gender embedded within their family and community. That is, gender was tied up with and very much done within the context of family and community. Women focused attention on how they could protect and support their children but also balanced this with their sense of belonging and obligation to their wider family networks and communities. Specifically, for five women who survived family violence and secured employment as Aboriginal health workers, this theme of serving their community was still strong, and they constructed themselves as rescuers in helping both men and women:

I know if I go to help a woman who is in domestic violence I can often get targeted by the men who would also actually ask for help and that would hurt me because I was funded to help the women and there was no men's health. So I would help the men because I am thinking the violence is not going to stop unless they, you know, look at some of their issues … I did have a few men come to my house after work and threaten and that is not real fun. I know it actually filtered into my family but I just couldn't separate it. I felt like I was a bit of a rescuer.

(Sally, 2007)

You are a jack of all trades. You are employed to do a job but you are really doing everything. We'll just do our best to get resources and if we can't we battle it on our own; we won't let the community miss out. I am not going to walk away and send her back for another flogging. So we usually just got to make it on our own and we make it within our own Indigenous workers.

(Kara, 2007)

I like obligations within the community, the obligations make you feel Aboriginal ... it is hard to brace the working and living relationships in the community and I know people take children home for safety and at that time it is the right decision. Because I am Aboriginal since the day I was born, it's been part of my life, whether it is at school, at work, home, and I just take that sort of stuff on and yeah it shouldn't be part of our lives, but we take it on.

(Dale, 2007)

Aboriginal women working together or the power of the collective experience of being a woman within Aboriginal communities was another construction we saw glimpses of in the women's interviews. Women were constructed and positioned as having the knowledge to respond to and help solve family violence. The women we interviewed often referred to the strength they gained from other women in their families and the practice of 'women helping women', offering comfort, insight, determination and healing. When Aboriginal women did not have access to other Aboriginal women, they felt and expressed sadness. Gender was therefore constructed in relation to women bonding (Puchala et al., 2010), that is, women's connectedness and identity within Aboriginal culture:

When I got back to Ceduna I had family there but then I was like door to door with my four kids and it's been hard going from cousins to aunties and they have kids too but I miss my mum, sisters and her daughters coming round for a visit and all the girls.

(Marg, 2010)

I had a white fella, like lots of women have got an Aboriginal partner ... but I wasn't going to leave because all my family lives in [names the town] and I didn't want to leave. That's why I am feeling flat, my family is still there.

(Audrey, 2010)

I have got the different generations sitting around together in my own family, grandmothers, mother, myself and my daughter and we sit there and have a most ripper conversation, the conversations and network is amazing.

(Sally, 2007)

I like our elders group and we can go to sources of information and they know the history, and we can speak to them about their knowledge and what's happened and their experiences of domestic violence.

(Kara, 2007)

We found gender was constructed from discourses that were specific to the Aboriginal women's groups, cultures and history, and that such discourses offered subject positions for Aboriginal women within associated cultural arrangements. The dominant discourses of femininity and associated subject positions of submissive, passive and sexually desirable that construct femininity in opposition and inferiority to masculinity that we see in Western cultural arrangements did not feature in Aboriginal women's stories. Discourses perpetuated by Australian culture of Aboriginal women being inferior to and servants for their men, who control them through violence and sexual exploitation (Atkinson, 1990a), did not feature in or get validation in the women's stories; instead, the interviews showed glimpses of and insight into the inherent power held by women in Aboriginal cultures (Watson, 2007). Despite enduring violence and abuse within their families and from partners, and the tension of juggling personal safety with familial and community obligations, the women positioned themselves as important carriers and maintainers of Aboriginal connections, identity and belonging for their children, and as potential teachers, healers and facilitators of change within their communities. Gender was not constructed or done in opposition or response to masculinity but was embedded within Aboriginal community and family.

## Conclusion

It is clear that we cannot understand women's experiences of family violence in Aboriginal communities without acknowledging the impacts of colonisation, dispossession and fragmentation of Aboriginal cultures, and the associated high unemployment, poor health, low educational attainment and poverty, and alcohol and drug abuse this has caused (Allan & Kemp, 2011). At the same time, we agree with Aboriginal (McGlade, 2012; Marchetti, 2010) and non-Aboriginal (Howe, 2009) writers that we cannot ignore gendered power relations in contexts of family violence because women and men are gendered (Eudine Barriteau Foster, 1992). But this is not to assume a universal sisterhood that focuses on the commonality of women's experiences of violence because the past has taught us that gender can become hijacked by privileged groups speaking for all women (Howe, 2009) and by patriarchal whiteness, which has demonised Aboriginal culture (Moreton-Robinson, 2005). In acknowledging these issues and in not wanting to inadvertently replicate them, in this chapter we have sought to recognise how Aboriginal women are gendered by interacting in their own social-cultural context and the context of colonisation. Aboriginal women have been arguing that gender matters in contexts of violence and abuse but we have not listened, recognised or understood the context from which they speak. In this chapter, we have aimed to open up this discursive space to see gender constructions that are possible, available and active through the stories of Aboriginal women. Gaining insight into gender relations through the stories of Aboriginal women themselves challenges assumptions of Aboriginal women being 'incapable' and 'needy', which have grown from patriarchal whiteness paradigms and from within feminism itself. As Irene Watson (2007, p. 107) argues, other narratives and images are needed to show a fuller range of Aboriginal experiences, and hence by drawing out Aboriginal women's subject positions from the discourses they draw on in their historical and local contexts, we are able to see glimpses of the power and potential of Aboriginal women in surviving and solving family violence. Finally, we have learned that, as non-Aboriginal women, we cannot fully retreat from these discussions; we just need to listen more carefully and at the same time remain responsible for our speaking so that we can be part of the different kind of conversation that will 'grow up the space' (Watson & Heath, 2004).

## References

Aboriginal and Torres Strait Islander Women's Taskforce on Violence (1999) *Aboriginal and Torres Strait Islander Women's Taskforce on Violence Report*, Department of Aboriginal and Torres Strait Islander Policy and Development, Brisbane.

Alcoff, L. (1991) The problem of speaking for others. *Cultural Critique*, 20, pp. 5–32.

Allan, J. & Kemp, M. (2011) Aboriginal and non-Aboriginal women in New South Wales non-government organisation (NGO) drug and alcohol treatment and the implications for social work: who starts, who finishes, and where do they come from? *Australian Social Work*, 64(1), pp. 68–83.

Arney, F. and Westby, M.A. (2012) *Men's Places Literature Review*, Centre for Child Development and Education, Menzies School of Health Research, Darwin, NT.

Atkinson, J. (1990a) Violence in Aboriginal Australia: colonisation and gender. *Aboriginal and Islander Health Worker Journal*, 14(2), pp. 5–21.

Atkinson, J. (1990b) Violence in Aboriginal Australia: part 2, *Aboriginal and Islander Health Worker Journal*, 14(3), pp. 4–27.

Atkinson, J., Nelson, J. & Atkinson, C. (2010) Trauma, transgenerational transfer and effects on community wellbeing. In N. Purdie, P. Dudgeon & R. Walker (Eds) *Working Together: Aboriginal and Torres Strait Islander Mental Health and Wellbeing Principles and Practice*, Commonwealth of Australia, Canberra, pp. 135–44.

Behrendt, L. (1993) Aboriginal women and the white lies of the feminist movement: implications for Aboriginal women in the rights discourse. *Australian Feminist Law Journal*, 27(1), pp. 27–44.

Bell, D. (1991) Intraracial rape revisited: on forging a feminist future beyond factions and frightening politics. *Women's Studies International Forum*, 14(5), pp. 385–412.

Bell, D. & Nelson, T. (1989) Speaking about rape is everyone's business. *Women's Studies International Forum*, 12(4), pp. 403–16.

Bennet, B. (1997) Domestic violence. *Aboriginal and Islander Health Worker Journal*, 21(4), pp. 11–14.

Berry, J., Harrison, J. & Ryan, P. (2009) Hospital admissions of Indigenous and non-Indigenous Australians due to interpersonal violence, July 1999–June 2004. *Australian and New Zealand Journal of Public Health*, 33(3), pp. 215–22.

Brownridge, D. (2003) Male partner violence against Aboriginal women in Canada: an empirical analysis. *Journal of Interpersonal Violence*, 18(1), pp. 65–83.

Cheers, B., Binell, M., Coleman, H., Gentle, I., Miller, G., Taylor, J. & Weetra, C. (2006) Family violence: an Australian Indigenous community tells its story. *International Social Work*, 49(1), pp. 51–63.

Coker, D. (2006) Restorative justice, Navajo peacemaking and domestic violence. *Theoretical Criminology*, 10(1), pp. 67–85.

Cossins, A. (2003) Saints, sluts and sexual assault: rethinking the relationship between sex, race, and gender. *Social and Legal Studies*, 12(7), pp. 77–103.

Cripps, K. (2008) Indigenous family violence: a statistical challenge. *Injury, International Journal of the Care of the Injured*, 39(S5), pp. S25–S35.

Cripps, K. & Davis, M. (2012) Communities working to reduce Indigenous family violence. *Indigenous Justice Clearinghouse*, Brief 12, pp. 1–8.

Cripps, K. & McGlade, H. (2008) Indigenous family violence and sexual abuse: considering pathways forward. *Journal of Family Studies*, 14(2–3), pp. 240–53.

Davis, K. & Taylor, B. (2002) Voices from the margins, Part 1: Narrative accounts of Indigenous family violence. *Contemporary Nursing*, 14, pp. 66–75.

Day, A., Jones, R., Nakata, M. & McDermott, D. (2012) Indigenous family violence: an attempt to understand the problems and inform appropriate and effective responses to criminal justice system intervention. *Psychiatry, Psychology and Law*, 19(1), pp. 104–17.

Dudgeon, P., Wright, M., Paradies, Y., Garvey, D. & Walker, I. (2010) The social, cultural and historical context of Aboriginal and Torres Strait Islander Australians. In N. Purdie, P. Dudgeon & R. Walker (Eds) *Working Together: Aboriginal and Torres Strait Islander Mental Health and Wellbeing Principles and Practice*, Commonwealth of Australia, Canberra, pp. 25–42.

Eudine Barriteau Foster, A. (1992) The construct of a postmodernist feminist theory for Caribbean social science research. *Social and Economic Studies*, 41(2), pp. 1–43.

Frederick, B. (2010) Reempowering ourselves: Australian Aboriginal women. *Signs: Journal of Women in Culture and Society*, 35(3), pp.546–50.

Greer, P. (1994) Aboriginal women and domestic violence in New South Wales. In J. Stubbs (Ed) *Women, Male Violence and the Law*, Institute of Criminology, Sydney, pp. 64–87.

Haaken, J. (2008) When white buffalo calf woman meets Oedipus on the road: Lakota psychology, feminist psychoanalysis, and male violence. *Theory & Psychology*, 18(2), pp. 195–208.

Howe, A. (2009) Addressing child sexual assault in Australian Aboriginal communities: the politics of white voice. *Australian Feminist Law Journal*, 30, pp. 41–61.

Huggins, J. (1994) A contemporary view of Aboriginal women's relationship to the white women's movement. In N. Grieve & A. Burns (Eds) *Australian Women: Contemporary Feminist Thought*, Oxford University Press, Melbourne, pp. 70–9.

Kennedy, M. (1999) Melva's story: an Aboriginal approach to preventing child sexual assault. In J. Breckenridge & L. Lain (Eds) *Challenging silence: innovative responses to sexual and domestic violence*. Allen & Unwin, Sydney, pp. 215–21.

Langton, M. (2007) Trapped in the Aboriginal reality show. *Griffith Review*, 19.

Lucashenko, M. (1994) No other truth? Aboriginal women and Australian feminism. *Social Alternatives*, 12(4), pp. 21–4.

Lucashenko, M. (1997) Violence against Indigenous women: public and private dimension. In S. Cook & J. Bessant (Eds) *Women's Encounters with Violence: Australian Experiences*, Sage, London, pp. 147–58.

Marchetti, E. (2010) Indigenous sentencing courts and partner violence: perspectives of court practitioners and elders on gender power imbalances during the sentencing hearing. *Australian and New Zealand Journal of Criminology*, 43(2), pp. 263–81.

McGlade, H. (2012) *Our Greatest Challenge: Aboriginal Children and Human Rights*, Aboriginal Studies Press, Canberra.

Memmott, P. (2010) On regional and cultural approaches to Australian Indigenous violence. *Australian & New Zealand Journal of Criminology*, 43(2), 333–55.

Moreton-Robinson, A. (2000) *Talkin Up to the White Woman: Indigenous Women and Feminism*, University of Queensland Press, St Lucia, Qld.

Moreton-Robinson, A. (2005) Patriarchal whiteness, self-determination and Indigenous women: the invisibility of structural privilege and the visibility of oppression. In B. Hocking (Ed) *Unfinished Constitutional Business? Rethinking Indigenous Self-Determination*, Aboriginal Studies Press, Canberra, pp. 61–73.

Nancarrow, H. (2006) In search of justice for domestic and family violence: Indigenous and non-Indigenous Australian women's perspectives. *Theoretical Criminology*, 10(1), pp. 87–106.

Price, B. (2009) 'I have seen violence towards women every day of my life': Australia 2009. *Australian Feminist Law Journal*, 30, pp. 149–50.

Puchala, C., Paul, S., Kennedy, C. & Mehl-Madrona, L. (2010) Using traditional spirituality to reduce domestic violence within Aboriginal communities. *Journal of Alternative and Complementary Medicine*, 16(1), pp. 89–96.

Purdie, N., Dudgeon, P. & Walker, R. (Eds) (2010) *Working Together: Aboriginal and Torres Strait Islander Mental Health and Wellbeing Principles and Practice*, Commonwealth of Australia, Canberra.

Taylor, J., Cheers, B., Weetra, C. & Gentle, I. (2004) Supporting community solutions to family violence. *Australian Social Work*, 57(1), pp. 71–83.

Watson, I. (2007) Aboriginal women's law and lives: how might we keep growing the law? *Australian Feminist Law Journal*, 26, pp. 95–107.

Watson, I. (2009) Aboriginality and the violence of colonialism. *Borderlands e-journal*, 8(1), pp. 1–8.

Watson, I. & Heath, M. (2004) Growing up the space: a conversation about the future of feminism. *Australian Feminist Law Journal*, 20, pp. 95–111.

Watson, N. (2011) The Northern Territory Emergency Response: has it really improved the lives of Aboriginal women and children? *Australian Feminist Law Journal*, 35, pp. 147–63.

Wendt, S. (2010) Building and sustaining local co-ordination: an Australian rural community responds to domestic and family violence. *British Journal of Social Work*, 40, pp. 44–62.

Wendt, S. & Baker, J. (2013) Aboriginal women's perceptions and experiences of a family violence transitional accommodation service. *Australian Social Work*, 66(4), pp. 511–27.

Wilson, T.J. (1996) Feminism and institutionalized racism: inclusion and exclusion at an Australian feminist refuge. *Feminist Review*, 52, pp. 1–26.

Zellerer, E. (2003) Culturally competent programs: the first family violence program for Aboriginal men in prison. *Prison Journal*, 83(2), pp. 171–90.

# 9   Lesbians

I think too for me it was very gradual … in the first two years of the relationship there was probably a couple of times where she put me down in front of other people or she didn't like what I said to her so she had a go at me in front of other people. But I just put that down as couples having an argument type thing. Then I think I really did dismiss a lot of it because she was ill so I just put it down to her being in a bad mood and I had the thing in my head that you hurt the ones you love type thing.

(Sonia, 2013)

## Introduction

In this chapter we explore the unique factors and circumstances that impact on lesbians' experiences of domestic violence. Our decision to include a chapter on lesbians in a book that is otherwise focused on heterosexual women's experiences of domestic violence is based on two main reasons. First, domestic violence does occur in lesbian relationships. While the 'true prevalence' of same-sex domestic violence is difficult to determine, it is clear that it does occur in same-sex relationships, that its occurrence is not anomalous and that, once it does occur, it is likely to re-occur and become increasingly severe over time (Renzetti, 1997). Second, it is our firm belief that we cannot fully engage with how gender features in women's experiences of domestic violence without attempting to understand how sexual orientation, as with other variables such as age, religion and motherhood, shapes what gender means for women in particular contexts of domestic violence. As with gender itself, sexual orientation is a fluid and continuous phenomenon, with the word 'lesbian' encompassing a range of internal experiences and social constructions of attraction, arousal, identity and affection (Brown, 1997). Yet, in a heterosexist and homophobic cultural landscape, lesbians are homogenised and stereotyped and this has implications for how they are positioned in contexts of domestic violence.

In addition, our understandings about domestic violence have traditionally been developed from and viewed through a heterosexual framework. Historically, attempts to understand same-sex domestic violence have involved super-imposing heterosexual models onto lesbian and gay relationships (Renzetti, 1997) and/or comparing same-sex relationship violence with male–female intimate violence (Ristock, 2002). According to Kanuha (2013), these lenses limit thinking on the ways that same-sex relationship violence are similar to or different from the prevailing, primarily feminist-based understanding of violence against women. Research has continuously shown that masculinity is associated with aggression and dominance within intimate relationships, and this has perpetuated the view that in same-sex relationships the perpetrator is the 'masculine' partner and the victim the 'feminine' partner (Renzetti, 1997). However, studies have shown little support for the theory that 'butch' women are more likely to perpetrate domestic violence or that lesbians engage in 'butch–femme' (or masculine–feminine) role-playing in their relationships (Balsam & Szymanski, 2005; Caldwell & Peplau, 1984; Renzetti, 1992). Nevertheless, domestic violence in lesbian relationships challenges the notion that women are inherently non-violent and problematises explanatory concepts such as patriarchy and gender inequality. In response, some researchers have moved away from a focus on social structural variables towards individual personality factors to understand and explain same-sex domestic violence (see for example, Dutton, 1994; Letellier, 1994). However, the latter approach is also problematic as it tends to pathologise victims and abusers, which has far greater implications for lesbian and gay communities than it does for heterosexual communities given the history of pathology associated with homosexuality (Renzetti, 1997).

What is clear is that there is still a need to understand lesbian domestic violence in ways that move beyond the parameters set by the heterosexual norm. As Kanuha (2013) points out, there is a political, deeply heteronormative agenda attached to research concerned with lesbian, gay, transgendered and queer communities, which posits that homosexuals are either as deviant as heterosexuals – that is, just as violent as male–female couples – or that they are quite the opposite – that is, same-sex abuse occurs less frequently in 'idealised', non-patriarchal relationships. We argue that the approach we have taken in this book allows us to look beyond the predominantly heterosexual paradigm of domestic violence because it involves setting aside those constructs that reflect a heterosexual reality, such as patriarchy and gender inequality, to look instead at how gendered discourses feature in different groups of women's lives and position them in particular ways in violent contexts. This means viewing lesbians' experiences in all their variability while, at the same time, identifying and weaving together the discursive threads of gender, sexual orientation and influences of heteronormativity that position lesbians in similar ways in contexts of domestic violence.

As heterosexual women, however, we acknowledge that we write this chapter from the comfort and privilege of being a member of the mainstream. That is, we cannot fully know what it means to be a lesbian, nor can we fully understand what it feels like to be defined or marginalised by our sexual orientation as ours is the norm and therefore we have never had to defend or justify it. As Brown points out:

> Lesbian experiences are seen as unique, offering little to the understanding of the norm. What occurs instead is that we are compared to the norm,

in the past to demonstrate our pathology and, more recently, to affirm our normalcy. Or we are simply categorized as an interesting variant of human experience, equal but still separate and always marginal.

(1997, p. 298)

Hence, we approach this chapter highly sensitive to the risk of inadvertently contributing to the 'otherness' so often experienced by lesbian communities. We have tried to reduce this risk, first by openly acknowledging that our writing is extremely limited by the fact that we have never experienced being a lesbian living in a heterosexist and homophobic society, and then by seeking the guidance of lesbian activists and academics to guide our thinking and to expand knowledge about domestic violence and gender. It should be noted, however, that any criticisms of this chapter should be levelled at us, the authors, and not those who have so graciously given their time and expertise.

Domestic violence in same-sex relationships is defined as 'a pattern of violent [or] coercive behaviours whereby a lesbian [or gay man] seeks to control the thoughts, beliefs, or conduct of [an] intimate partner or to punish the intimate partner for resisting the perpetrator's control' (Hart, 1986, cited in Renzetti, 1997, p. 286). As this definition implies, same-sex domestic violence is similar to heterosexual domestic violence because both acknowledge and draw on ideas of power and control. However, there are factors that make domestic violence in same-sex relationships unique and in this chapter we explore these factors. For example, lesbians live in a society where their lives and relationships are not the norm (Balsam & Szymanski, 2005), and as a result they may be subject to behaviours that are unsympathetic to or even antagonistic towards their identities and relationships. As well as exploring the factors and contexts that make the experience of domestic violence unique for lesbians, we also examine how dominant gendered discourses and practices that stem from heteronormative and often homophobic cultural practices shape and influence how lesbians are positioned as gendered subjects in contexts of domestic violence. These discursive repertoires and subject positions have implications for how lesbians understand and respond to domestic violence in their lives.

We draw on data collected during a small qualitative study conducted in 2013 that examined lesbians' experiences of domestic violence in same-sex relationships. As the study was advertised in an Australian lesbian magazine and using Facebook and Twitter, participants came from a range of states and territories across Australia as well as from overseas. The women interviewed ranged in age from twenty-nine to forty-nine years and none were still living in a situation of domestic violence. The length of women's violent relationships ranged from eighteen months to six years. For some women, the violent relationship had ended many years ago and for others it had ended more recently. In all cases, however, the women spoke candidly and in detail about their experiences, often with a great deal of lament that they had experienced abuse in what they had understood to be a loving and caring relationship.

# Domestic violence and lesbians

The majority of studies on domestic violence have focused on violence in heterosexual relationships. Like for other groups of women, reported prevalence rates for lesbian relationship violence are contradictory, with some studies reporting similar rates of violence for lesbian couples as for gay and heterosexual couples (Burke & Follingstad, 1999) and others reporting that being homosexual increases interpersonal violence risk for both men and women (Messinger, 2011), with lesbians reporting experiences of violence (within a relationship and with strangers) in significantly higher proportions than heterosexual women (Moracco et al., 2007). The types of violence reported, including sexual, physical, financial and emotional abuse, have also been found to be similar across lesbian, gay and heterosexual relationships (McClennen, 2005; Renzetti, 1992), with violence in all cohorts increasing in frequency and severity over time (McClennen, 2005). Several studies have been concerned with identifying the factors contributing to domestic violence in lesbian relationships, with many of these studies focusing on the variables suggested by research in heterosexual relationships such as family-of-origin violence, power imbalance and dependency of intimate partners.

For example, several researchers have investigated the link between family-of-origin violence (either experienced as a child in the form of physical abuse or witnessed as a child in terms of observed inter-parental violence) and violence in a later lesbian relationship. The findings were mixed regarding the relationship between abuse history and later same-sex relationship abuse. Some recent studies suggest that, due to cultural heterosexism and pervasive homophobia, homosexual individuals are more likely to experience emotional, physical and child sexual abuse than their heterosexual peers (McDonald, 2012). Although some studies have identified a relationship between family-of-origin violence and violence in later lesbian relationships (e.g. Lockhart et al., 1994; Margolies & Leeder, 1995), other studies did not find such an association (e.g. Coleman, 1991, cited in Burke & Follingstad, 1999; Renzetti, 1992).

Power imbalance has also been propounded as a contributing factor in physical violence within lesbian relationships (Lockhart et al., 1994). According to Renzetti (1992), however, the results of studies that would lead to such a conclusion are often contradictory and inconclusive. According to Waldner-Haugrud, Gratch and Magruder (1997), the kind of gender-derived social power evident in heterosexual relationships is not the fulcrum around which power differentials are organised within lesbian relationships. They suggest that status and power in lesbian relationships would have to come from other indicators of power such as physical size, physical attractiveness and conventionality, or economic and job status. However, Renzetti's (1992) research found that differences in power-giving resources such as social class, intelligence and earning power were not significant predictors of relationship violence, and that dependency is a more important variable than power. Furthermore, power imbalance was not clearly associated with physicality or masculine role-playing (Renzetti, 1992). Lesbian relationships may also demonstrate shifting relations of power between partners.

For example, in Ristock's (2003) study, women spoke of less predictable and even fluctuating power dynamics within their relationship. Power was not something that resided fully within one person but was relational. Ristock (2003) argued that dominant discourses of victimhood create an image of the victim as pure, innocent and blameless, which makes it difficult to speak about agency, strength, resiliency or revenge. Consequently, the women in her study tended to situate their experiences of abuse within the binary categories of victim–perpetrator, even when they described fighting back with the intent to harm their partner and acts of self-defence, because the victim element of the binary is constructed as passive and innocent no matter what. Ristock (2003) concluded that shifting relations of power inherent in lesbians' experiences of violence do not constitute mutual abuse because such a term assumes symmetry in the relationship with equal power, motivation and intent to harm, which misrepresents the variable relations of power in lesbian relationships.

Several researchers have investigated the role of dependency in domestically violent lesbian relationships. Renzetti's (1988) study found that lesbians who were abusive were particularly dependent upon their partners, which also appears to be the case with heterosexual perpetrators. Renzetti (1992) found that the greater the lesbian perpetrator's dependency and the greater the victim's desire to be independent, the more likely the perpetrator is to inflict more types of abuse and with greater frequency. Lockhart et al. (1994) reported that when lesbian partners feel a need to share all recreational and social activities, and express a need to do everything together, abuse is more likely to be part of the relationship. According to Waldner-Haugrud, Gratch and Magruder (1997), over-dependency in lesbian relationships is probably fuelled by the heterosexual structure of society, which encourages lesbian couples to fuse or create 'closed' relationships in the absence of social support mechanisms offered by normative institutions like 'marriage' or 'the family'. While this sort of prejudice-imposed isolation may also encourage over-dependency and subsequent violence in gay male couples, lesbians are more noted for creating closed systems than gay men (Waldner-Haugrud, Gratch & Magruder, 1997). The high dependency needs of abusers also supports a psychodynamic enmeshment theory of abuse, which poses that lesbians are likely to experience merger through over-identification with each other (Ohms, 2008). Subsequently, they may experience conflict resulting from the loss of their sense of individuality in the relationship.

A number of unique factors associated with domestic violence in lesbian relationships were identified in the literature. First, the most influential difference between heterosexual domestic violence and same-sex domestic violence is that those who experience the latter are living as an oppressed minority in a heterosexist and homophobic society (Brown, 2008). Being both women and lesbians means that they experience violence in 'the context of a world that is both misogynistic *and homophobic*' (Pharr, 1986, cited in Renzetti, 1997, p. 286). The impact of this oppressive cultural context on the individual has often been referred to as 'minority stress' (Balsam & Szymanski, 2005). Minority stress is psychosocial stress derived from being a member of a minority group that is stigmatised and marginalised.

For lesbian, gay and bisexual people, minority stress can result from external stressors, such as hate crimes and discrimination, as well as internal stressors, such as internalised homophobia (Balsam & Szymanski, 2005). According to Renzetti (1998) societal homophobia produces internalised homophobia, which in turn may generate, among other outcomes, partner abuse in homosexual relationships. Minority stress can also result from experiences related to self-disclosure, including the stress of 'coming out' and the stress of self-concealment (Balsam & Szymanski, 2005, p. 259).

Second, the pervasiveness of assumptions about women's non-violence may contribute to the seeming inexplicability and unexpectedness of violence and abuse in woman-only contexts (Barnes, 2010). Heterosexist assumptions can lead to victim blaming and invisibility for lesbians who are abused by their female partners (Brown, 2008). There are myths in society surrounding lesbian relationships that compel women to keep silent about abuse, including the myth that lesbian relationships are egalitarian, lesbians do not oppress or beat each other and, even if they did, women are not big enough to really hurt each other (McLaughlin & Rozee 2001, cited in Brown, 2008). There is a danger therefore that those women experiencing violence in lesbian relationships may encounter disbelief upon disclosing abuse by female partners or may fear disbelief upon disclosure and therefore make the decision to suffer in silence (Barnes, 2010).

Third, lesbian victims' responses to and subjective negotiations of their abuse experiences are often markedly different to heterosexual victims. It has been suggested that this difference is largely due to the dominance of theories that situate men as perpetrators and women as victims of violence (Brown, 2008). Giorgio (2002) found that dominant discourses of domestic violence, which tend to foreground male violence, do not allow lesbian victims to view or define their status as a victim. The gender bias inherent in heterosexual domestic violence discourse creates ambivalence for the lesbian victim in terms of acknowledging her own victimhood. This ambivalence is reinforced by the responses of others to whom she may disclose or seek help for the abuse. According to Giorgio (2002), without the definitive markers of gender revealing the perpetrator and victim in the situation, the community often denies, minimises or ignores the abuse. Giorgio (2002) also contends that the myth of 'mutual abuse' remains an obstacle for abused lesbians, who struggle with their understandings of relationship violence.

Fourth, victims of same-sex partner abuse experience the added threat of social isolation on a much larger scale than do victims of opposite-sex partner abuse. That is, although they experience all of the same threats as heterosexual victims (lack of friends and support) they can also experience being 'outed' by their partner. Their partner may reveal or threaten to reveal the victim's sexual orientation to employers, friends and family members, which can lead to greater isolation and fear (Renzetti, 1998). According to Renzetti (1998), in our homophobic society, where 'outing' may result in being shunned by relatives and friends, the loss of a job, and a range of other discriminatory consequences with little or no legal recourse for victims, homophobia is indeed a powerful weapon of coercion and control.

Fifth, lesbians may elicit very different responses from formal and informal support systems than heterosexual women when they attempt to report or disclose abuse. Those who have concealed, or partially concealed, their sexual identity may have a particularly difficult time reaching out to family and friends, thereby reducing available social support and financial and alternative housing resources. The isolation and helplessness that lesbian victims of domestic violence experience is often exacerbated by being a member of a sexual minority population (Allen & Leventhal, 1999). According to Ohms (2008), lesbian victims are reluctant to seek support for violence outside the lesbian community because they want to protect their violent partners from experiencing discrimination on the grounds of their sexual orientation and are afraid of being re-victimised themselves. Lesbians may also face other barriers, either perceived or actual, when seeking help for abuse. Court systems do not always afford lesbian victims the same rights as heterosexual women affected by domestic violence (Renzetti 1998). This inconsistency of protection restricts the options lesbians have available to them, such as restraining orders or potential prosecution of perpetrators (Eaton et al., 2008).

Sixth, when lesbians are visible in the public space, their relationships are often depicted as ideal or perfect. This idealisation of lesbian relationships not only makes it more difficult for lesbians to admit to relationship conflict or problems, but it prevents lesbians affected by domestic violence from learning about the experiences of other lesbians in similar circumstances as their experiences are often hidden from public view. Consequently, some lesbians may be unable to understand or define their experiences of domestic violence or may feel that they are alone in dealing with such experiences. As several of the women we interviewed noted:

> I didn't really know how it was supposed to go and maybe that was why I sort of didn't … it didn't sort of appear to be a problem or that it wasn't right, because I guess I didn't know what a lesbian relationship was supposed to be like.
>
> (Benita, 2013)

> I guess seeing my mother being in such an unhealthy relationship always made me want a healthier relationship. Obviously here in Australia we don't have much on TV that's going to influence you as you're growing up. You don't see it, so it's not really spoken about, just being a lesbian. So I think LOTL [Lesbians on the Loose] magazine does a lot to try to get a bit of information and stuff out there, which is good, but I think it's all been, for me, trial and error, having relationships and seeing what works and what doesn't. I can't say that there's been any outside influence.
>
> (Joanne, 2013)

> I think it just can be much more subtle when it's the same-sex relationship. I think because you grow up seeing stuff on TV and in the media and stuff and it really is heavily focused on hetero couples. So you see it always gives the impression of

this mousey tiny beat down woman and this overbearing husband. That's kind of … I almost can't translate that into a same-sex relationship because I just don't see them as that … so I think it's a lot more subtle than that.

(Sonia, 2013)

## Domestic violence, lesbians and gender

Feminist analyses have tended to invoke theories about male gendered power to explain violence in intimate relationships. However, in lesbian relationships where there is no male perpetrator to define as the abuser, explaining domestic violence becomes more challenging. Some research has suggested that the abuser in a lesbian relationship is 'borrowing' male authority, as this role encompasses dominance and control, and legitimises power (Kimball 2001, cited in Eaton et al., 2008). Accordingly, the abuser in a lesbian relationship may take on qualities that are typical of the male gender role as it has been defined in Western societies (Eaton et al., 2008). However, as we noted earlier in this chapter, there is little support for the notion that lesbians who are abusive are taking on 'masculine' roles in their relationships (Balsam & Szymanski, 2005; Caldwell & Peplau, 1984).

Consequently, some researchers have turned their attention to non-gender-related theories, such as those relating to the personality of individuals, to explain violence across genders and sexualities. Personality theories focus more on the individual than on culturally defined gender roles. Personality disorders such as antisocial personality disorder are commonly associated with being abusive for both women and men (Renzetti, 1998). However, these theories do not eliminate the issue of power because power is not only attributed to the male gender but can also be attributed to certain personality characteristics. Just as between opposite-sex partners, the principal correlate attributed to the existence of same-sex partner abuse is power imbalance (Renzetti, 1992). Determining the composition of this imbalance is more challenging than with opposite-gender abuse where, historically, men have been imbued with power over women, and a differential in physical size results in women more often being harmed by the abuse. For lesbian partners, the correlate of power imbalance has been attributed to the combined factors of perpetrators' lack of communication and social skills, perpetrators experiencing intergenerational transmission of violence, and exhibiting substance abuse and faked illnesses, victims' internalised homophobia and couples' status differentials (McClennen, 2005).

According to some theorists, theories about patriarchy, with their focus on men's domination of women, cannot explain the existence of same-sex partner abuse. Four theoretical approaches have been proposed to explicate the phenomenon of abuse in same-sex relationships. Originally, Island and Letellier (1991) attributed partner abuse to perpetrators' personality disorders. Renzetti and Miley (1996) asserted that feminist theory elucidates same-sex intimate partner violence because it emphasises the socio-political oppression of at-risk populations, which is a pivotal factor in same-sex abuse. Integrating the former two theories, Merrill (1996, cited in McClennen, 2005) proposed the social-psychological theory, which attributes violence in same-sex relationships to oppression, learned behaviours and individual choices. Although agreeing with the social-psychological theory as underlying gay male violent relationships, McClennen (2005) proposed that, when referring to violence in lesbian relationships, the *patriarchal* social-psychological theory is more illuminative of the phenomenon, as the addition of this feminist term emphasises the sexism and gender socialisation experienced by all women regardless of their gender orientation. However, Balsam and Szymanski (2005) suggest that it is no longer sufficient to view domestic violence through a patriarchal or gendered lens: other forms of oppression need to be incorporated into an understanding of domestic violence in both same-sex and opposite-sex relationships. They suggest that identifying the external and internal minority stressors, such as experiences of discrimination and internalised homophobia (Meyer, 2003), which can have a negative impact on relationships, should direct future violence prevention and intervention efforts among diverse populations of women and men (Balsam & Szymanski, 2005). Overall, it is likely that the complexity of lesbian domestic violence means that it is almost impossible to encompass all relevant factors in a single theory.

The literature concerned with domestic violence in lesbian relationships has also pointed to fears that acknowledging woman-to-woman partner abuse could disrupt the feminist focus upon male violence, thus destabilising the much needed gender-based analysis of domestic violence (Ristock, 2003). The threat to a gender-based analysis has raised concerns about resources being directed away from women abused by male partners (Morrow & Hawxhurst, 1989). Further, within lesbian communities, there have been fears that, akin to other minority communities, disclosures of woman-to-woman abuse could draw attention to community problems and subsequently fuel further prejudice against lesbians (Morrow & Hawxhurst, 1989; Ristock, 2003).

What is clear from the literature and from women's stories is that lesbian violence adds several layers of complexity to questions of gender and power in contexts of domestic violence. One of the most notable complexities relates to how dominant gendered discourses reinforce the deviancy of homosexuality because these discourses are inherently heterosexual. Gender is so bound up with heterosexuality that to consider them separately is akin to studying human behaviour in a social vacuum. Moreover, it is impossible to talk about homosexuality without invoking its heterosexual opposite, even if only implicitly. Hence, dominant gendered discourses assume, imply and require that a 'true' femininity is performed and lived out by women engaging in intimate relationships with men; that fundamental to gendered intimacy is the pairing of the masculine and the feminine. Because lesbians are engaged in intimate relationships with women, there is no feminine–masculine duality characterising such relationships, making a lesbian femininity appear unintelligible and chaotic or as going against the 'natural order of things'. These gender constructions are powerful and all-consuming and, as such, lesbians have little choice but to confront them in living out their sexuality. Hence, the gendered discourses surrounding lesbianism and lesbian relationships work hand in hand with homophobic discourses and practices to offer lesbians certain harmful subject positions such as 'immoral', 'deviant' and 'pathological'. These subject positions cause women to feel a strong sense of shame and discomfort in admitting to being and living as a lesbian:

> It was really hard for me. I guess regarding my own sexuality I think when it did come out about my dad [abusing me] and stuff I was actually in a relationship with a girl and my mum didn't like that. So I was in a girls' school and she took me out of the girls' school and put me in a co-ed school. I guess it was really hard for me because as a young person and a young adult, you want to please your parents. That's what you want to do. When you get told that what you're doing isn't okay but you don't ... and you don't really understand why. Everyone makes you question ... 'What's wrong with me? Why aren't I good enough?' So it took me a while to get over that.
>
> (Elena, 2013)

> I also felt like I needed to be with a man, because that's what you did. You went to school. You grew up. You got with a man and you had a family. That was just the way you did it, whether you were happy or not. Those were my influences, definitely.
>
> (Sadie, 2013)

> I didn't come out until I was seventeen and pretty much had left school, so in terms of talking about intimate relationships with my peers, I didn't, really ... I guess I observed what they were doing, but in terms of myself, that didn't happen until I was at university, because I withdrew so much from the whole thing because I wasn't comfortable coming out. I wasn't comfortable with my sexuality.
>
> (Kayla, 2013)

The subject positions of 'immoral', 'deviant' and 'pathological' contribute to lesbians staying silent about the occurrence of violence and abuse in their relationships. These positions are set up by heterosexual norms, positioning femininity as only engaging with and serving masculinity:

> I think, also, I don't know, as someone in a same-sex couple, you almost want to portray to other people that you have a great relationship; that everything is good in your relationship and that it's really great to be in a same-sex relationship, because you've battled to get there and to get that acceptance. You don't want to admit that there's something wrong with the relationship that you have now got, because we spend so much of our time defending our relationships and saying it's okay to be in a same-sex relationship and trying to educate people that it's okay to be in a same-sex relationship, to then actually acknowledge that something's not going so well, then it almost feels like you're admitting that it's not that great.
>
> (Kayla, 2013)

I think it's a lot harder for us to pull ourselves out of it [domestic violence] because of the stigma behind it. It's bad enough that we're gay and now we have to turn around and say that someone is being violent towards us, just to face it.

(Tara, 2013)

I think definitely if you're not out to the world then that's something that your partner can hold over your head, threaten to out you and stuff like that.

(Sonia, 2013)

As the above narratives illustrate, in dealing with the challenge they present to a 'true' or heterosexual femininity, lesbians are positioned to hide violence and conflict in their relationships because to admit to violence and conflict is to declare the unacceptability of their sexuality and, by extension, their femininity. In other words, unlike heterosexual women, lesbians are put in the position of having to prove to themselves and others that their relationships are intimate, loving and caring because they are living in a world where heterosexual intimacy is not only dominant but archetypal. Moreover, the removal of the 'masculine' assumes the removal of the 'aggressor' in intimate relationships. Hence, violence in lesbian relationships is viewed as so unlikely that its appearance is considered particularly deviant or 'completely outside the natural order of things', thereby reinforcing the subject positions of immoral, deviant and pathological. This situation raises the stakes for lesbians in terms of the need to present to the world an idyllic relationship, and therefore to stay silent about relationship violence and conflict. Moreover, unlike heterosexual women in domestic violence contexts, lesbian victims and perpetrators of violence share in the feminine subject positions offered by gendered discourses. Hence, domestic violence for lesbians is saturated in the feminine, regardless of how such femininity is expressed and lived out.

This sharing of feminine subject positions has implications for how lesbian victims understand and respond to domestic violence. Most notably, the notion that lesbian partners share their femininity with each other is reinforced by the lesbian discourse that woman-to-woman relationships epitomise a feminine utopia. Irwin (2008) states that values of egalitarianism, non-violence and non-hierarchical practices replaced the dominant values of patriarchy that have shaped and limited women's lives, generating discourses of a lesbian utopia in which lesbian relationships are characterised as peace loving, nurturing, non-competitive and idyllic. These powerful discourses served to close the space for any discussion of the possibility of violence in lesbian relationships.

Moreover, this lesbian discourse is given further power and legitimacy through the dominant heterosexual gendered discourse that women are inherently non-violent and therefore not capable of inflicting violence in intimate relationships. And, even if woman-to-woman violence does exist, women are not physically strong enough to cause any real or long-lasting harm. While this discourse has some basis in empirical evidence and has afforded a much needed focus on men's violence towards women and other men, it has served to restrict lesbians' identification with the subject position of victim in the context of intimate relationships, and this has implications for lesbians experiencing domestic violence. Sadie, a forty-nine-year-old woman who was in an abusive lesbian relationship nearly twenty years ago, stated that members of her own family did not believe her when she told them she was being victimised by her partner:

> There was a lot of 'you're equal physically, so why couldn't you fight back? She doesn't look any stronger than you.' She was beautiful. She wasn't masculine at all, so it was very much like you couldn't take her, for lack of a better term. Why couldn't I fight back? She doesn't look any stronger than you. She's not any bigger than you, so why didn't I? I did reach out to my sister actually, and she didn't believe me.
>
> (Sadie, 2013)

We found that the discourse of women as inherently non-violent was most strongly evidenced in how lesbian victims described the motivations and behaviours of their abusive partners. In many cases, lesbians rationalised their partner's violent behaviour as resulting from mental illness or some other disorder:

> I guess my partner at the time was diagnosed with a mental illness. So yeah, it's just a bit; it was just so full on. It was but it wasn't. At the time it didn't seem full on but looking back I'm thinking 'wow, that was pretty full on …' If they're not in a good headspace then things like this can happen because they don't know how to handle their own problems correctly. Maybe when I told my ex when we were together that this was domestic violence, she just, I don't know, I guess she wasn't even expecting it. Yeah and I think it was a bit of a shocker for her and at that point she wasn't getting help.
>
> (Elena, 2013)

> It hadn't ever happened to me in previous relationships. So at the beginning I was just pushing it out of my mind, saying 'oh don't be silly it's just little things, she may have a bit of baggage that she's carrying around', as I used to call it. Like anyone has a bit of baggage.
>
> (Tara, 2013)

> The other thing was that she was addicted to codeine, and I believe she was bipolar. She would have manic situations, manic personality, and then it would change. A lot of it had to do with if she had her codeine.
>
> (Sadie, 2013)

> I wish I would have got help right then, at that point, to get out from there. But I just thought okay, maybe … obviously she was unstable. Maybe I'd done something to set her off or whatever, which is ridiculous thinking now, when you look back. It's like it would have been nothing that I would have done. It was just her way of coping.
>
> (Joanne, 2013)

My partner has been ill for, well my ex-partner I should say, has been ill for the majority of our relationship with different illnesses. So there was probably a period of close to three years in total where she wasn't working so the financial burden fell on me. So I think I cut her a lot of slack because she was ill. So the embarrassing me in front of other people and putting me down and all of that kind of stuff, I tried to let it just wash over me and I tried to excuse her behaviour.

(Sonia, 2013)

I think one of the main components or one of the main factors with this person was that she suffered from anxiety, and quite debilitating anxiety, to the point of social isolation or things like that at times. So she always presented herself as a very vulnerable person and she was from a huge history of abuse and those other things. So there was always this vulnerability with her, and the explanation of her wanting to have control of things was her trying to nurture her anxiety.

(Kayla, 2013)

Hence, the discourse that women are inherently non-violent gave legitimacy and power to constructions of female perpetrators as mentally ill or unstable rather than consciously or deliberately violent and controlling. Consequently, perpetrators are positioned as 'blameless' in contexts of domestic violence. While violent men in heterosexual relationships often attempt to shift blame for their use of violence onto the victim by suggesting provocation by their female partners, the subject position of the 'blameless' perpetrator could be seen to be even more insidious in lesbian relationships because it requires no defence at all by perpetrators who are viewed by victims as 'helpless' and not in control of their actions. In this way, the responsibility of perpetrators in lesbian relationships is absolved or significantly diminished by the actions and defences of victims themselves. Hence, victims become the defenders of their own attackers. Lesbian victims have a vested interest in viewing their partner's violent behaviour as arising from mental health or other issues beyond their control, rather than as a deliberate or conscious act, because to see it as the latter is to give credibility to homophobic discourses that view lesbianism and lesbian relationships as morally wrong and unnatural, and therefore inherently dysfunctional. A corollary of this position, however, is that constructions of mental illness in lesbian relationships can also be exploited by homophobic discourses that perpetuate the view that mental illness is a symptom or extension of the deviance of homosexuality. At the same time, the discourse that women are inherently non-violent positions victims as 'victimless', which makes it difficult for them to recognise abusive behaviours from partners, particularly emotional abuse and controlling behaviour, as constituting domestic violence:

Yeah I guess when there weren't a lot of incidents where it happened. I guess when it did happen it was more of a verbal harassment type and then also things were thrown and broken. Then my partner made me unlock my phone so she could read all my messages because she was convinced I was cheating on her … that sort of intimidation basically. I guess I really didn't think that that was domestic violence.

(Elena, 2013)

I wasn't aware that it was domestic violence. It's only now that I'm with a police officer that I'm much more understanding of domestic violence. I always thought it was physical rather than anything else. I actually … it was emotional with this particular girl … and it was more just mind games really.

(Benita, 2013)

I guess I didn't really recognise it as domestic violence probably because it was mostly mental and emotional.

(Sonia, 2013)

I work with people who have been experiencing domestic violence. Actually, at the time when things turned physical, I was on a committee, a domestic violence awareness committee in my local area. Even with all that information around me, I still didn't want to acknowledge that there was that significant power imbalance. I think I failed because of the types of control that she was using. Even though all that information was there in front of me, I still didn't want to believe that that's what was going on.

(Kayla, 2013)

The difficulties expressed by lesbians in being able to identify emotional and psychological abuse in their relationships may have a great deal to do with the association of femininity with emotionality. The view that women are emotional and men are rational is a ubiquitous element of Western sex stereotypes (Fischer, 1993). As Lutz (1990) points out, everyday discourse on emotion draws links among women, subordination, and rebellion. Gender is intrinsically bound up in emotional expression because gender determines the significance, applicability and social implications of particular emotional behaviours (Fischer, 1993). Emotions have traditionally been viewed as the province of the feminine and, while women's inherent emotionality has historically been used to support their inferiority to men, feminist scholarship has argued that emotionality is not an innate and distinctly feminine trait, and some feminist scholars have suggested that women's emotionality is a positive characteristic associated with their capacity to see and define themselves in relation to others (e.g. Chodorow, 1974; Gilligan, 1982). As lesbians are just as exposed to these gendered discourses as heterosexual women, and perhaps doubly so in the context of their relationships given that both partners share a feminine identity, it is likely that lesbians experience gender in ways that minimise or make invisible particular forms of domestic violence, such as emotional or psychological abuse. In other words, if emotionality is viewed as women's domain and strength, it is much easier for emotional abuse in lesbian relationships to be mistaken for the 'natural' demonstration of heightened emotion, particularly as both partners are women and therefore viewed as being equally imbued with emotional superiority. In such a context, it is difficult, if not impossible, to decipher victimisation or to make a distinction between victim and perpetrator. Hence, the victim becomes invisible or is positioned as 'victimless'.

The discourses of a feminine utopia and women as non-violent and emotionally superior also position women as inherently nurturing and indelibly connected to one another. These discourses are given verisimilitude through a range of biological functions belonging to all women and only women, such as pregnancy, childbirth, lactation and menstruation. Women's connectedness to each other has been illustrated in the metaphysical (e.g. witches' covens); the social (e.g. the mother–daughter bond); the political (e.g. the women's movement); and the biological (e.g. synchronicity in the menstrual cycles of women in close proximity). Historically, dominant discourses of femininity have attributed to women the qualities of empathy, nurturance, cooperativeness and connectedness to others and to nature, most of which have had their basis in women's reproductive capacity (Plumwood, 1993). Hence, women are connected to each other, not just because they share the same qualities but also because the very nature of these qualities encourages and facilitates female bonding, sharing and caring. For women in lesbian relationships, these subject positions are strengthened by the intimacy of a sexual relationship. Hence, there is not just the sharing of biological functions and social roles: there is also the sharing of bodies at an intimate level, which reinforces the subject positions of nurturer and carer. Consequently, lesbian victims of domestic violence are often deeply shocked and hurt by their partner's abuse because it shatters the cherished female bond that is developed through the sharing of feminine activities, thoughts and feelings as well as bodies. Abuse therefore becomes a betrayal of the highly valued subject positions of lover, nurturer and carer of women:

> I think that you're blindsided because you feel like ... I don't know how to say this. It's like this is your friend. You feel like it's a girlfriend. Do you know what I mean? She's a friend of yours, you are the same, and she wouldn't do anything to hurt you.
>
> (Sadie, 2013)

> I think there has been a lot of ... you feel like you've got a really strong, emotional connection with someone and you talk about everything and it's not just ... I don't quite know how to articulate it, but that really close connection that you perceive as having with the person, that same-sex couples really get one another and that sort of thing. That is almost like a bit of a barrier to recognising that [domestic violence] is going on and that's changed the dynamic of it.
>
> (Kayla, 2013)

In its betrayal of the subject positions of lover, nurturer and carer of women, lesbian domestic violence becomes a significant source of shame and humiliation for lesbians because it makes them feel as if they are being disingenuous or living a lie:

> It was even hard when the police … the police were called because it was a violent attack. I couldn't have looked them in the eye. I was so embarrassed, even though I should have been more focused on my own safety and wellbeing. I'm not even sure if we actually had a lesbian and gay support police officer at that time, who may have come in afterwards, but at that particular time I had two male policemen, which made the situation even more, for me, uncomfortable. I think even if there was one straight woman there, I think I would have felt a little bit more … not so alien.
>
> (Joanne, 2013)

The presentation of lesbians as disingenuous or as living a lie reinforces the subject positions of immoral, deviant and pathological, which plays into the hands of homophobic discourses that lesbian relationships are 'unnatural' and therefore dysfunctional:

> Well most people in general say, 'It's not going to happen to me', which is wrong. Then the next thing is, 'well it's not going to happen to me someday because lesbians don't do that'. But I think it's different because girls can get very jealous and they … I don't know … you've probably heard of lesbian drama where people just get so involved in stuff and they do. They can get physical, they can get violent … My partner was very jealous of me, did not trust me, and thought that I was sleeping with everyone when I wasn't.
>
> (Elena, 2013)

In addition, perpetrators can also exploit women's subject positions of lover, nurturer and carer to control and abuse their partners:

> It was like a catch-22 situation for me because if I said that I wasn't doing that and then later on admitted to doing that she would call me a liar. The last probably six months of our relationship was very bad in that respect because I had, I guess, started to find strength in me where I felt like I really had to be honest … because she kept saying to me, 'I want you to be honest with me.' So every time I would she would just completely lose it because it was not what she wanted to hear. So then she'd call me a liar because I'd said something different in the past.
>
> (Sonia, 2013)

> It happened in a way that I wasn't really picking up on it because part of the cycle was the really deep, in-depth conversations about emotions and history and unpacking all of that, and really working through it and feeling like you

had worked through it in a way where, maybe if she'd come home with a bouquet of flowers, I probably would have gone 'that's the cycle I know … I know what that's about.'

(Kayla, 2013)

Paradoxically, while dominant gendered discourses position women as inherently nurturing, caring and indelibly connected to one another, they also position them as 'bitchy' and intrinsically antagonistic towards each other. Like nurturance, empathy and care, bitchiness is viewed as the province of femininity. Moreover, while the 'nurturing goddess' seems far removed from the 'nasty bitch', what they have in common is that both sit within the discursive ambit of women as highly emotional and closer to nature than men. In popular culture and in everyday life, men and women use 'bitch' as an epithet against women and 'the etymology of "bitch", as applied to women, indicates that the word was linked to suppressing images of women as powerful and divine and equating them with sexually depraved beasts' (Kleinman, Ezzell & Frost, 2009, p. 51). While the term 'bitch' is commonly used to denigrate women and girls, Chesler (2009) makes the point that bitchiness is a painfully lived experience for many women and girls. She argues that it is not unusual for members of oppressed groups to take their anger out on each other because they are unable to express anger towards the source of their oppression. Women, argues Chesler (2009), see power as a limited resource and a desperate need for respect in a man's world can manifest itself as a fierce, often denied form of competition with and/or punishment of women who show superior ability or competence. Or, it can be expressed as girl-on-girl humiliation and shunning. Unfortunately, she argues, this kind of female sexism, which is fuelled by patriarchy, actually serves to entrench the patriarchal status quo (Chesler, 2009). Hence, patriarchal discourses and practices create a lived experience for women in which reactions to powerlessness may well be interpreted as bitchy because such reactions themselves are limited by women's powerlessness in relation to men. In this way, a cycle is created in which the discourse of the 'bitch' becomes a lived experience and through this lived experience the discourse becomes truth. As Butler explains, language is 'a set of acts, repeated over time, that produce reality-effects that are eventually misinterpreted as "facts"' (1990, p. 147). Hence, it is almost impossible for lesbians to pull free from the subject position of 'bitch' because such a positioning is so entangled in feminine lived experience:

I spoke to a counsellor … it got to the stage at part of the relationship I thought if I could try to fix it and using my knowledge from before and saying to her 'look we need to see a counsellor', or 'you need to go and see a counsellor, I need to go and see a counsellor'. We actually did go and see a counsellor together. That just wasn't right … That counsellor actually started to say 'because you're two females, this is to be expected that you're going to have this sort of relationship and you'll always come to heads …' So that was a bad experience for me and for the situation because I felt it probably made it worse at the time.

(Tara, 2013)

When I was in a heterosexual relationship there was no way I would let a male dominate me like that, but I guess, the gender difference, where women are more sensitive and I guess can be more bitchy, I guess I have a natural peace-keeping nature so I kind of ... I guess I kind of stepped back and let her be the ... I don't know, be the girl, the more female personality and sort of get what she wanted, sort of thing.

(Benita, 2013)

I think there's a lot more emotional domestic violence because with two women, you get the two bitchy natures, sort of thing. Whereas I think in a heterosexual relationship you're probably more inclined to get the physical, if it's male towards female.

(Tracey, 2013)

I think it's probably more emotional than physical ... I mean that's certainly been my experience. But I think in general I think women know how to get to each other like that.

(Sonia, 2013)

Within such a discourse, violence between women is constructed as a symptom or extension of women's 'bitchiness', and therefore it is less likely to be considered 'real' violence or anything 'out of the ordinary'. Hence, even when it does become visible, domestic violence in lesbian relationships is constructed as different to or not as serious as male-to-female violence because, like emotionality, bitchiness is viewed as the domain of women and therefore part of their 'natural' and 'normal' behaviour. Such a discourse appeared to prevent women from understanding or conveying to others the gravity of their experiences of domestic violence:

I think when you get two females that closely together, you're going to get a bit of ... quite a bit of the arguing ... I don't know whether that makes sense ... I told friends and they were just, they just said to me, 'I don't know why you bother staying', but they couldn't see that it was that big of a problem ... like me, they were just not thinking that that would be domestic violence and something to feel worried about or report, I guess. A lot of people do think that unless it's physical it's not an issue.

(Benita, 2013)

I feel like it [the abuse] was minimised, firstly by myself, but then by the people that I was talking to, because of the fact that we were two females.

(Kayla, 2013)

So I agreed to go to a hospital. At that point I was diagnosed with post-traumatic stress disorder because of my abusive situation. I had to go to an outpatient program for a couple of months. It helped me a lot. It really, really helped me. We addressed what happened, and I addressed it with my family.

I did ask my sister why she didn't help me. She told me that she ... they had thought I was overreacting. So I think that's the general consensus: 'Oh, you had an argument; you're overreacting.'

(Sadie, 2013)

Hence, the somewhat contradictory gendered discourses of women as inherently non-violent, nurturing and loving but intrinsically bitchy work hand in hand to remove the potentially helpful subject position of 'victim' and to replace it with the potentially unhelpful subject position of 'bitch'; a woman who is mutually antagonistic and therefore has no claim to the status of victim. Moreover, as these subject positions are lived by both partners in lesbian relationships, the binary of victim–perpetrator that characterises violence in heterosexual relationships becomes blurred and indiscernible, both for women themselves and outsiders. This has implications for victims because to be viewed as a 'bitch' rather than as a 'victim' is to garner little sympathy or credibility in responses to disclosures of violence. Moreover, the subject position of 'bitch', which is implicitly petty, serves to minimise the abusive behaviours of perpetrators as well as the deleterious effects of violence on victims, even in contexts of extreme violence. For example, several of the women we interviewed reported episodes of severe violence and discussed the grave impact of violence on their mental and physical health:

It was probably six months into the relationship. We were driving along a freeway and she was driving and I was in the passenger's seat. She went to try to grab me around the neck and push me out of the vehicle.

(Joanne, 2013)

So I was lying in bed and she came and lay on top of me and I was trying to push her shoulders off me but she's a lot stronger than me. She grabbed my wrists and pinned them to the bed and refused to let me go, and just kept tightening her grip until it was physically hurting so I was crying. She's like, 'Oh your tears won't work for me bitch.' It was just like she was this whole other person. It's like she had completely lost her mind.

(Sonia, 2013)

It got to the stage I was getting hospitalised and it happened quite a few times and authorities actually started to get involved and that. Yeah, and I felt that for me personally, I felt that I was pushing my children further and further away and that was hurting me deep inside because I was very close to my children, and I suppose having ... my daughter moved out of my home, away from me. Even though she was safer away, I felt ... I thought I was starting to lose control and I was at that point, I suppose, in the relationship that I was thinking things that I would normally not be thinking; to hurt myself. I had got to that stage; even though she was hurting me enough, I wanted to hurt myself and just finish it.

(Tara, 2013)

I've had depression and anxiety before, my own separate issues, but this was completely different. I could not eat, I could not sleep, I didn't feel safe anymore and it was just, I just wanted to vomit. I couldn't function. Again, I thought it was something that I did. But just realising because my body's saying you're not safe here, you need to get out. Even though nothing happened, I just ... I guess I've got to trust my body. I never felt anything like that ever before in my life.

(Elena, 2013)

Even though many years ago I was out of the situation, I can't tell you how many times it has ... this is a little hard for me, I'm sorry ... it has reared its ugly head. With my son ... my son was also abused, so I had that guilt once we got out. I had ... I don't know if it was a nervous ... I suffered some depression and I went into a hospital because I had a very bad bout with depression. I was suicidal.

(Sadie, 2013)

Everything that went on really did have a massive impact on me, which I got to the point where I realised that I was ready to start working that through. But I honestly felt like I had to bring the counsellor or the psychologist that I was speaking to back to that point and go, it was actually quite a serious ... it was one of the most significant times in my life, in terms of having an impact on me and my emotional wellbeing.

(Kayla, 2013)

In addition, the subject position of 'bitch' compels victims to dismiss their victim status and to question how their own 'bitchiness' may have invited or provoked their experiences of violence. Again, it is the sharing of feminine subject positions that makes the difference between victim and perpetrator in lesbian relationships almost indistinguishable:

I felt, and for a while even after we broke up, that it was my fault that ... because we were in a relationship and I wasn't meeting her expectations that that was part of it, that I contributed to it and it was just her retaliation for me not being what she wanted or who she needed. So I guess it was really hard to say 'that's domestic violence' without going 'oh actually I feel like I'm partly to blame, what I created by not being what she wanted or what she needed'.

(Elena, 2013)

When it was ... I guess I kept second guessing myself. So when certain things would happen, say we'd agree on something as basic as paying a phone bill, when the phone bill would come, then she would say, 'Oh, I never said that. I never said I would pay it.' So you second guess yourself and think, 'Oh, goodness, how can this be?' and it would cause an argument.

(Joanne, 2013)

As the subject positions of immoral, deviant, pathological and bitchy are ubiquitous and continually reinforced, lesbians are motivated to search for more positive identities. Throughout our interviews with women, it became apparent that lesbians gained power and self-affirmation from being positioned as strong and assertive women. Moreover, this subject position appeared to have validity in both heterosexual and lesbian contexts. That is, the dominant gendered discourse of femininity as submissive and passive, and masculinity as assertive and strong, intersects with homophobic discourses that position lesbians as 'butch'. This intersection makes the subject position of the strong and assertive lesbian intelligible and truthful in a heterosexual context because it is more easily aligned with 'butch' than the positioning of weak and passive, thus generating a lesbian identity that is plausible, and therefore valid in such a context. Domestic violence, however, poses a serious threat to this valued subject position because it not only makes women feel vulnerable and powerless; it also shows as deceptive one of the few subject positions available to them that has legitimacy and value in both the heterosexual and lesbian communities, leading to a double shame or a double loss of identity. Consequently, many lesbians chose to stay silent about their experiences of abuse:

> Because everyone knowing me as such a strong person in myself, because I was always quite active within the community itself, out there with other women helping other women get from child abuse and so forth, I guess, to a lot of younger lesbians and gay boys. So I suppose I was putting on a different face. I suppose I came across as I was fine, everything was good. I would carry on like normally around other people that knew me, or at work, but then really underneath I wasn't feeling so good about myself. That all started to break down eventually and people then started to notice and started asking questions and then I would start making excuses.
>
> (Tara, 2013)

> In the lesbian community it feels like you're already on the back foot. So to bring any negative attention to yourself, on to your relationship, I guess, it tended to make me more embarrassed and shameful for the lesbian community in general because I was bringing it shame, I guess.
>
> (Joanne, 2013)

Notwithstanding, none of the lesbians we interviewed were still living in a domestic violence situation, and most were currently living in healthy and happy same-sex relationships. It was clear that, while domestic violence had left an indelible mark in women's lives, it had not permanently affected their positioning as strong and assertive women.

We found that constructions of gender and power dominated lesbians' stories about domestic violence but that these constructions did not follow the butch–femme dichotomy that is so commonly referred to in everyday representations of lesbian relationships. In other words, the lesbians we interviewed rarely invoked the idea that, as victims, they played the feminine role, or that their abusive partners played the masculine role. Our interpretation is that both partners are saturated in the feminine, and so both are expected to live and experience femininity in the same ways: for example emotional, nurturing, bitchy, strong and assertive. This creates a space within which it is very difficult to talk about power and control because feminine subject positions hide the dynamics of power and control, and both lesbian and homophobic discourses prevent them from being spoken about at all. However, this does not mean that power and control cease to exist in lesbian relationships; they are still there but lesbians experience them in different ways and in different contexts than heterosexual women:

> I've spoken to other women since I've come out of that relationship to help my own recovery, because I don't class myself as a victim anymore, I class myself as a survivor. I've talked to other females, women in that way and they're both heterosexual and lesbians. I've even heard of boys, men having the same thing so I don't think it's very different at all. I think it starts off exactly … it may start off differently but there's still the similarity … It's definitely about the power. It's an ego boost for them and I learnt that I didn't actually lose the power, I just put it away. I guess she was just a bit stronger than me, I thought, at the time. But really deep inside, I was actually stronger because I actually got out before I was … I hate to say the word, but before she killed me.
>
> (Tara, 2013)

> Sometimes the dominant personality can shift depending on what the situation is. I thought that was very much the case with us. I thought we were very even footed at the beginning and the dominance would change depending on the situation. But as things got worse in the relationship she became more dominant and I became more submissive. For me, that was about keeping the peace and not rocking the boat, walking on eggshells, that kind of thing. So I definitely became more submissive.
>
> (Sonia, 2013)

> So I think while I was in the relationship, I always thought that she was the vulnerable one and I actually had the power, but probably, looking back on what happened after we separated, I realised just how much of myself I'd given up in order to appease what she needed, which was power. The power that she was actually wanting was power over me. It wasn't over other things. That seemed to be what she needed, and it happened in such a gradual progression that I wasn't even aware of how much she actually was creeping up and up and up and up, until like I said, there was … even when it got to the point where I couldn't even talk to my parents on my own because she wasn't comfortable with that. Even that frustrated me, but I didn't see it as a power thing, probably, until after the relationship was over.
>
> (Kayla, 2013)

As with heterosexual women in domestic violence situations with men, lesbian victims engaged in submissive forms of femininity to 'not rock the boat' and to 'appease' their abusive partners. However, unlike heterosexual women, lesbian victims seemed to understand their submissiveness in terms of choice; a subject position that they could step in and out of as needed. The perception that they could choose to be submissive to violent partners is consistent with their view that domestic violence involves the exchange of power between themselves and their partners. It is also likely, however, that victims' perceptions of agency in contexts of violence may be the result of sharing feminine subject positions with perpetrators, making distinctions of power and control murkier or less clear cut than in heterosexual relationships, where discourses of masculinity and femininity construct very different experiences of power and control between men and women. In addition, while lesbians saw their partners' abuse as an indicator of wanting or taking power in the relationship, these power relations were viewed as fluid and changeable, and neither masculine nor feminine. That is, lesbian victims saw themselves as having as much power as the perpetrator but choosing to use this power differently, such as renouncing it to 'keep the peace' or 'putting it away'. Even though victims perceived power and control to be constantly fluctuating and mutable between themselves and their abusive partners, it was also clear that power was not equal between victims and perpetrators, and that victims were extremely vulnerable in contexts of domestic violence:

> Yeah, it was like in the beginning it was mainly the mental and emotional manipulation. It was probably starting as manipulating me, making me feel that I was misunderstanding what she was saying, or she was putting me down quite a bit. I was ... before I met her I was actually quite an active person in the community, very outgoing, very assertive, and very confident within myself. So she slowly started breaking me down.
>
> (Tara, 2013)

> You were constantly on ... the smallest thing would make you second guess yourself all of the time. I think that led to a lack of confidence because I was quite a bubbly and confident and strong young woman. So there was no way that I thought that I would ever be in that sort of situation. When I did find myself in that situation, I was incredibly ashamed. I was very embarrassed and, yeah, it was just awful.
>
> (Joanne, 2013)

> There were times it surprised me because I'm physically so much bigger than her, and emotionally, I thought I was so much stronger and all that sort of thing, but that got lost along the way. I didn't recognise it until after the relationship was over.
>
> (Kayla, 2013)

# Conclusion

Dominant gendered discourses are inherently heterosexual and consequently they work in tandem with homophobic discourses and practices to pathologise lesbian sexuality and relationships, offering lesbians very negative subject positions such as immoral, deviant and pathological. Lesbians are just as exposed to and subjected by dominant gendered discourses as heterosexual women, and may even have a greater consciousness of their femininity due to the scrutiny of their sexuality. Moreover, given that there is no masculine opposite in lesbian relationships, it is also likely that lesbians are even more powerfully positioned by dominant gendered discourses. In this way, lesbian couples are saturated by the feminine, leading to both victims and perpetrators sharing the subject positions of emotional, non-violent, nurturing, caring and bitchy. Such subject positions restrict lesbians' identification with the subject position of victim in contexts of domestic violence, making their experiences invisible or indiscernible. Moreover, abuse becomes a betrayal of the highly valued subject positions of lover, nurturer and carer, leading to experiences of shame, humiliation and deceitfulness. Domestic violence also threatens the highly valued subject position of the strong and assertive woman, an identity that is accepted in the mainstream culture and embraced in the lesbian community, leading to lesbians hiding or staying silent about their experiences of domestic violence. Like heterosexual relationships, violent lesbian relationships involve dynamics of power and control but lesbian victims experienced these as mutable and exchangeable between themselves and their abusive partners, a perception that may be fuelled by the sharing of feminine subject positions with perpetrators, making it difficult for lesbians and others to identify the differentials of power and control in abusive lesbian relationships. Notwithstanding this, it was clear that power was not equal between victims and perpetrators in contexts of lesbian domestic violence, and victims became extremely vulnerable over time.

# References

Allen, C. & Leventhal, B. (1999) History, culture, and identity: what makes GLBT battering different? In B. Leventhal & S. Lundy (Eds) *Same-Sex Domestic Violence: Strategies for Change*, Sage, Thousand Oaks, CA, pp. 73–81.

Balsam, K. & Szymanski, D. (2005) Relationship quality and domestic violence in women's same-sex relationships: the role of minority stress. *Psychology of Women Quarterly*, 29(3), pp. 258–69.

Barnes, R. (2010) Suffering in a silent vacuum: women to women partner abuse as a challenge to the lesbian feminist vision. *Feminism and Psychology*, 21(2), pp. 233–9.

Brown, L.S. (1997) New voices, new visions: toward a lesbian/gay paradigm for psychology. In M.M. Gergen & S.N. Davis (Eds) *Toward a New Psychology of Gender: A Reader*, Routledge, New York, pp. 295–310.

Brown, C. (2008) Gender-role implications of same-sex intimate partner abuse. *Journal of Family Violence*, 23(6), pp. 457–62.

Burke, L. & Follingstad, D. (1999) Violence in lesbian and gay relationships: theory, prevalence and correlational factors. *Clinical Psychology Review*, 19(5), pp. 487–512.

Butler, J. (1990) *Gender Trouble: Feminism and the Subversion of Identity*, Routledge, London.

Caldwell, M. & Peplau, L. (1984) The balance of power in lesbian relationships. *Sex Roles*, 10(7–8), pp. 587–99.

Chesler, P. (2009) *Woman's Inhumanity to Woman*, Lawrence Hill Books, Chicago, IL.

Chodorow, N. (1974) Family structure and feminine personality. In M.Z. Rosaldo & L. Lamphere (Eds) *Woman, Culture, and Society*, Stanford University Press, Stanford, CA, pp. 43–66.

Dutton, D. (1994) Patriarchy and wife assault: the ecological fallacy. *Violence and Victims*, 9, pp. 167–82.

Eaton, L., Kaufman, M., Fuhrel, A., Cain, D., Cherry, C., Pope, H. & Kalichman, S. (2008) Examining factors coexisting with interpersonal violence in lesbian relationships. *Journal of Family Violence*, 23(8), pp. 697–705.

Fischer, A.H. (1993) Sex differences in emotionality: fact or stereotype? *Feminism & Psychology*, 3(3), pp. 303–18.

Gilligan, C. (1982) *In a Different Voice: Psychological Theory and Women's Development*, Harvard University Press, Cambridge, MA.

Giorgio, G. (2002) Speaking silence: definitional dialogues in abusive lesbian relationships. *Violence Against Women*, 8(10), pp. 1233–59.

Irwin, J. (2008) Challenging the second closet: intimate partner violence between lesbians. In B. Fawcett & F. Waugh (Eds) *Addressing Violence, Abuse and Oppression: Debates and Challenges*, Routledge, London, pp. 80–92.

Island, D. & Letellier, P. (1991) *Men Who Beat the Men Who Love them*, Harrington Park, New York.

Kanuha, V.K. (2013) 'Relationships so loving and so hurtful': the constructed duality of sexual and racial/ethnic intimacy in the context of violence in Asian and Pacific Islander lesbian and queer women's relationships. *Violence Against Women*, 19(9), pp. 1175–96.

Kleinman, S., Ezzell, M.B. & Frost, A.C. (2009) Reclaiming critical analysis: the social harms of 'bitch'. *Sociololgical Analysis*, 3(1), pp. 47–68.

Letellier, P. (1994) Gay and bisexual domestic violence victimisation: challenges to feminist theory and responses to violence. *Violence and Victims*, 9, pp. 95–106.

Lockhart, L., White, B., Causby, V. & Isaac, C. (1994) Letting out the secret: violence in lesbian relationships. *Journal of Interpersonal Violence*, 9(4), pp. 469–92.

Lutz, C.A. (1990) Engendered emotion: gender, power, and the rhetoric of emotional control in American discourse. In C.A. Lutz & L. Abu-Loghod (Eds) *Language and the Politics of Emotion*, Cambridge University Press, Cambridge, pp. 69–84.

Margolies, L. & Leeder, E. (1995) Violence at the door: treatment of lesbian batterers. *Violence Against Women*, 1, pp. 139–57.

McClennen, J. (2005) Domestic violence between same gender partners: recent findings and future research. *Journal of Interpersonal Violence*, 20(2), pp. 149–54.

McDonald, C. (2012) The social context of woman to woman intimate partner abuse. *Journal of Interpersonal Violence*, 27(7), pp. 635–45.

Messinger, A. (2011) Invisible victims: same sex IPV in the National Violence Against Women Survey. *Journal of Interpersonal Violence*, 26(11), pp. 2228–43.

Meyer, I. H. (2003) Prejudice, social stress, and mental health in lesbian, gay, and bisexual populations: conceptual issues and research evidence. *Psychological Bulletin*, 129, pp. 674–97.

Moracco, K., Runyan, C., Bowling, J. & Earp, J. (2007) Women's experiences with violence: a national study. *Women's Health Issues*, 17(1), pp. 3–12.

Morrow, S. & Hawxhurst, D. (1989) Lesbian partner abuse: implications for therapists. *Journal of Counselling and Development*, 68(1), pp. 58–62.

Ohms, C. (2008) Perpetrators of violence and abuse in lesbian partnerships. *Liverpool Law Review*, 29(1), pp. 81–97.

Plumwood, V. (1993) *Feminism and the Mastery of Nature*, Routledge, London.

Renzetti, C.M. (1988) Violence in lesbian relationships: a preliminary analysis of causal factors. *Journal of Interpersonal Violence*, 3(4), pp. 381–99.

Renzetti, C.M. (1992) *Violent Betrayal: Partner Abuse in Lesbian Relationships*, Sage, Newbury Park, CA.

Renzetti, C.M. (1997) Violence in lesbian and gay relationships. In L.L. O'Toole & J.R. Schiffman (Eds) *Gender Violence: Interdisciplinary Perspectives*, New York University Press, New York, pp. 285–93.

Renzetti, C.M. (1998) Violence and abuse in lesbian relationships: theoretical and empirical issues. In R. Kennedy Bergen (Ed) *Issues in Intimate Violence*, Sage, Thousand Oaks, CA, pp. 117–27.

Renzetti, C.M. & Miley, C.H. (1996) *Violence in Gay and Lesbian Domestic Partnerships*, Harrington Park, New York.

Ristock, J.L. (2002) *No More Secrets: Violence in Lesbian Relationships*, Routledge, New York.

Ristock, J.L. (2003) Exploring dynamics of abusive lesbian relationships: preliminary analysis of a multisite, qualitative study. *American Journal of Community Psychology*, 31(3–4), pp. 329–41.

Waldner-Haugrud, L., Gratch, L. & Magruder, B. (1997) Victimisation and perpetration rates of violence in gay and lesbian relationships: gender issues explored. *Violence and Victims*, 12(2), pp. 173–84.

# 10 Women with intellectual disabilities

Women are looking for a romantic notion of intimacy, they are looking for closeness with someone and having somebody alongside of you … keeping on trying to find that thing that's elusive … I think it is intimacy and closeness … we have intimacy with other people in different ways that don't have sexual components but the women we are talking about haven't had those very ordinary things to try and figure out because of childhood abuse, child protection systems, institutional settings … there is a lack of opportunity or that kind of normative process of learning about relationships and learning about intimacy.

(Fran, social worker, 2012)

## Introduction

In this chapter we will explore the unique factors that impact upon the domestic violence experiences of women with intellectual disabilities. Intellectual disability rather than physical disability is the focus, as the former has been under-researched and under-theorised globally. We will explore the contexts that increase the complexity of domestic violence for this group of women, such as being abused by multiple perpetrators over long periods of time, being less likely to report or disclose abuse, and heightened vulnerability to abuse because of dependency on partners. These factors are often compounded by a poverty of relationships and social isolation, whereby women with intellectual disabilities are more likely to 'normalise' abusive relationships because of their desire for intimacy and social contact.

We understand intellectual disability as a social construct. As Rapley (2004) points out, intellectual disabilities are constructed in both official discourses, such as medical or psychological, and in everyday common sense, as disorders of competence affecting individual people, hence requiring professional diagnosis, treatment and management. This viewpoint highlights how social structures, attitudes and behaviours create disabling environments in which we are all embedded and these environments prevent people with disabilities from accessing human, health and justice services, transport, housing, employment, education and social networks (Healey, Humphreys & Howe, 2013). In Australia, the preference has been to 'put the person before' the disability and impairment, using the term 'people with disabilities'; hence in this chapter we use the terminology 'women with intellectual disabilities', showing the intersection of gender and disability (Healey, Humphreys & Howe, 2013).

This chapter is informed by a small number of interviews with women with intellectual disabilities and human-service workers employed within the disability and domestic violence sectors of Australia. Over the course of a year, we held information sessions with workers located at various disability services and asked for their assistance to enable women to participate in an interview. This method of recruitment was undertaken because, as Booth and Booth (1994) argue, research needs to be introduced to vulnerable participants by a person they know and trust. Furthermore, workers were able to recommend women with intellectual disabilities who were emotionally ready and safe to participate. Intellectual disabilities were assumed to be a common understanding between us as researchers and human service workers to mean a range of developmental, intellectual and cognitive impairments, including traumatic brain injury (Cockram, 2003), hence we did not seek 'proof' of a professional diagnosis before interviews.

Extensive literature reviews on women with intellectual disabilities and domestic violence revealed a scarcity of studies that include women's personal stories. Research epistemology has been dominated by assumptions that women with intellectual disabilities do not have the capacity to tell their life story (Ellem et al., 2008). With this in mind, it was our purpose to be sensitive to what women with intellectual disabilities were saying, and what they were doing in their own terms and in their own lives (Rapley, 2004). As described above, we were reliant on the goodwill of organisations involved in women's lives to enable interviews to take place. Workers were more than willing to be interviewed about their insights, views and concerns regarding the experiences of women with intellectual disabilities and domestic violence. In fact, workers greatly encouraged our endeavour to include women in the research process. Simultaneously, we experienced gatekeeping from workers, particularly after ethics approvals were granted. The encouragement we originally received turned to reluctance, with conversations reflecting hesitation about women with intellectual disabilities being involved in interviews. For example, 'I don't think she is ready', 'I don't want to jeopardise my relationships with her by naming domestic violence in her life' and 'I don't want to distress her' were common reasons workers gave for not assisting with recruitment practices. This disjunction expressed from workers was consistent over time in our efforts to speak with women with intellectual disabilities. We acknowledge our difficulties not as excuses for the small number of women with intellectual disabilities represented in our interview data over time or to lay blame on potential gatekeeping practices, but to highlight the ethical challenges of research with people with intellectual disabilities. In contrast, workers themselves were keen to be interviewed, and their interviews about women's experiences of domestic violence were rich, valuable and extremely insightful. We concur with Nixon (2009b) when she states that, even though the voices of women with intellectual disabilities themselves are rarely heard or heeded, this does not diminish the efforts of those activists who are working to establish the issue of domestic violence in the lives of women with intellectual disabilities. As Rapley (2004, p. 18) argues, intellectual disability is a social construct, and if we wish to discover where, when, how and why such identities are relevant to persons, we must look at doing the interactional business in a variety of ways. We conducted this interactional business with both women and workers to explore unique factors of intellectual disabilities and how these shaped women's experiences of domestic violence. We present women's stories from their own personal narratives,[1] women's stories told by workers, and workers' own insights and understandings of gender, intellectual disability and domestic violence. We bring these three storylines together to help illuminate the personal and social realities of intellectual disability and domestic violence.

## Domestic violence, women and disability

Over the past two decades, there has been growing recognition of the need to include women with disabilities in domestic violence research. Studies have aimed to determine the rate of physical and sexual abuse of women with disabilities and, even though statistics vary, it is clear that at the very least women with disabilities experience abuse at the same rate as non-disabled women, and at worst they experience higher rates of abuse, incidents of disability-related violence and sexual assault (Martin et al., 2006; Plummer & Findley, 2012). In addition, studies suggest that women with disabilities are abused for extended periods of time, are at greater risk of abuse by multiple types of perpetrators, and experience abusive tactics that target their disability (Plummer & Findley, 2012; Healey, Humphreys & Howe, 2013).

Women with disabilities can and do experience the same kinds of abuse as other women but their experiences are amplified by disability-specific abuse (Hague, Thiara & Mullender, 2011). For example, perpetrators can make use of and exploit a woman's impairment or condition through emotional degradation and humiliation. A perpetrator can increase hurt and damage if the woman is immobile or frail. Destruction or withholding of needed equipment, manipulation of medicines, and reliance on the abuser for personal and intimate care and assistance with daily tasks related to a woman's disability add many dimensions to domestic violence (Martin et al., 2006; Hague, Thiara & Mullender, 2011; Lund, 2011). In efforts to understand disability-specific abuse and domestic violence, we also need to examine dominant perceptions or images of women with disabilities (Nixon, 2009b). For example, the construction of helpless and passive means disabled women are encouraged to be endlessly compliant to health care workers, doctors, carers, family members, and so on; hence, this identity exposes them to multiple potential abusers, and this perceived vulnerability can be exploited by certain predatory individuals. Women with disabilities are also often portrayed as non-sexual or as incapable of having intimate relationships with either non-disabled or disabled people (Nixon, 2009b). Consequently, women with disabilities may experience high rates of low self-esteem, and be more likely to tolerate actions and behaviours out of fear of being abandoned and alone (Hassouneh-Phillips & McNeff, 2005; Hague, Thiara & Mullender, 2011; Plummer & Findley, 2012).

Instead of focusing on the disability itself, other explanations have pointed out that domestic violence experiences are different for women with disabilities because they experience higher incidence of poverty and unemployment than people without a disability. Women with disabilities are more likely to experience economic disadvantage and marginalisation, which is pertinent for women with a disability experiencing domestic violence (May, 2006). Furthermore, with the lived experiences of group homes, institutions and medical settings, women with disabilities are more likely to experience domestic violence in wider community settings; that is, while spouses are most frequently the perpetrators, women with disabilities are more vulnerable to abuse from a range of people including personal care assistants where the categories of 'partners' and 'carers' can overlap (Nixon, 2009c). The social context of disability, such as reliance on support services, poverty, inaccessibility and isolation, increases the risk of domestic violence for women with disabilities, and contributes to the complexity of addressing abuse (Powers et al., 2009; Curry et al., 2009).

In summary, in understanding domestic violence in the lives of women with disabilities, the unique forms of abuse, lack of accessibility, mobility and social isolation are common features and, together with being taught to comply with others' wishes and demands, create an atmosphere of fear, inability and/ or reluctance to identify and talk about domestic violence. Limitations in functional capacity to independently perform activities to navigate work, home and community environments place women with disabilities at considerable risk of domestic violence (Gilson, Cramer & DePoy, 2001; Lund, 2011; Plummer & Findley, 2012).

## Domestic violence and women with intellectual disabilities

The factors identified in the literature that impact on domestic violence experiences for women with disabilities are equally relevant to women with intellectual disabilities. However, we note with Brownridge (2006) that the experiences of women with intellectual disabilities are particularly absent amongst the growing number of studies into disability and domestic violence. Consultations with workers from the disability and domestic violence sectors reiterated this concern and encouraged us to focus on the needs of women with intellectual disabilities. For example, a woman who had worked in disability, domestic violence and sexual assault across her career commented:

> There's a sense of being powerless over certain areas of their lives and often they're not offered choices because it's not thought that they're capable of making choices and society sees them as not equal to other non-disabled people.
>
> (Jane, 2012)

Similarly, a woman who had worked in disability services for her entire career of approximately twenty years said:

> There's just this other level when you look at women with intellectual disabilities compared to other women … I'm not saying that I blame women in any way but when a woman has the intelligence to make a choice to leave, access support networks … and I fully understand the fear behind leaving and the entrapment for all women but with a woman with an intellectual disability, they're not even aware of that … especially for someone that doesn't have really good literacy skills, it is a very, very difficult concept to teach and support that person to understand.
>
> (Michelle, 2013)

The absence of women with intellectual disabilities in domestic violence research may be the result of societal myths that women with intellectual disabilities are single and asexual and therefore do not have intimate partner relationships (Brownridge, 2006). Or it may be, as Martin et al. (2006) argue, perpetrators feel that such women will be relatively powerless to resist, thinking that these women may be more easily manipulated into dangerous situations where violence can occur; hence women with intellectual disabilities are less likely than other women to report assaults, particularly to authorities. Despite this absence in the literature, Lin et al. (2010) found rates of domestic violence to be particularly high for women with intellectual disabilities. They examined the Taiwanese Domestic Violence Report System and found the average increase in the annual reported prevalence of domestic violence for people with disabilities was 3.7 times that of the general population. Furthermore, intellectual disability increased the most on average between 2006 and 2009. Similarly, Lin et al. (2009) found that the rate of sexual assault reported among people with disabilities was 2.7 times that of the general population, and people with intellectual disabilities accounted for the largest proportion of reported sexual assault cases among the disabled. We focus in this chapter on women with intellectual disabilities because, as Sobsey (2000) points out, many women with developmental disabilities experience violence perpetrated by spouses, dates or sexual partners, yet little is known about this abuse. Furthermore, stereotypes and myths such as being asexual, single, undesirable, naïve and dependent (Cramer, Gilson & DePoy, 2003) pervade constructions of women with intellectual disabilities, and this leads to assumptions that they are much less likely to be married, live in a common law relationship or participate in dating (Sobsey, 2000).

When searching for studies that focus on women with intellectual disabilities and domestic violence, very little emerges; however, researchers do draw attention to unique factors associated with intellectual disabilities that need to be considered. For example, Brownridge (2006) argues that disabled women with fewer relative education resources may be more dependent, less powerful and thus more prone to violent victimisation. A social worker who had a background in disability and statutory services concurred with this argument:

> There is definitely a level of predatory [behaviour]. I have seen one man have a relationship with three women with intellectual disability to access their children. There is a level of vulnerability that he seems to target. The

men seem to be a bit higher functioning than the woman but sometimes even significantly more so like I remember a man, he was studying a PhD and he was from overseas and it was an online relationship and she was supporting him to come over here ... these men seem to be higher in terms of their IQ but have their own perhaps mental health and control and anger management type issues. That seems to be the picture anyway.

(Amy, 2013)

Taking this a step further, Doughty and Kane (2010) discuss the challenges of establishing sexual-abuse protection and other life protection skills for people with intellectual disabilities, pointing out that it is much more difficult for this group of individuals to discern the sexual abuse confrontation as dangerous, and then respond in a way that allows them to escape from the situation. This difficulty arises particularly for women because they often have limited understandings of sexual and other forms of abuse, and often have an extensive history of reinforcement and compliance with requests. Furthermore, reporting abuse becomes much more difficult for women with intellectual disabilities because of impaired social skills, decision-making skills and communication skills. Workers we spoke with reaffirmed similar themes about the difficulties they encountered in trying to teach women with intellectual disability protection skills and safety plans. For example:

> I think it's harder for women with intellectual disability to find men that are not violent, that sounds really generalising but it seems more difficult for them to find good men. It's difficult for all of us to find good men but I think for these women particularly ... the sort of blokes that are attracted, a bit predatory in nature or exploitative in nature ... I think it's very hard for them to break out of that cycle and to even realise and perhaps if they've had poor relationships with their own parents as children then it's just – well that's normal.

(Amy, 2013)

> Over the past five years, we've worked with her, for her to understand her rights, her right to have this relationship, but it's also your right to be safe and not put up with this violence, and his abuse. When he comes home in a bad mood, for example, she is saying I'm not putting up with that, and goes out and has a walk. But her dedication to staying committed to the relationship is, well ... Then there is another woman who needs to and wants to have a man involved in her life, and will continually look for somebody else. It takes years to actually support somebody with an ideal – this has been my experience – and to actually read the signs for the next relationship ... it has been very difficult to teach that woman, to learn from mistakes. You know, do you really want to go down that road again?

(Michelle, 2013)

And then being able to imagine and intellectualise around safety and all sorts of things and perhaps having some experience of it – you can't teach this – because there is a learning impact of intellectual disability there is no incidental stuff happening that might field one's sense of what this is or what might be safe and what might not be.

(Ruth, 2012)

Both Nosek et al. (2001) and Barranti and Yuen (2008) argue similar themes, including that limitations of developmental, intellectual or cognitive disabilities make it extremely difficult to escape or recognise domestic violence. This difficulty especially arises when the perpetrator is providing particular emotional, social, financial and care needs, which makes it even more confusing for women with intellectual disabilities. More specifically and directly, Zweig, Schlichter and Burt (2002) argue that women with learning disabilities have the barrier of limited ability to understand what is happening in their case of domestic violence; they are less able to articulate their pain, and experience the cultural bias that allows society to view their victimisation as less traumatic than the victimisation of women with average or above average intelligence. In summary, we point to the interactions amongst disability, functional capacity and abuse as significant and unique factors in the lives of women with intellectual disabilities who are experiencing domestic violence. Positioning women as having below average intelligence attracts labels of 'stupid' and 'dumb', which constructs dominant discourses that domestic violence for women with intellectual disabilities does not exist or is not as serious as other women's experiences of violence and abuse. A worker said:

There is a view that because they have an intellectual disability, they are promiscuous and they don't know they are promiscuous because they have been abused throughout their lives. Workers, people assume naively that the woman is consenting to everything in that relationship and that is not always the case. There is a lot of vulnerability there and add power differentials with their partner or someone that is taking advantage of them – informed choice is not clear cut. Sometimes these relationships are forced on them but workers, people think this is not our issue to deal with. People can't deal with or think about it.

(Amy 2013)

Only a few researchers have actually interviewed women with intellectual disabilities about their experiences of abuse within the context of intimate partner relationships. These studies provide great insight into the unique circumstances for this group of women. For example, McCarthy (1998) interviewed women with learning difficulties about their experiences of sexuality and sexual abuse perpetrated by peers, boyfriends, family members or staff members. She argued that women with learning difficulties find it difficult to name and recognise abuse when it is in the context of an ongoing valued relationship, and when they do recognise abuse they are often reluctant to report it due to fear of repercussions for their partner and potential loss of the relationship. She also found that in institutional settings women are often paid for sex, and so sex is seen as a commodity and a one-way exchange. She argues that the power of men to pay brings with it power and control and women learn through engaging in this process not to value their own bodies, feelings and instincts, which potentially leaves them vulnerable to abuse. Aggressive and forced behaviour therefore often forms the expectations of women around sex and what intimate relationships have to offer them, making it more difficult for women to distinguish between what is abusive and what is not, and what is consensual and what is not. Eastgate et al. (2011) also interviewed women with intellectual disabilities about sexuality and sexual abuse experiences, arguing that women with intellectual disabilities are highly vulnerable to abuse in their relationships because they often do not understand their rights in a relationship, including the right to decline unwanted sex. They found that women were often quite confused about refusing sex with an established partner, and struggled in negotiating the often complex nuances of an intimate relationship.

Women with intellectual disabilities have particular difficulty understanding and recognising different forms of domestic violence, particularly abuse that is insidious, subtle and manipulative; however, this difficulty is not unique to those with intellectual disabilities. In addition, this group of women often experience abuse across their life span from a variety of perpetrators, while simultaneously living with societal judgements about their sexuality such as asexual and non-existent or the complete opposite, promiscuous and flirtatious. This context creates a societal perception that abuse cannot happen to these women because they could not possibly have intimate relationships or these women are desperate and consensual. These complexities collide in the experiences of domestic violence for women with intellectual disabilities and, within this context, particular constructions of gender become visible:

> Vulnerability and naivety and so not understanding ... I know a woman who is so lonely and she likes company and so she lets these men into her house and they have sex with her. She doesn't feel good about it afterwards and tells me 'I didn't want that to happen', but she just doesn't know how to tell them to leave, to stop ... And then there is a misconception too around women with intellectual disability being flirtatious, promiscuous.
>
> (Michelle, 2013)

Dominant constructions of women with intellectual disabilities as being asexual or promiscuous create an apathetic and unresponsive service system. For example, Walter-Brice et al. (2012) interviewed women with learning disabilities about their experiences of domestic violence and found that, although women sought help from services to leave their abusive partners, it was either denied or inappropriate to their needs. They argued that women with intellectual disabilities internalise oppression from their partners and from services that fail them, and this results in immense feelings of powerlessness and self-blame. This physical and psychological isolation commonly experienced by women with intellectual disabilities underpins and shapes the way they make sense of their worlds.

In summary, the interplay between intellectual disabilities and the perceived functional limitations of this label must be taken into consideration when understanding domestic violence for women with intellectual disabilities. Domestic violence is embedded in contexts of inherent vulnerability of living with learning, cognitive and intellectual difficulties, as well as living with dominant gendered constructions of being either asexual or promiscuous (Gilson, Cramer & DePoy, 2001).

## Domestic violence, intellectual disability and gender

Examining and naming the unique experiences of domestic violence for women with intellectual disabilities exposes how their specific impairment can increase vulnerability to abuse, in particular how their disabilities can be exploited or used by perpetrators in domestic violence. The many stories we heard over the span of a year from workers in disability and domestic violence services painted a dominant background context of women experiencing childhood sexual abuse or other forms of abuse and neglect, institutionalised care, poverty and social isolation. This context together with the dependence it creates can be identified as a risk marker for domestic violence against women with intellectual disabilities (Brownridge, 2006). Furthermore, workers raised significant concern and suspicion about the intentions of the male partners of women with intellectual disabilities, often using expressions such as 'men targeting', 'men exploiting' and 'bees to a honeypot' to describe their perceptions of women's intimate relationships. We raise this concern not to create the assumption that all women with intellectual disabilities have these experiences or do not have positive family, friendship or relationship networks, but to recognise vulnerability and that the workers we interviewed were embedded into systems and agencies that are asked to respond, support and advocate for women in need of assistance. On the other hand, Brownridge (2006) argues that patriarchal dominance, sexual possessiveness and sexual jealously are linked to significantly increased odds of violence for women with and without disabilities but have a considerably stronger impact on women with intellectual disabilities. Women with intellectual disabilities are often perceived by men who espouse a patriarchal ideology as being easier to dominate, which may include domination through violence. Pointing out this vulnerability is not to suggest that it is a cause for domestic violence or that it is an avenue for blame. Rather, naming this vulnerability exposes the unique gendered experiences for this group of women. For example, workers said:

> They are more vulnerable. But because vulnerable tends to focus on the nature of the women's characteristics, we say they're much more likely to be targeted because that focuses on the characteristics of the perpetrator. Because women are only vulnerable because a perpetrator sees them as someone that they can behave outrageously with. That's the characteristics of the perpetrator.
>
> (Kelly, 2012)

> The men I have seen, perhaps he's wanting to maybe do a bit of rescuing or has a traditional kind of view of the male role with women ... I guess people

are bringing different things to the relationship but from my perspective it looks exploitative in terms of what the woman is getting out of it or not getting out of it but we know what the man is getting out of the relationship. The woman perceives she's getting a sense of stability and security and challenging that with her is quite difficult. It's always this level of exploitation around the finances and sexually as well.

(Amy, 2013)

Feminist researchers have called for an integration of feminist and disability theory to further explanations of domestic violence for women living with disabilities (Wendell, 2006; Nixon, 2009a; Hague, Thiara & Mullender, 2011). However, Nixon (2009a) argues that there are possible tensions around defining domestic violence as it relates to women with disabilities in terms of intimacy, caring and gender. To increase understandings of domestic violence and how gender shapes women's experiences, examining criss-crossing constructions of gender and intellectual disability is particularly useful.

As the literature in this chapter has demonstrated, discourses of intellectual disability offer women particular subject positions such as non-sexual, undesirable, incapable of having intimate relationships, helpless and passive (Foster & Sandel, 2010). Seeking out a socially desirable status synonymous with partnering in an intimate relationship and wanting to perform gender roles associated with partnering is a way for women not to be perceived as different or intellectually disabled (Chenoweth, 1997). We found in our interviews with women and workers that seeking out the position of intimate partner was particularly important to women with intellectual disabilities. For example, two women with an intellectual disability said the following:

He just makes me feel ... he makes me feel special, um, makes me feel ... Even though he doesn't love me the same way cause he's told me that. It makes me feel special, it makes me feel wanted, you know, it makes me feel as though someone does care about me ... Yeah, that somebody does think about me in that way.

(Claire, 2012)

When I got older I thought, well, where are they going to put us, cause I was ten years old when I went into [names the institution], yeah, ten years old and I thought 'oh I just want to get out of here' so I thought 'I'll just get married'.

(Gloria, 2012)

The subject position of intimate partner can be seen as a way that women can resist the dominant subject positions that surround intellectual disability. In particular, we found that women with intellectual disabilities positioned themselves as having some kind of status because they were a mother, a girlfriend or wife, and they used these positions to make meaning in their lives, to demonstrate they belonged in a relationship, family and society. A worker said:

Women with intellectual disability aren't afforded any valued roles … they don't have the role of student, family member, workers, etc. and so wife and partner they are absolutely the only available ones … so even though they are very unavailable they are also the only available ones … roles for women have been limited historically and traditionally around wife and mother, and so women try and grow self-esteem around 'I am wife', 'I am a mother' and so escape the only label they have got … 'I am the person that receives services', 'I am a person with an intellectual disability … I can shift that a little by grabbing some of those other normal roles at all costs' … and often the only available relationships are with vulnerability.

(Fran, 2012)

Such subject positions allow women with intellectual disabilities to engage with a range of dominant discourses and access language to show they are part of something that is valued by society. The discourses of love and romance surrounding intimate relationships provide particular meaning for women with intellectual disabilities. These discourses are used to conform to a range of discursive constructions of gender, particularly traditional subject positions of masculinity and femininity. Many workers expressed that women with intellectual disabilities take particular notice of media representations of intimate relationships, love and romance because the social circumstances of intellectual disability perpetuate impoverished relationship experiences and social isolation. The women's magazines and the television soaps provide women with intellectual disabilities with images, hopes and dreams of what it might be like to experience love and happiness with a man. For example, workers said:

The television is the primary teaching tool in the women's lives because you live in isolation, you're not getting an education; you haven't got your peers to teach you. Your experience of normal is what you can access on the television. I advocate for a young woman that had an intellectual disability as well as being in a wheelchair and if she spotted a guy that she thought was good looking, she would just drive the wheelchair at him … she might have some seconds of having him in her space. She loved magazines of people and would get fixated on a good-looking man. A lot of the intimacy is with celebrity figures and we get that good-looking bloke type stuff which is a big conversation point for some of the women we work with … And they ask me most times 'So are you in relationship? What's he like? Does he treat you well' and so there are questions about that, I suppose trying to find commonality in some way – a camaraderie that's what probably more it is.

(Ruth, 2012)

I think women with intellectual disability that maybe find it more difficult to navigate social media and to navigate just the messages that the world sends us is even tougher – love can mean, mmm, they have such impoverished social systems and social networks.

(Erin, 2013)

Similarly, Sammy, a twenty-one-year-old woman with an intellectual disability, talked about her experiences of intimate relationships through discourses of love and romance:

> I made up a song, it was like because I didn't know what love is, so I can – [sings the following] 'can you show me what love is, I don't know what love is' [stops singing]. My heart's been broken so many times. [Sarah/interviewer asks, 'Can you tell me about a time?'] I had a boyfriend ... me and my two brothers were playing at the playground together and he came with my sister, he came with us and then he grabbed a ring and asked me to marry him ... I thought he was joking but he wasn't ... he was hot, sexy, he made my heart melt.
>
> (Sammy, 2013)

As the interview progressed, Sammy talked about why she did not like boys anymore:

> They weren't boyfriend material. [Sarah/interviewer asks, 'What is boyfriend material?'] It means they will respect her and take their girlfriend's side and not their friends ... and treat them right and not flog into it ... like won't flog into women. They're nice to the lady and nice person to his girlfriend, give her flowers and chocolates.
>
> (Sammy, 2013)

Discourses of love and romance enable traditional subject positions of masculinity and femininity, and these gendered positions featured predominantly in the narratives of women with intellectual disabilities. Workers named traditional gender roles consistently in the interviews:

> I notice very conservative views of relationships, I think it is about normalising, it's probably the ultimate expression in our society that I am a part of – this is legitimate, now I am like other women, roles are very important.
>
> (Ruth, 2012)

> There seems to be a theme that women with intellectual disability view the male in a very traditional sense, like in the 1950s, of the way a woman would see a man as being the provider and the strong person, the person that looks after them.
>
> (Amy, 2013)

> I don't know if this is just about disability, but one of the things I have experienced is there appears to be much more traditional roles in these relationships ... the woman at home, and doing the home duties.
>
> (Michelle, 2013)

Men are positioned as potential protectors in the lives of women with intellectual disabilities perhaps because masculinity is positioned in gendered discourses as being strong, assertive, powerful and rational. These dominant constructions have historically existed and been maintained through various iterations with which all women in society have been bombarded, but women with intellectual disabilities particularly invest hope in this image. Hope is significant because these women are positioned as passive and weak, subject positions that dominate constructions of women and disability (Begum, 1992). The impacts of these socially constructed classifications collide in the lives of women with intellectual disabilities when navigating intimate partner relationships. Louise, a woman with an intellectual disability, reflected on her relationships when she was younger:

> I was happy. Gary was older, I was 18 he was 31, and he showed me the love and respect that I needed. He was more like a father figure I guess. But it wasn't until there was trouble. Oh, there was trouble in our relationship. I used to jump to his command you know, 'yes sir, no sir'. He modelled me to be, if you remember Elvis and Priscilla Presley, he modelled her to do what he wanted her to be. Well, Gary was like that and that's what he'd do to me.
>
> (Louise, 2012)

Sammy's hope was to find a rich man:

> Don't go with a boy who flogs the hell out of women, don't go with a woman basher ... go for a rich man ... that's what my mum said ... Don't marry a bad guy for his, umm ... marry the, marry a rich man.
>
> (Sammy, 2013)

Begum (1992) argues that there are certain aspects of women's oppression that may be the same for all groups of women but the impact of disability means that the implications or effects may differ. Women without intellectual disabilities are also influenced by and engage with discourses of gender, love and romance that surround traditional heterosexual relationships; however, women with intellectual disabilities are constructed as being weak, passive and inferior by both gendered and disability discourses. These discourses compel women with intellectual disabilities to over-invest in taking up particular subject positions of femininity because of the historical and social contexts of their lives. Women with intellectual disabilities are more likely to be marginalised, excluded and powerless than other groups of women, and these experiences are often reinforced by unemployment, poverty and being denied a 'real' education. This marginalisation and devaluation constructs women with intellectual disabilities as being asexual or gender free (Chenoweth, 1997). The position of partner or wife to a strong man is a way of engaging in common normalised gendered roles and enables the removal of at least one label that positions them as inferior (Scior, 2003). The influences of traditional gender roles cannot be underestimated for women with intellectual disabilities because, as Begum (1992) argues, gender roles can be a source of great relief and sense of liberation, representing meanings of womanhood. Despite men predominately being the perpetrators of their childhood sexual abuse and their adult domestic violence experiences, women with intellectual disabilities continue to look to men to protect them. This hope in men comes from a society that idealises female perfection and beauty, romance and seduction from males. Within such discourses the sexuality and self-respect of women with intellectual disabilities become possible. These gendered discourses influence women's social relations and the ways in which women with intellectual disabilities can make meaning of their lives, because other avenues of meaning-making through education and employment opportunities are so often absent. Women with intellectual disabilities often remain in relationships because they construct their identities around particular gendered roles that they perceive as having value and status in society; they can access these gendered roles – girlfriend, wife and mother – more easily than other roles. A social worker working in the domestic violence field said:

> I think there are some differences for women with intellectual disability but there are a lot of things that are basically the same for all women, all the messages we get as women. But our interpretation of it, that can vary across – all sorts of factors come into that including if there is an intellectual disability. I guess that might make that understanding of it perhaps more basic … a bit more of a need for – to have somebody that cares for them. There's nothing wrong with that and it's a basic human need but it's often about that male protective figure for women with intellectual disability … it is the interpretation of our society – the fairy tales, the – how families are presented in the media, in books, on TV, all of that. It's the protective male, the knight in shining armour; I guess women cling onto that … And I think men have a tendency to be controlling and consciously but the women don't see it that way.
>
> (Sue, 2012)

Women with intellectual disabilities' hope for and embrace of traditional gender roles can be exploited and used by perpetrators in domestic violence relationships. Sexual and financial forms of abuse by male partners provide unique contexts where gender and intellectual disability intersect in situations of domestic violence. Sexual and financial abuse dominated the stories of women's experiences. Louise recalled being raped by her partners' friends on a regular basis, and talked about the confusion she felt around sex and relationships.

> Gary was letting his male friends sleep with me … So if you know what I mean. Gary had all these male friends and one particular guy used to say, 'Can I sleep with your missus?' He'd say, 'You know where she is, go for it' and then never asked my permission but asked his permission. So when he come in my room he never asked me 'can I have sex with you?' or whatever … he went straight to Gary and Gary said 'go for it …' I didn't know what to do. I had to let him do it. This was one of Gary's best mates and Gary used to let him take me for a drive and say to him 'do whatever and dump her' … You see my no's were no's but his was yes, meaning my no's meant yes to him so I

was raped a few times by him. He used to dump me in front of Gary's place on the gutter so of course Gary used to call me 'gutter slut'.

(Louise, 2012)

Louise's story was replicated in many similar examples from workers whereby women with intellectual disabilities often find it difficult to name and recognise sexual abuse when it is in the context of an ongoing valued relationship. For example:

She was gang raped and sadly by other clients, that were supported by the same service. And she's seen that that wasn't her husband's issue. It wasn't his fault – because he actually wasn't in the room doing it. But he invited the men into their home. But she couldn't connect at all – that he actually set her up – because he was getting paid by these other people, to do this to her. But she couldn't understand that it was actually him being involved. She said 'But no, he didn't hurt me … It was these other four people that hurt me.'

(Michelle, 2013)

The gendered positions of boyfriend, husband, girlfriend and wife make it more difficult for women with intellectual disabilities to distinguish between what is abusive sexual behaviour and what is not; that is, to identify manipulative and coercive sexual behaviour by male partners. For many women with intellectual disabilities, it is often the accepted public displays of affection that give them considerable joy and intimacy, not sexual intercourse. Sources of pleasure such as kissing, hand holding and caressing are often absent in the lives of women with intellectual disabilities, and sexual experiences with men are generally vaginal/anal penetrations (McCarthy, 2002). For example, Yvonne, a woman with an intellectual disability, said:

It was alright from the start and we were holding hands and everything … I also had butterflies and stuff.

(Yvonne, 2012)

Similarly, Michelle provided the following example:

Some men see women's vulnerability and exploit it … I know a woman who is available to this man 24/7 … when he wants her and then she will be hurt and not understand why he's not around at other times when she would actually like to do something … she is struggling to join the connection, that he actually only comes into her life for physical needs, and there's none of those other niceties that go with it. There is no going out for a meal, there's no going to a movie, it is purely he comes to visit her for a physical relationship. And she continues to do this because she believes that he loves her and she wants that other stuff.

(Michelle, 2013)

Similarly, the subtle, manipulative and coercive tactics often embedded in financial abuse are also difficult for women with intellectual disabilities to identify. The subject position of 'traditional male providing for his wife and family at home' can be reinforced through financial abuse by male partners because it invokes the social and emotional desires of intimacy for women with intellectual disabilities. Women with intellectual disabilities can be easily manipulated into giving over their money to their male partners because it represents a construction of the provider position that they have been longing and searching for. For example a worker told the following story:

> I know a woman who had some money that was left to her by her grandfather so she had about $100,000 and the Public Trustee were looking after it. In a meeting she said to me, 'I believe that I should give my partner all of my money' and I was sitting there looking at her, like, 'but that's your money'. And she said, 'but I've got the right to give my partner my money if I want to and I don't see why the Public Trustee should make decisions about that. It's my money.' The number of times women present with the idea that perhaps they will just hand over the finances to the man to deal with … I find this really hard to address because they see it as normal and why are you having an issue with it. And even when they leave that partner and go on to someone else it's still the same kind of – if they give that money then they get the emotional connection, I don't know, it's a trading maybe.
>
> (Amy, 2013)

Women with intellectual disabilities often understand intimate relationships in simple and innocent ways by subscribing to the dominant messages of traditional masculinity and femininity, whereby two people fall in love and the man protects and provides for the woman. This specific context enables sexual and financial exploitation in particular, but also positions women with intellectual disabilities as being emotionally vulnerable to perpetrators. The theme of emotional vulnerability also gives us insight into how discourses of intellectual disability criss-cross with gendered discourses in domestic violence in two main ways. First, the backgrounds of abuse often experienced by women with intellectual disabilities from childhood to adulthood leads to an accumulation of trauma that women do not heal from, hence such backgrounds reinforce a sense that abuse is acceptable or normal in intimate relationships. The abuse of women with intellectual disabilities becomes so common that it is often not noticed:

> When you've got an intellectual disability, your ability to process information and work through stuff there is a barrier there. So, I think when it comes to this emotional trauma that people have experienced over their life and because of DV, it's even more difficult for them to take that step to heal, and we just currently don't have a system that actually recognises or funds that.
>
> (Michelle, 2013)

I guess that extra level of intellectual and emotional vulnerability. I was trying to make domestic violence really clear to a woman one time and she said, 'I don't know what you're talking about. I don't know those words.' Working with women with intellectual disabilities in particular, it is about that. Not in a patronising way, not to put them down or to think that they're, but I was thinking about the fact that these women who are experiencing domestic violence, the greater and more often and more severe, the harder it is.

(Sue, 2012)

Second, perpetrators of violence and abuse take advantage of women with intellectual disabilities, perceiving them as emotionally naïve and therefore exploiting their own simple and uncomplicated understandings of intimate relationships. Many women with intellectual disabilities have little experience of social relationships or ordinary community life and so chatting with complete strangers, giving addresses and phone numbers, and misinterpreting predatory approaches of interest and friendliness make it difficult for women with intellectual disabilities to brush someone off (Chenoweth, 1997). As one worker noted:

We get constant reports of taxi drivers who tell women that they're their girlfriends and then will stop along the way and have sex and that's it. It's really sexual assault. But the women put up with it because they don't know any better and because they think that the taxi driver's their boyfriend and they've got a boyfriend and that's status. Likewise, we hear reports of carers in accommodation services who will abuse women, sexually assault women on a regular basis. Women think that's normal. They mightn't like it, but they think they haven't got any choice.

(Kelly, 2012)

Emotional manipulation and financial and sexual abuse feature in domestic violence relationships for many different groups of women, but abusive men often target the backgrounds of trauma and the innocent emotional naivety of women with intellectual disabilities. When we spoke to women and workers about experiences of intimacy and domestic violence it became apparent that these unique factors were particularly exploited in women's lives. The stories of financial and sexual abuse were extreme, so much so that workers disclosed personal vicarious traumatisation and we, as researchers, felt overwhelmed by the excessive amounts of violence and abuse women with intellectual disabilities endure. Stories of domestic violence were filled with severe sexual abuse and degradation including bestiality, gang rapes, pimping, vaginal, anal, oral penetrations and experimentations, and children being removed from their mothers because this sexual violence and abuse spilled over to their children, with the perpetrator often being a known paedophile. Naming these forms of violence and abuse is not to compare or enter into arguments about which group of women experiences more violence and abuse because all forms of abuse are dangerous and impact on women's lives; however, we found through listening to experiences of women with intellectual disabilities that they are often used, degraded and exploited in the most extreme ways by men. The construction of women with intellectual disabilities as 'already damaged' and 'less than human' are powerful and dominant modes of social and cultural operation because they view women as non-gendered, non-powerful and non-citizens (Robinson & Chenoweth, 2011). These constructions allow society to ignore the extreme forms of abuse that are common in the lives of women with intellectual disabilities, particularly when it is perpetrated in the privacy of domestic violence. Men are able to target and abuse women with intellectual disabilities because they exploit their hopes and dreams of being a girlfriend or wife; they are able to emotionally manipulate this need and want to belong in society. They can perform violence and abuse at the extreme because women with intellectual disabilities are positioned as undervalued, undesirable, naïve and intellectually incapacitated. The criss-crossing of gender and intellectual disability increases the likelihood of extreme abuse in domestic violence, especially sexual violence (Smith, 2008). Social workers said:

> Whereas if you're a woman with an intellectual disability – a man who knows damn well what he is doing and has seen you coming and they do – they see the woman coming directly in front of them and they know that she has a cognitive impairment and the level of exploitation is much more darker – its intent is different.
>
> (Erin, 2013)

> There is a theme of financial exploitation that happens in almost every single case. Often women very easily give over their money or pensions whether it is to a parent, partner and friend. There is also a level of sexual exploitation … there is kind of like an underbelly of society where our clients are really exploited and that's almost like a trading of using anything to trade. So if they're a sixteen year old girl, people are trading her for sex, favours for money and she thinks she is being thought of positively by someone in a higher power situation. Our clients don't have a lot of things to trade except their disability pension, sex, and there is a level of ignorance or gullibility that is exploited over and over again.
>
> (Amy, 2013)

Women with intellectual disabilities not only experience extreme forms of abuse but they do so for long periods of time. Perpetrators know it is easier to escape criminal conviction for such acts because women with intellectual disabilities often do not conform to the constructions and requirements of being good witnesses. Workers often expressed their frustration and disappointment in legal systems that could not accommodate women's different abilities; for example, statements being disregarded because a woman could not recall a specific time. Extreme forms of abuse and little social justice results because gender and intellectual disability criss-cross, which constructs devaluation and vulnerability. And perpetrators target this perceived difference of having less power (Hollomotz, 2012).

In offering explanations for why women with intellectual disabilities experience significant amounts of severe abuse over periods of time, workers raised the lack of networks associated with having a group of female friends as a contributing factor. Unlike other women, the opportunity to chat, socialise, gossip and confide was seen as rare for women with intellectual disabilities. They are more likely to experience unbalanced friendships such as relationships with family carers and support workers to fulfil some of their social and emotional needs. Such relationships are by their nature less balanced than friendships (Hollomotz, 2012). For example:

> I have been fortunate in my life to have had a very loving family around me and I know that it hasn't been the same for many of the women we work with. I have had opportunities for different kinds of relationships and have figured out over time about relationships and had many conversations with other women about relationships, whereas we know the women we are talking about don't often get those opportunities for conversations with other women because there aren't any other women in their sphere at all. So to have strong relationships with other women is not an easy thing anyway but when you're a woman with an intellectual disability who has experienced lots of rejection and lots of isolation, that's even harder. We as women learn from each other, check with each other. The pool of other women around women with intellectual disabilities is often smaller.
>
> (Fran, 2013)

> There is no girlfriend thing; there is no mother–daughter thing that builds that stuff about what it is to be a woman. I think this is very powerful and critical in how we then approach our relationships with men. This has robbed, she doesn't have the intellectual capacity to understand what a period is and the sight of blood sends her hysterical. This is becoming less prevalent – perhaps a bit more sneaky. Women with intellectual disability lose normal friendships and sibling relationships, lack of family and so there is a lot there I think in what's done to the bodies of girls as they're growing to women.
>
> (Ruth, 2012)

The subject positions of 'girlfriend', 'daughter' or 'sister' – the positions that find meaning through bonding with other women, that is, chatting, gossiping, giving advice about relationships, bodies, sexuality, intimacy – are often non-existent for women with intellectual disabilities. This lack of female friendship or bonding is another unique factor that can be exploited by men who use violence and abuse (Hollomotz, 2012). Social abuse is a facet of domestic violence where perpetrators isolate women from their family and friends and/or make it difficult for women to have close relationships with others by being rude and aggressive. Despite the severity of abuse experienced by women with intellectual disabilities in the context of intimate relationships, many workers noted that the women are particularly loyal to their male partners. For example:

Absolute loyalty and loyal to like the nth degree and if we do anything that is perceived to undermine the relationship in any way you're out the door and we are the enemy.

(Ruth, 2012)

Patriarchal protection … I don't think women even know the notion that you deserve to be safe … I wanted to say that before, around women we know in some ways choosing who the abuser is because this 'may not be so good this relationship' – or 'this is the bloke that I will be with because if he's not here I am then at risk of many men rather than just one man'. So in some ways it's always a deficit choice. Better the devil you know than the one you don't. It's kind of making decisions around protecting herself from other things – even though that is a dangerous or unsafe relationship in a sense – she is also making decisions around protecting.

(Fran, 2012)

We argue that women's investment in being valued through being a wife, girlfriend or mother, together with a lack of social networks, particularly female networks, enables severe social abuse which breeds a loyalty to the male partner, the symbol of protection and strength for women with intellectual disabilities. As Begum (1992) argues, if women with disabilities do not conform to conventional gender roles then the fight to gain access to valued institutions such as the family becomes extremely difficult, if not impossible. Women with intellectual disabilities often value conventional gender-role distinctions because they are constructions that can potentially classify them as 'real women'. The sexist and ableist constructions of gender consistently remind women with intellectual disabilities of their limitations and position them as lifelong dependent, burdensome, asexual and undesirable (Plummer & Findley, 2012). Women battle this devaluation and marginalisation, and thus they seek out gendered subject positions that they perceive to be valuable in society. However, the paradox is that when women with intellectual disability engage with such subject positions they are then labelled promiscuous, unrestrained and wanton. This social devaluation and isolation enables men to exploit and degrade women with intellectual disabilities in their search for belonging and intimacy at the most extreme levels.

## Conclusion

Women with intellectual disabilities struggle with both the oppressions of being women in male-dominated societies, and the oppressions of being labelled as intellectually impaired. Sobsey (1994) has long argued that the first step toward reducing risks for people with disabilities is to understand how and why abuse and violence occurs in their lives. In this chapter we have explored the specific contexts of domestic violence for women with intellectual disabilities by identifying some of the unique factors and differentiated experiences of gender relations for this group of women. Constructions of sexless or unrestrained sexuality, negative feminine image and restricted gendered roles expose gender in the experiences of domestic violence for women with intellectual disabilities. The various dimensions of gender and their interrelationship with intellectual disability are manipulated and abused in domestic violence (May, 2006). Attitudes around intellectual disability consolidate established hierarchies of power and influence already manifested in gendered relations and feed social inertia and lack of awareness about the extreme forms of abuse women experience (Healey, Humphreys & Howe, 2013). Women with intellectual disabilities value, seek and fulfil subject positions that will give them a gendered identity. However, the subject positions embedded in discourses of intellectual disability and traditional heterosexual relationships combine to perpetuate extreme isolation and powerlessness, and the invisibility of domestic violence in their lives (Healey, Humphreys & Howe, 2013).

## Note

1   We would like to thank Katrina Pestka from Disability SA, who conducted interviews with four of the women in this chapter about their experiences of domestic violence. These interviews were part of her honours thesis in the Bachelor of Social Work at the University of South Australia, supervised by Sarah Wendt.

## References

Barranti, C. & Yuen, F. (2008) Intimate partner violence and women with disabilities: towards bringing visibility to an unrecognised population. *Journal of Social Work in Disability and Rehabilitation*, 7(2), pp. 115–30.

Begum, N. (1992) Disabled women and the feminist agenda. *Feminist Review*, 40, pp. 70–84.

Booth, T. & Booth, W. (1994) The use of depth interviewing with vulnerable subjects: lessons from a research study of parents with learning difficulties. *Social Science and Medicine*, 39(3), p. 415.

Brownridge, D. (2006) Partner violence against women with disabilities: prevalence, risk, and explanations. *Violence Against Women*, 12(9), pp. 805–22.

Chenoweth, L. (1997) Violence and women with disabilities: silence and paradox. In S. Cook & J. Bessant (Eds) *Women's Encounters with Violence: Australian Experiences*, Sage, London, pp. 21–39.

Cockram, J. (2003) *Silent Voices: Women with Disabilities and Family and Domestic Violence*, People with Disabilities (WA), Perth.

Cramer, E., Gilson, S. & DePoy, E. (2003) Women with disabilities and experiences of abuse. *Journal of Human Behaviour in the Social Environment*, 7(3/4), pp. 183–99.

Curry, M., Renker, P., Hughes, R., Robinson-Whelen, S., Oschwald, M., Swank, P. & Powers, L. (2009) Development of measures of abuse among women with disabilities and the characteristics of their perpetrators. *Violence Against Women*, 15(9), pp. 1001–25.

Doughty, A. & Kane, L. (2010) Teaching abuse-protection skills to people with intellectual disabilities: a review of the literature. *Research in Developmental Disabilities*, 31(2), pp. 331–7.

Eastgate, G., Van Driel, M., Lennox, N. & Scheermeyer, E. (2011) Women with intellectual disabilities: a study of sexuality, sexual abuse and protection skills. *Australian Family Physician*, 40(4), pp. 226–30.

Ellem, K., Wilson, J., Chui, W. & Knox, M. (2008) Ethical challenges of life story research with ex-prisoners with intellectual disability. *Disability & Society*, 23(5), pp. 497–509.

Foster, K. and Sandel, M. (2010) Abuse of women with disabilities: toward an empowerment perspective. *Sexuality and Disability*, 28(3), pp. 177–86.

Gilson, S., Cramer, E. & DePoy, E. (2001) Redefining abuse of women with disabilities: a paradox of limitation and expansion. *Affilia: Women and Social Work*, 16(2), pp. 220–35.

Hague, G., Thiara, R. & Mullender, A. (2011) Disabled women and domestic violence: making the links, a national UK study. *Psychiatry, Psychology and Law*, 18(1), pp. 117–36.

Hassouneh-Phillips, D. & McNeff, E. (2005) 'I thought I was less worthy': low sexual and body esteem and increased vulnerability to intimate partner abuse in women with physical disabilities. *Sexuality and Disability*, 23(4), pp. 227–40.

Healey, L., Humphreys, C. & Howe, K. (2013) Inclusive domestic violence standards: strategies to improve interventions for women with disabilities. *Violence and Victims*, 28(1), pp. 50–68.

Hollomotz, A. (2012) Disability, oppression and violence: towards a sociological explanation. *Sociology*, 47(3), pp. 477–93.

Lin, J., Lin, L., Lin, P., Wu, J., Li, C. & Kuo, F. (2010) Domestic violence against people with disabilities: prevalence and trend analyses. *Research in Developmental Disabilities*, 31, pp. 1264–8.

Lin, L., Yen, C., Kuo, F., Wu, J. & Lin, J. (2009) Sexual assault of people with disabilities: results of 2002–2007 national report in Taiwan. *Research in Development Disabilities*, 30, pp. 969–75.

Lund, E. (2011) Community-based services and interventions for adults with disabilities who have experience interpersonal violence: a review of the literature. *Trauma, Violence and Abuse*, 12(4), pp. 171–82.

Martin, S., Ray, N., Sotres-Alvarez, D., Kupper, L., Moracco, K., Dickens, P., Scandlin, D. & Gizlice, Z. (2006) Physical and sexual assault for women with disabilities. *Violence Against Women*, 12(9), pp. 823–37.

May, J. (2006) Feminist disability theory: domestic violence against women with a disability. *Disability & Society*, 21(2), pp. 147–58.

McCarthy, M. (1998) Sexual violence against women with learning disabilities. *Feminism & Psychology*, 8(4), pp. 544–51.

McCarthy, M. (2002) Sexuality. In P. Noonan Walsh & T. Heller (Eds) *Health of Women with Intellectual Disabilities*, Blackwell, Oxford, pp. 90–102.

Nixon, J. (2009a) Defining the issue: the intersection of domestic abuse and disability. *Social Policy & Society*, 8(4), pp. 475–85.

Nixon, J. (2009b) Domestic violence and women with disabilities: locating the issue on the periphery of social movements. *Disability & Society*, 24(1), pp. 77–89.

Nixon, J (2009c) Exploring interaction between two distinct spheres of activism: gender, disability and abuse. *Women's Studies International Forum*, 32, pp. 142–9.

Nosek, M., Foley, C., Hughes, R. & Howland, C. (2001) Vulnerabilities for abuse toward women with disabilities. *Sexuality and Disability*, 19(3), pp. 177–89.

Plummer, S. & Findley, P. (2012) Women with disabilities' experience with physical and sexual abuse: a review of the literature and implication for the field. *Trauma, Violence, and Abuse*, 13(1) pp. 15–29.

Powers, L., Renker, P., Robinson-Whelen, S., Oschwald, M., Hughes, R., Swank, P. & Curry, M.A. (2009) Interpersonal violence and women with disabilities: analysis of safety promoting behaviours. *Violence Against Women*, 15(9), pp. 1040–69.

Rapley, M. (2004) *The Social Construction of Intellectual Disability*, Cambridge University Press, New York.

Robinson, S. & Chenoweth, L. (2011) Preventing abuse in accommodation services: from procedural response to protective cultures. *Journal of Intellectual Disabilities*, 15(1), pp. 63–74.

Scior, K. (2003) Using discourse analysis to study the experiences of women with learning disabilities. *Disability and Society*, 18(6), pp. 779–95.

Smith, D. (2008) Disability, gender and intimate partner violence: relationships from the behavioural risk factor surveillance system. *Sexuality and Disability*, 26(1), pp.15–28.

Sobsey, D. (1994) *Violence and abuse in the lives of people with disabilities*, Brookes, Baltimore, MD.

Sobsey, D. (2000) Faces of violence against women with developmental disabilities. *Impact*, 13(3), pp. 2–3, 25.

Walter-Brice, A., Cox, R., Priest, H. & Thompson, F. (2012) What do women with learning disabilities say about their experiences of domestic abuse within the context of their intimate partner relationships? *Disability and Society*, 27(4), pp. 503–17.

Wendell, S. (2006) Towards a feminist theory of disability. In L. Davis (Ed) *The Disability Studies Reader*, 2nd edition, Routledge, New York, pp. 243–56.

Zweig, J., Schlichter, K. & Burt, M. (2002) Assisting women victims of violence who experience multiple barriers to services. *Violence Against Women*, 8(2), pp. 162–80.

# 11  Conclusion

This book stemmed from what we saw as a need to think again about the role of gender in women's lives in contexts of domestic violence. We argue that gender is of central importance in domestic violence because such violence occurs in contexts of intimacy wherein gender has one of its greatest meanings and impacts. Recent feminist theorising about domestic violence has highlighted how the intersection of gender, race, class, ethnicity, disability, sexuality, geographical location and so on has impacted on women's experiences of violence, and such theorising has been vital to understanding violence in women's lives from an intersectional perspective. The point of such theory, however, is to understand gender in the context of other social variables, which means that gender itself is not the focus in understanding women's experiences of violence. The recent move away from gender as a central factor in theories about domestic violence has compelled us to re-examine its role and significance, but we do so with the knowledge that gender is understood and lived differently by different groups of women.

In this book, we have focused on particular communities of women to explore their differentiated experiences of gender in specific contexts of domestic violence. We contend that a better understanding of what gender looks like across different communities of women will provide a new way forward in understanding domestic violence from a feminist and gendered perspective. A new way forward is timely and necessary given that there has been very little reduction in the incidence and prevalence of domestic violence in women's lives across the globe, despite decades of feminist theorising. This is not to suggest that feminism has not made great inroads in improving the lives of women and girls affected by domestic violence as the last several decades has created unprecedented scholarship and political awareness of domestic violence, as well as a range of services to respond to the problem. Nonetheless, domestic violence remains a significant and ubiquitous issue, and thus we sought to illuminate the role and investment of gender in the lives of diverse communities of women in order to advance feminist theory and knowledge in the area of domestic violence.

We see post-structuralist theory as providing a way to expose the complexities and nuances of gendered positioning in contexts of domestic violence. We use this theory to build on and extend feminist understandings of gender and domestic violence by exposing how gender is taken up, used and organised in intimate everyday lives, and how gender features in and influences domestic violence. In simple terms, our book interrogates how gender matters in understanding domestic violence. The chapters have provided a rich tapestry of gender constructions, particularly femininities, and how they impact on women's own, their partners', families' and communities' understandings and responses to domestic violence. This interrogation of gender shows us how women's unique social and cultural contexts facilitate understandings of domestic violence, as well as how gender is done in women's everyday lives. We argue that gender is different for different women but certain expectations and ways of doing gender, that is, femininity for women, are similar for all women. In other words, while it is clear that women's lives have changed remarkably over time and women live in diverse contexts, the stories in this book show that there are dominant discourses of femininity that seem intractable and similar for all women. These discourses are persistent and common in women's lives because they offer women a sense of belonging, identity and fulfilment within intimate relationships but, at the same time, these discourses heighten their risk of domestic violence.

In conceptualising this book, we realised that we were entering relatively unknown territory as very few feminists have developed and/or applied post-structuralist theory to domestic violence. We understand that the under-utilisation of post-structuralism, with its focus on specificity, difference and diversity, stems from feminists' concerns about its potential to diminish the political elements of domestic violence theory, which relies heavily on the construct of 'woman' as a unified and distinct group within which members share similar experiences of oppression and violence. However, our book has shown that feminist post-structuralist theorising of domestic violence allows a balance between a focus on specificity and diversity, and consideration of patterns and commonalities across women's experiences of gender. In this way, we have been able to show how particular gendered discourses and feminine subject positions resonate similarly across women's lives. Hence, feminism is still able to maintain its political grasp of gender in domestic violence even when it engages in post-structuralist ideas. While we acknowledge that there will be some feminists who do not agree with our perspectives and arguments in this book, we argue that post-structuralism offers feminism a new way to show both the diversity and commonality of gender constructions across women's lives, and hence a way of arguing that gender must be a central consideration in studies of domestic violence. Hence, we adopt a post-structuralist position in this book *despite* the potential for criticism, but also *because* of it.

In this book, we have used the concepts of discourse and subjectivity to expose the ways that gendered discourses are generated and/or re-shaped through the different local contexts of women as well as how the feminine subject positions offered through these gendered discourses impact on women's experiences of domestic violence. Hence, we have used the understanding of subjectivity as constituted in discourse to inform our analyses of how different communities of women live, think and 'do' gender in contexts of domestic violence. At the same time, the concepts of discourse and subjectivity have enabled us to demonstrate the similarities in how gender is taken up by women, irrespective of their unique contexts.

While we have established throughout this book that gender looks different refracted through the lenses of age, intellectual disability, religion, Aboriginality, sexuality and so on, our analysis demonstrates that there are dominant gendered discourses and feminine subject positions that transcend the diversity of women's lives. For example, discourses surrounding the sanctity of marriage, exclusive mothering and mother blaming, women's inherent emotionality and capacity for nurturance, and women's sexuality as either unrestrained or non-existent appeared to surpass the diversity and unique contexts of women's lives. The pervasiveness of these gendered discourses meant that particular subject positions were shared by most, if not all, women. For example, the subject positions of weak, passive, submissive and subservient, of dutiful and obedient wife, of carer and nurturer, of lover and servant, of protector of family and culture, of needy and incapable, of emotional and bitchy, of sexless or hyper-sexualised, and of immoral, deviant, damaged and dishonoured appeared to saturate women's lives, irrespective of their unique contexts. Of course, many of these subject positions had greater significance in some women's lives than in others, but they resonated to a greater or lesser degree in all women's lives.

These common discourses and subject positions, we argue, provide fertile ground for domestic violence because they can make domestic violence appear a normal, inevitable and acceptable element of women's lives. That is, discourses and subject positions that are valued by women can be used by perpetrators to abuse women and exploit constructions of masculinity and femininity. Domestic violence becomes an extension or exaggeration of this exploitation of gendered positioning. Gender is lived in everyday intimate lives, which makes domestic violence possible but at the same time invisible or downplayed. For example, through living out subject positions such as submissive, dutiful, obedient, emotional, bitchy, hyper-sexualised and deviant, domestic violence comes to be seen as inevitable and even warranted, making it invisible or seemingly normal when such constructions of femininity are seen as inferior to masculinity. Or, through living out the subject positions of submissive and dutiful wife, for example, women are more likely to accept and succumb to violence because it is seen by them and others as the successful fulfilment of their femininity.

However, as we have shown, women themselves do not construct discourses of femininity as something less than, weak or deviant; this occurs when constructions are viewed through a masculine gaze or compared to masculinity. In fact, the women we interviewed valued femininity highly and strived to fulfil femininity in all its richness, value and worth. For example, refugee and Aboriginal women saw themselves as protectors and maintainers of culture, rural women positioned themselves as vital players in the survival of farming life, lesbians told stories of strength and caring, mothers spoke about protection and their centrality in ensuring the wellbeing of children, and women with intellectual disabilities showed us that they seek recognition and value in society within femininity. In fact, we found that women predominantly aimed to 'do' femininity well, and they valued it highly, even in extremely difficult contexts. We argue that it is the need for power and control inherent in domestic violence that positions femininity in negative ways. That is, femininity becomes something to be feared, or something that is in need of control, or exploitable. Hence, femininity is not the 'cause' of domestic violence; it is the abuse of gender, particularly of the feminine, that permits and supports domestic violence. While the abuse of gendered discourses and feminine subject positions permit and support domestic violence, domestic violence also becomes a mechanism by which to reinforce and maintain these discourses and subject positions. For example, for religious, rural and refugee women, and for mothers in particular, domestic violence was often constructed in terms of punishment of women for not living up to the subject positions of sexual purity, devoted wife and subservient to men. In accepting that gendered discourses and domestic violence produce each other, we must also accept that there are no boundaries between gendered discourses and domestic violence; both flow in and out of each other in a circuitous and symbiotic fashion.

Moreover, because most gendered discourses position women as inferior to men, they often work hand in glove to reinforce male superiority and domestic violence. For example, when the subject position of subservient becomes entangled with discourses of dutiful wife and mother, it becomes further entrenched because subservience is lived out by women as integral to the fulfilment of their constructed pre-ordained roles of wife and mother. Subject positions of subservience and submissiveness have been shown to extend women's suffering in contexts of domestic violence because women view the acceptance of such violence as testament to their submissiveness and loyalty to partners and families. Gendered discourses sanctifying marriage and demonising divorce, particularly when children are involved, also contributed to women's submissiveness in contexts of domestic violence because it resulted in their enduring in abusive relationships for decades. Similarly, when rape and sexual assault become entangled with discourses of the sanctity of marriage, they can become hidden because they are lived out by women as fulfilling their loyalty and duty to husband or partner. Women also have a vested interest in such discourses and subject positions because failure to live up to what is often perceived by women and men as the 'natural' and pre-ordained roles of women represents a failure of women's femininity.

As the women's stories in this book have shown, most gendered discourses construct femininity within the context of home, family and community life. Consequently, women's roles within these realms are far more heavily scrutinised than men's, leaving the door open for women to face much of the blame and responsibility when these domains become fractured or broken. As domestic violence occurs in the home, women's behaviour rather than men's becomes the focus, and women often blame themselves for violence or for staying or leaving the abusive relationship. Hence, the ways that women engage with gender in intimacy is far more scrutinised and judged by society than the ways that men do with gender in this context because femininity is so entangled with the wellbeing of husbands, family and children. For example, this scrutiny is even present in the lives of women with intellectual disabilities where vulnerability is often eclipsed by positions of promiscuity or 'knowing no better'. In another example, in rural contexts, femininity is constructed as essential to the survival of rural and family life; hence women, men, family and extended family look to them for explanation and answers about domestic violence, leaving the perpetrator's actions invisible. Similarly, for religious women, masculine authority and feminine submission is constructed as divinely ordained and this reinforcement of gender positions women as the subordinate, yet it is given status and the spotlight in the realm of home life.

We acknowledge that women look for power and status within the realms of femininity and intimacy because these realms are given value and legitimacy by dominant discourses of gender that are valued by society, for example mothering, nurturing family, serving community, but it is within these realms that domestic violence occurs and where femininity is exploited and abused. We argue that these are also the realms in which domestic violence is more easily hidden and trivialised because women occupy a paradoxical space that constructs femininity as submissive and weak, but which simultaneously gives femininity its status and power. This paradox of femininity enables domestic violence to become invisible and insignificant because women are coerced into navigating the contradictions and mixed messages that inhere in such a paradox. For example, gendered discourses position lesbians as inherently non-violent, emotional and bitchy, making domestic violence appear unlikely to occur in lesbian relationships and less serious when it does. For refugee women, the subject position of protector of family and culture, which is situated in experiences of trauma, loss and vulnerability, allows refugee women to exert agency and strength in contexts where they are likely to have very little power and control. However, this subject position can prevent women from seeking help for domestic violence as they also share with their partners the positioning of 'other', suspect and untrustworthy, which is set up by refugee discourses in Australia. Similarly, Aboriginal women, who do gender in contexts of colonisation, dispossession and fragmentation of their cultures, are positioned as important carriers and maintainers of Aboriginal connections, identity and belonging for their children, and as potential teachers, healers and facilitators of change within their communities. As such, they were often put into a position of having to juggle their own safety from violence with their obligations to their culture and community. Women with intellectual disabilities value, seek and fulfil feminine subject positions because they can potentially classify them as 'real women'. However, their social devaluation and isolation enables men to exploit and degrade them in their search for belonging and intimacy. In summary, these constructions of femininity are persuasive and seductive for women because, on the one hand, they afford women value, identity and belonging but, on the other, these highly valued constructions of femininity are open to exploitation in contexts of domestic violence.

We found that women wanting to do femininity well along with particular subject positions available to women contributed to their enduring domestic violence for long periods of time, and to their reluctance to name their experiences as domestic violence. For example, older women who experienced domestic violence in their youth had tolerated abuse for many years because the particular feminine subject positions embedded in discourses of marriage, divorce and mothering were so dominant that it was difficult for them to see an alternative. Moreover, alternative subject positions were unavailable or devalued, making gender for older women rigid and monolithic. Similarly, for mothers, the cultural messages and expectations of good mothering can exacerbate women's feelings of anxiety, frustration, guilt, low self-esteem and inadequacy because the danger, hostility and fear embedded within domestic violence can make social and personal perceptions of good mothering difficult, if not impossible, to achieve.

We argue that women's desire to do femininity well can be used by perpetrators to compound the fear they already experience in contexts of domestic violence where there is often ever-present physical and sexual danger. As the stories showed, women fear they are not good enough mothers, wives, carers, protectors and nurturers. Women doubt their femininity and live in fear of not performing it well enough because its performance is largely situated in home and family life, which is still considered to be the cornerstone of a functional society. As such, women conduct femininity in spaces that are highly scrutinised, judged and pressured, and perpetrators take advantage of this context to abuse women. For example, protecting children affected by domestic violence almost always puts the gaze on the mother. Similarly, protecting family and culture nearly always requires women to compromise their own safety, as is shown by Aboriginal, rural and refugee women. In summary, we argue that it is those subject positions that are valued by women, families and society, for example, wife, mother, helper, homemaker, carer, nurturer, lover and protector of family and culture, that are targeted and exploited in contexts of domestic violence.

However, in closing, we need to be careful in how we make such an argument. First, we need to be clear that women are not responsible for 'taking up' particular feminine subject positions that are ostensibly not in their best interests. While women are active agents within discourse – that is, they are able to take up available subject positions and discard others – dominant gendered discourses show that there are particular subject positions that many women take up and from which they gain fulfilment and status. However, we have argued and shown throughout this book that discourses also present the ultimate paradox. On the one hand, women exhibit agency as they construct themselves by taking up available discourses and, on the other, they are simultaneously *subjected* – forced into subjectivity – by those same discourses (St Pierre, 2000). Second, and following on from the previous point, we are not suggesting that women are 'locked in' by a particular set of restricted gendered discourses to lives of inferiority, powerlessness and violence. Instead, we suggest that it is the targeting and exploitation of feminine subject positions that needs to be recognised; it is the abuse, devaluation and exploitation of femininity that needs to change across families, community and society to stop domestic violence as well as examining and critiquing constructions of masculinity.

Hence, it is not power itself that is the problem – it is *what* is considered to be powerful. Second-wave feminists have focused on the power–powerless division between men and women, and this has served a great purpose in demonstrating the ways that men's power allowed for and permitted domestic violence in women's lives. Post-structuralist understandings extend this work and we want our book to be an example of this. Our book has demonstrated how gender positioning and power is played out in domestic violence, permitting an understanding of the complex ways in which gendered power relations are exercised through discourse, providing fertile ground for domestic violence and its continuation and, in some cases, justification. While everyday intimacy has different meanings and significance in different contexts, such as mothering, ageing, religiosity, refugee, rurality, Aboriginality, sexuality and disability, it is the investment in particular gendered discourses and subject positions, and the abuse of femininity in particular, that needs to be questioned and changed to stop domestic violence.

## Reference

St Pierre, E.A. (2000) Poststructural feminism in education: an overview. *Qualitative Studies in Education*, 13(5), 477–515.

# Index